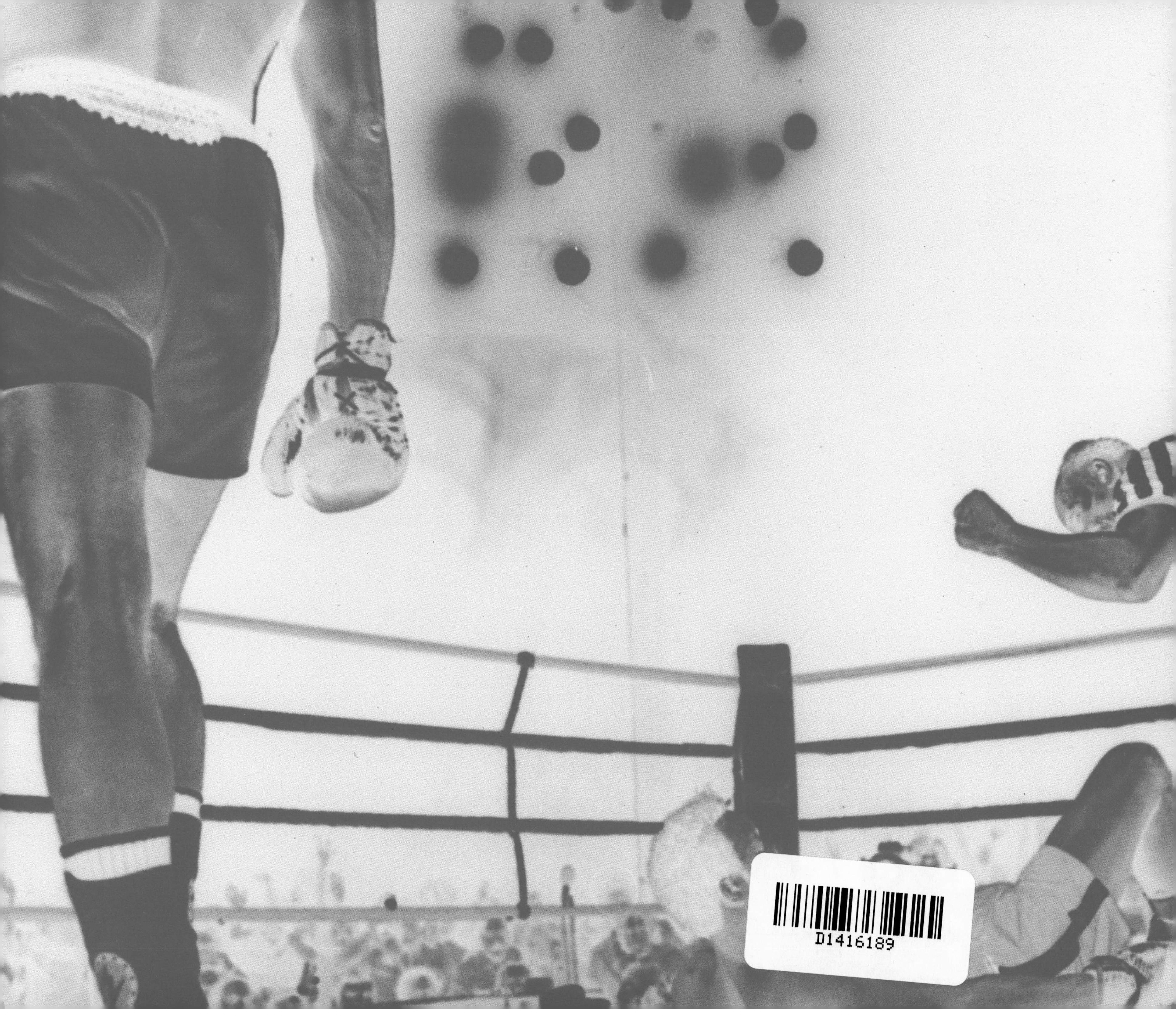

cover image
Muhammad Ali vs. George Foreman, Zaire, 1974.
Courtesy: The Ring Magazine.

The Institute of International Visual Arts
London, England

The MIT Press
Cambridge, Massachusetts

An Anthology of Writings on Boxing and Visual Culture
BOXER

FIRST MIT PRESS edition, 1996.

Kirkman House, 12-14 Whitfield Street,
London W1P 5RD, United Kingdom.

Specially illustrated from the archives of *The Ring* magazine.
London Publishing Co.
PO Box 750
Fort Washington, PA 19034
USA

ISBN 0-262-53143-7

Library of Congress Catalogue Card Number: 96 – 75615

Edited by David Chandler, John Gill, Tania Guha and Gilane Tawadros

Published by the Institute of International Visual Arts

Design
Simon Kennedy

Print Production
Uwe Kraus GmbH

Color separations
Sele Offset Torino

Printed in Italy by Tipolitografia Petruzzi, Città di Castello

This publication has been made possible by the generous financial support of the Arts Council of England and London Arts Board.

institute of international visual arts

LONDON ARTS BOARD

Funded by THE ARTS COUNCIL OF ENGLAND

Registered Charity
no.103172

Acknowledgements

Gilane Tawadros
Director, Institute of International Visual Arts

The exhibition *Boxer*, curated by John Gill and produced by Walsall Museum & Art Gallery in association with the Institute of International Visual Arts (29 July – 10 September 1995), emerged out of a conversation between John Gill, Malcolm Bacon and myself about Joyce Carol Oates' insightful reflections on the sport in *On Boxing*. Oates' ambivalence about boxing and her perspective as a working class woman who is both attracted and repelled by the sport, suggests that boxing is a discursive and representational space which lies beyond simplistic morality on the one hand or uncritical celebration on the other. The heated discussion which ensued about the ambivalence of the sport and its status as an arena in which issues of race, class and sexuality are staged/acted out became the starting point for both the exhibition and the book.

John Gill's exhibition, which included the artists The Douglas Brothers, Andrew Heard, Glenn Ligon, Kurt Marcus, Jane Mulfinger with Graham Budgett, Keith Piper, Ingrid Pollard and Bruce Weber, raised questions about the figure of the boxer as a cultural icon and placed the boxer at the centre of debates around class, race, masculinity and eroticism. The essays in this book negotiate the same complex terrain as they encompass a broad sweep of historical space and time and a range of media from painting and sculpture through photography, video, installation and film, tracing the relationship between boxing and visual culture.

The exhibition *Boxer* and this publication are far from comprehensive surveys of a subject which has elicited countless writings and art works, ranging from Norman Mailer to Jean-Michel Basquiat and from Gerald Early to Francis Bacon. Both projects should be seen as contributions to an ever-growing field of production and debate in which no exhibiton and no volume can claim to be either exhaustive or conclusive. In the course of preparing this book, we have come across numerous artists and writers whose work touches on themes explored here but whom we were unable to include. No doubt there are many others of whose work we are ignorant but we hope that this volume will provide the stimulus for other books and projects in this area.

This book would not have been possible without the vision and commitment of my fellow editors David Chandler, John Gill and Tania Guha. We would also like to thank the participating artists, Peter Jenkinson and Deborah Robinson of Walsall Museum & Art Gallery for making the exhibition possible. We are grateful to all those who have assisted and supported us in the preparation of this book: in particular, Roger Conover of MIT Press for his personal and passionate interest in the project and David Gerhardt of London Publishing Co., publishers of *The Ring* magazine for allowing us access to and use of *The Ring*'s extraordinary archive. Our thanks also to Hou Hanru, Anne Tallentire, Ian Geraghty, Martine Barrat, Simon Kennedy, Russell Ferguson, Chris Hall, Elizabeth Smith, Fiona Duncan, Kit Taylor and Uwe Kraus.

Finally, special thanks are due to the artists and writers who have contributed to this volume, Roger Lloyd Conover, Jean Fisher, Jennifer Hargreaves, Sarah Hyde, Nick James, Ian Jeffrey, Glenn Ligon, David Allan Mellor, Joyce Carol Oates, Keith Piper and Marcia Pointon whose ideas and insights map out the intricate relations between boxing and visual culture.

Jack Dempsey vs. Gene Tunney, Chicago, September 1927. The Stanley Weston Collection.
Courtesy: The Ring Magazine.

If the gym is a mesmeric space of shrouded identities, the ring irradiates the body and exposes fine detail, it casts individual boxers as the sharp focus of attention and brings them under the power of the watchers. In the ring boxing is a luminous concentration of the energies directed by its audience. Consider the picture of a darkened stadium with thousands of shadowed spectators poised on the edge of violence. The brightly lit ring at the centre symbolically glows with their urgency, their expectation and anticipation of what might 'unfold in the fighting'. For in contrast to most sports boxing has retained its scent of the illicit, and the boxers in that ring carry the projected weight of the crowd's ambiguous desire. The boxer is both isolated, within himself, and connected, at the charged but fragile centre of an entire nervous system.

The boxer is a figure formed on this high-wire tension, caught between the experience of his immediate physical contest – his *living* in the ring – and the inner struggles of the individual and collective will. It is this interplay of forces – this image – that, during the early twentieth century, helped boxing become, arguably, the ultimate modernist spectacle and that conditioned the boxer's emergence as one of the most clearly delineated of all existential figures. Since the 1950s the boxer and the spectacle of boxing have been increasingly subsumed in and diffused by television. Boxing now exists, for the most part, in a virtual space mediated by television. Framed and re-framed by the ring and screen, it is a picture of itself, an encrusted conglomeration of mythologies dramatised through global networks for maximum profit.

The transformation of boxing into a virtual spectacle of televised entertainment laden with trappings of commercialisation, has increased its visibility and may have turned it into 'the world's most popular spectator sport' but has also, in the opinion of many, severed its connection with a grass-roots culture in which its higher aspirations were bred. In the process the shift has also cast boxing adrift from its most solid metaphors and meanings, distancing the sport from its historic perception as a rigorous and honourable discipline, 'the embodiment of transcendental courage, strength and chivalry', the noble art, the sweet science.[9]

The profits that individual boxers might accumulate from this more commercialised system are undoubtedly greater than ever before and would seem to confirm the social mobility offered by the boxer's success. The rags to riches narrative, in which the deprived, marginalised figure traverses the barriers of class and race through physical prowess to assume hero status and vast wealth is a central pillar of boxing lore. Yet the class tensions embedded in so many representations of boxing highlight how this mobility is illusory and racked with conflicts and uncertainties.

This is manifest in the boxer's often haunted presence in visual culture, and especially in film, as a figure of profound melancholy; at once hero and malleable victim, at the mercy of both conspiring promoters and managers and a fickle, braying public. There is an acute poignancy to his efforts as a fighter. He only wins to fight again; in transcending temporarily the exigencies of the physical contest he is also propelled towards eventual defeat. There is an inevitability about his decline, physically, mentally and socially. As Joyce Carol Oates has said: "Outside the ring they [boxers] inhabit an alarmingly accelerated time."[10] The boxer's time, it seems, is always running out. But this popular, romantic image of the boxer is reinscribed by an even more tortured condition, that of the many losers who never win a fight, the unknowns, the nameless 'opponents' who serve to bolster the records of aspiring champions, the main investments. Again there is a recurrent image of this lost boxer, a hunched, bloated, brain-damaged and permanently scarred figure, a member of a special underclass whose physical erosion is matched by pyschological erasure.

Throughout its history boxing has engendered passionate responses across a broad social spectrum, but those responses have been equally differentiated and justified according to a given code of social value. For the well-to-do enthusiasts of eighteenth and nineteenth-century England, for example, the base thrill of brutal violence or the tentative signs of homoerotic attraction had to be qualified by an overlay of classical references and associations befitting the recognisable taste and education of a gentleman. The development of boxing is uniquely formed around such tensions, between the physical, intellectual and aesthetic that exist within a realm of constantly shifting moral opinion. Even now as these formative tensions seem to have evaporated into promotional excess, provocative images of boxing and boxers proliferate in our visual culture, perhaps as never

Muhammad Ali vs. George Foreman, Zaire, 1974.
Courtesy: The Ring Magazine.

before, and remain a focus for the ambiguities and contradictions which trail through boxing history.

Boxer explores these tensions; it investigates boxing as a form of representation in itself and as a source of complex imagery traced back into the early eighteenth century. The book does not attempt to document or provide a history of the relationship between boxing and visual culture but rather offers a number of perspectives that consider boxing as an arena in which aspects of race, nation, class and sexuality are staged and acted out. The essays brought together here are mostly new and commissioned by the Institute of International Visual Arts, and to an extent the book has tapped a 'hidden' store of ideas, giving the authors an opportunity to write for the first time about a subject which has long been of interest to them. Their writing is accompanied by a selection of boxing imagery which not only specifically illustrates the texts but also offers a sense of the dynamic space that boxing has claimed in visual culture, both as reported sporting spectacle and as a focus for the work of artists.

The essays intentionally do not follow any chronological sequence, the approach has been to allow the book to move freely back and forward through history, over subject areas and critical approaches. The essays shift similarly from the consideration of historical moments, artists and cultural figures, to the analysis of a single work of art. They make references to painting, sculpture, photography, film, video and the printed media, but all see boxing and its images as a field of representation which crosses and confuses social and artistic hierarchies.

The essays are preceded by an extract from Joyce Carol Oates' seminal text *On Boxing*, both as an acknowledgement of that book's inspirational role in the formation of this anthology and to prepare the intellectual ground for the writing that follows. Oates' ideas rise to the surface repeatedly through these texts, as they do in this introduction; her fascination and her perspective as a woman overlooking and probing the determinedly male domain of boxing is especially relevant in a book that contains essays by four other women as well as the work of women artists.

In their essays both Sarah Hyde and Marcia Pointon consider the complex negotiations between the spheres of boxing and art in England at important moments during the early eighteenth and nineteenth centuries respectively. The essays provide a historical context for the class tensions and the aesthetic, intellectual discourses around the boxer's body which, though transformed, remain essential to contemporary debates about boxing and find echoes throughout this book. Importantly these essays look at representation, and propose visual culture as a key site in which these ideas were originally developed and contested.

Roger Lloyd Conover exposes another critical dialogue between boxing and art, this time from the early twentieth century. His essay, drawing on years of research, concerns the iconoclastic but elusive figure of Arthur Cravan, self-styled poet and boxer and tormentor of the Parisian art world c.1910-17. Cravan's quest for outrage, his violent polemic and his flamboyant physicality take up the threads that link boxing to aesthetics and spin them into an orbit of bizarre theatre. If Cravan was the precursor and embodiment of Dada, then, as Conover forcefully argues, he also used boxing in his degenerate strategy as an active symbol of confrontation and transgression.

As Cravan disappeared mysteriously off the face of the earth in November 1918 his more legitimate counterparts in the professional boxing ring were increasingly visible to a mass public and some were being lauded as national heros. Looking back at that historical moment, and specifically to a fight of 1927 between American Jack Dempsey and the Irish World Heavyweight Champion Gene Tunney, the artist James Colemen used the fight as a vehicle with which to explore elements of the ancient hero myth and investigate the role of representation in the formation of identity. Jean Fisher's essay offers an insightful analysis of Colemen's complex video work, *Box (Ahhareturnabout)*, 1977, placing it in the context of his other work of the 1970s and within the broader aesthetic debates of the period.

In their related essays, Ian Jeffrey and David Alan Mellor consider the perceived 'descent' of boxing from its high modernist ideals and position as an 'authentic' cultural phenomenon into the 'slam-bang brawls' favoured by new television audiences of the 1950s and later into a public relations exercise, increasingly determined by corporate interests. Jeffrey's essay examines how boxing was mediated by the images and poetic journalism of the American magazine *The Ring*

Andrew Heard, *Here we go, here we go*, 1988.
Installation photograph by David Catchpole.
Courtesy: Chris Hall.

Ingrid Pollard, *Contenders*, 1995. Commissioned by the Institute of International Visual Arts for the touring exhibition *Boxer*, curated by John Gill and organised by Walsall Museum and Art Gallery.
Installation photograph by David Catchpole.
Courtesy: The Artist.

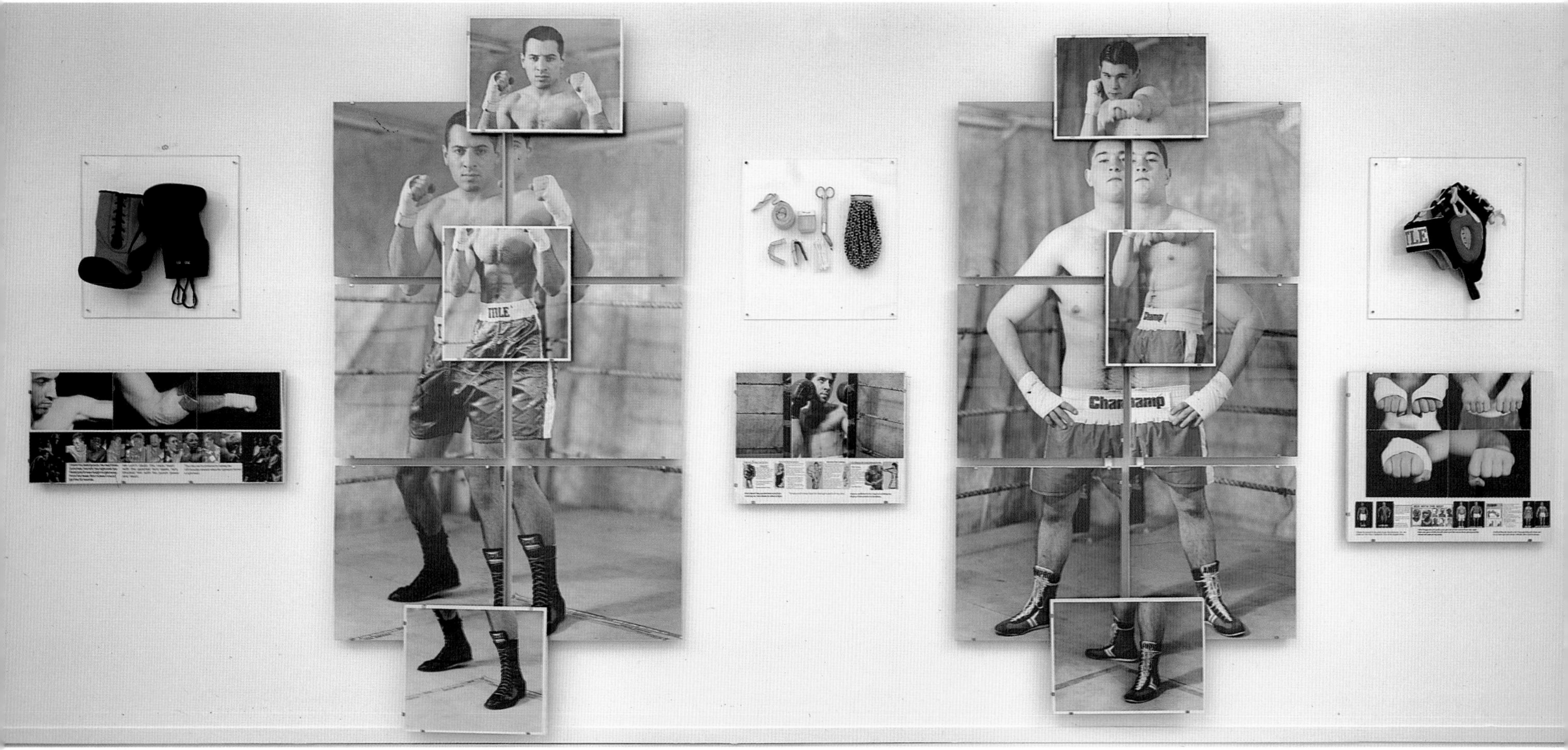

RANDY TURPIN
GENE FULLMER
CARMEN BASILIO
DICK TIGER
NINO BENVENUTI
CARLOS MONZON
RODRIGO VALDEZ
SONNY LISTON
LEON SPINKS
MIKE TYSON

BOXER

Jane Mulfinger and Graham Budgett, *A Grey Area*, 1995.
Commissioned by the Institute of International Visual Arts for the touring exhibition *Boxer*, curated by John Gill and organised by Walsall Museum and Art Gallery.
Courtesy: The Artists.

during the 1930s to 1950s, and how boxing's decline in the face of television's postmodern public was sorely lamented. *The Ring's* troubled script revolved around a detailed appraisal of the tested boxer figure as principal carrier of the sport's heroic mantel. David Alan Mellor uncovers similar narratives in the shadowy frames of post-war boxing films and his essay focuses on more recent cinematic attempts to 'recover' these films' 'authenticity' and to reinstate the boxer as an image of 'existential man in all his bleak grandeur'.

Nick James also delves into the often contradictory images of boxing films and looks at their particularly ambiguous representation of male sexuality. In Joyce Carol Oates' opinion the sexuality of boxing is exclusively homoerotic, something that for filmmakers anxious to construct model heterosexual heroes has created visual problems, narrative confusion and the side-stepping of overt eroticism in most boxing movies. As James has argued, when sex *is* invoked it is through the male body's relation to (heterosexual) power or impotence, and even when that power is lost the boxer's fall is associated with nostalgia for the 'pre-impotent lethal fist-fighter version of masculinity'.

For Jennifer Hargreaves this 'natural' identification of the boxer with the physical and psychological conditions of maleness is historically inaccurate, testifying to the denial of female physical power and to the overall repression of women in society. In her essay, Hargreaves reveals a largely unknown history of women's boxing (equally as violent and punishing as that of the male sport) as background to a cultural analysis of the recent rapid expansion of boxing related activities practised by women. Accompanying the growth of this new subculture have been an array of media images, particularly in advertising, depicting female boxers or women wearing boxing gloves. Hargreaves looks closely at some of these images and considers the tensions implicit in the broadening of femininity which they both confirm and deny.

As this book consistently shows, the image of the black boxer fuels the critical resonance of boxing in contemporary visual culture. If boxers carry the projected weight of many conflicting desires and expectations, generated throughout boxing's discursive spaces, then for the black boxer their representative meanings are even more accutely poised and potentially profound.
The conflicts and tensions embodied in the figure of the black boxer are especially charged, here the polarities of winner and loser, hero and victim, power and powerlessness, control and impotence are shot through with an entire history of struggle and oppression. In an essay which forms a textual background to his work *Four Corners* (1995), artist Keith Piper explores these tensions through the differing public images of four of the most celebrated black heavyweight champions, Jack Johnson, Joe Louis, Muhammad Ali and Mike Tyson. Piper considers the trangressive and iconic significance of these boxers who, in different ways and at different points in the twentieth century, had a profound influence on debates about race and in particular on perceptions of black masculinity.

For American artist Glenn Ligon the image of Muhammad Ali was an important catalyst in the formation of his racial pride in the late 1960s and 1970s and also in the awakening of his sexual identity. In the short autobiographical introduction to his work *Skin Tight*, Ligon, like Keith Piper, again confirms the impact of black boxers across a broad social front, as bringing a sense of empowerment to the disenfranchised communities from which they have emerged and, in the process, taking on a more historic role as cultural signifiers in the development of black consciousness.

Making a distinction between Sonny Liston, a boxer reknowned for his air of uncontrolled menace, and Floyd Patterson, often perceived as a cultured stylist in boxing terms, Joyce Carol Oates has said: "Sonny Liston was [...] so different in spirit from Floyd Patterson as to seem to belong to another sub species; to watch Liston overcome Patterson in tapes of their fights in the early 1960s is to watch the defeat of 'civilisation' by something so elemental and primitive it cannot be named."[11]
The vision of Liston conjured by LeRoi Jones (aka Amiri Baraka) however denotes a very different perspective. Jones has no illusions about 'naming' Liston's image: "Sonny Liston is the big black Negro in every white man's hallway, waiting to do him in, deal him under for all the hurt white men, through their abitrary order, have been able to inflict on the world [...] Sonny Liston is 'the huge Negro', the 'bad nigger', a heavy-faced replica of every whipped

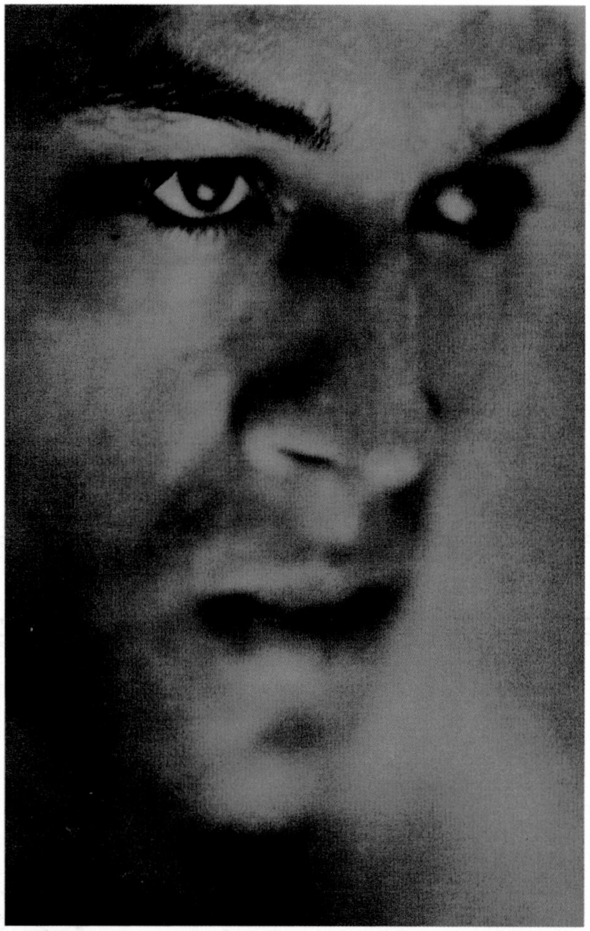

up woogie in the world. He is the underdeveloped, have-not (politically naive), backward country, the subject people, finally here to collect his pound of flesh."[12] Similarly for Eldridge Cleaver, writing in 1970, images of black boxers were tied intimately to an awareness of African American history and a developing black radical politics. In his view: "What America demands in her black champions is a brilliant, powerful body and a dull bestial mind." In contrast to Joyce Carol Oates, Cleaver saw Floyd Patterson as: "The symbolic spearhead of a counterrevolutionary host, leader of the mythical legions of faithful darkies who inhabit the white imagination." Cleaver looked on Patterson's fight with Muhammad Ali therefore as necessarily symbolic, because for him Ali was "the first 'free' black champion ever to confront white America [...] a genuine revolutionary, the black Fidel Castro of boxing."[13]

However, in his more recent book, *The Culture of Bruising*, Gerald Early has questioned this heroic definition of Ali and other black fighters since, arguing that: "Every black fighter, sooner or later, represents white interests of some sort." Early's overall view of the boxer is of a figure more fractured, less able to sustain the physical demands and moral dilemmas of his 'elevated' position: "Boxing, finally, for the black fighter is an apolitical, amoral experience of individual esteem, which the black fighter purchases at the expense of both his rival's health (and often his own) and his own dignity."[14]

Early cites a passage from Ralph Ellison's novel *Invisible Man* which sketches in a lyrical elaboration of the boxer's forlorn, tragic role. It is one significantly bound up with the interplay of race and vision, proposing a delicate exchange between boxing, boxers and their images: "I went across the room to a torn photograph tacked to a faded wall. It was a shot, in fighting stance, of a former prizefight champion, a popular fighter who had lost his sight in the ring [...] The photograph was that of a man so dark and battered that he might have been of any nationality. Big and loose-muscled, he looked like a good man. I remember my father's story of how he had been beaten blind in a crooked fight, of the scandal that had been supressed, and how the fighter had died in a home for the blind."[15]

The Douglas Brothers, *Boxer, Miami*. Included in the touring exhibition *Boxer*, curated by John Gill and organised by Walsall Museum and Art Gallery.
Courtesy: The Artists.

1 Joyce Carol Oates, *On Boxing*, [New Jersey, The Echo Press, 1994], pp.8.
2 Elliott J. Gorn, *The Manly Art: The Lives and Times of the Great Bare Knuckle Champions*, [London, Robson Books, 1989], pp.205.
3 William Hazlitt, 'The Fight', *William Hazlitt Selected Writings*, (London, Penguin, 1982), pp.89.
4 Joyce Carol Oates, op. cit., pp.15.
5 Elliott J. Gorn, op cit, pp.205.
6 Ibid, pp.205.
7 Joyce Carol Oates, op. cit., pp.8.
8 Budd Schulberg, *The Harder They Fall*, [New York, Random House, 1947], pp.89-90.
9 Vernon Scannell, see Jennifer Hargreaves' essay in this book.
10 Joyce Carol Oates, op. cit., pp.17.
11 Joyce carol Oates, op. cit., pp.74-75.
12 LeRoi Jones, 'Home: Dempsey–Liston Fight", *Social Essays*, [London, MacGibbon & Kee, 1968], pp.155-6.
13 Eldridge Cleaver, 'Lazarus, Come Forth', *Soul on Ice*, [London, Jonathan Cape, 1970], pp.92-93.
14 Gerald Early, 'The Black Intellectual', *The Culture of Bruising*, [New Jersey, The Ecco Press, 1994], pp.28.
15 Ibid, pp.30.

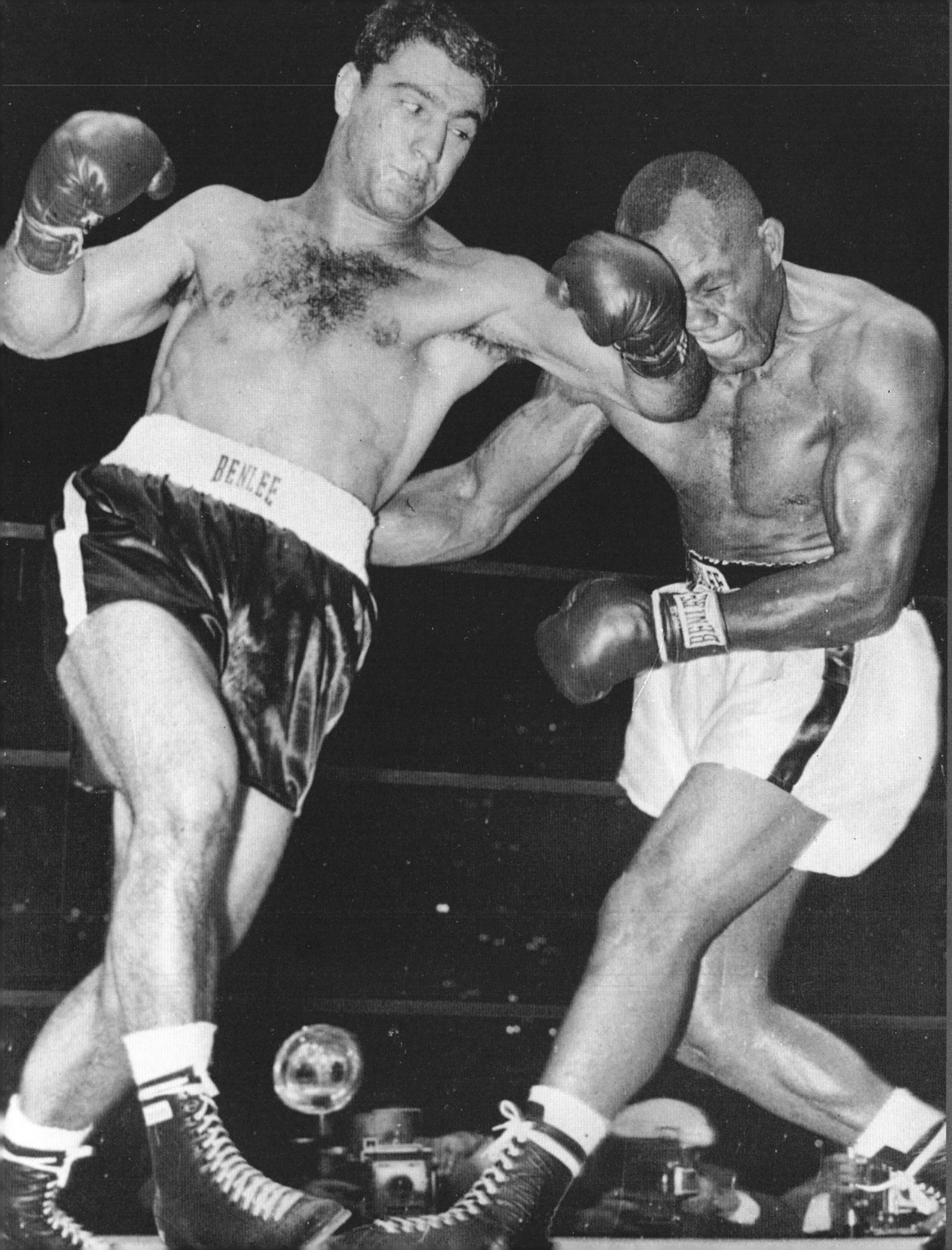
BENLEE
BENLEE

Rocky Marciano KO's Jersey Joe Walcott, February 1953.
Courtesy: The Ring Magazine.

On Boxing

Joyce Carol Oates

Each boxing match is a story – a unique and highly condensed drama without words. Even when nothing sensational happens: then the drama is 'merely' psychological. Boxers are there to establish an absolute experience, a public accounting of the outermost limits of their beings; they will know, as few of us can know of ourselves, what physical and psychic power they possess – of how much, or how little, they are capable. To enter the ring near-naked and to risk one's life is to make of one's audience voyeurs of a kind: boxing is so intimate. It is to ease out of sanity's consciousness and into another, difficult to name. It is to risk, and sometimes to realise, the agony of which *agon* (Greek, 'contest') is the root.

In the boxing ring there are two principle players, overseen by a shadowy third. The ceremonial ringing of the bell is a summoning to full wakefulness for both boxers and spectators. It sets into motion, too, the authority of Time.

The boxers will bring to the fight everything that is themselves, and everything will be exposed – including secrets about themselves they cannot fully realise. The physical self, the maleness, one might say, underlying the 'self'. There are boxers possessed of such remarkable intuition, such uncanny prescience, one would think they were somehow recalling their fights, not fighting them as we watch. There are boxers who perform skilfully, but mechanically, who cannot improvise in response to another's alteration of strategy; there are boxers performing at the peak of their talent who come to realise, mid-fight, that it will not be enough; there are boxers – including great champions – whose careers end abruptly, and irrevocably, as we watch. There has been at least one boxer possessed of an extraordinary and disquieting awareness not only of his opponent's every move and anticipated move but of the audience's keenest shifts in mood as well, for which he seems to have felt personally responsible – Cassius Clay-Muhammad Ali, of course. 'The Sweet Science of Bruising' celebrates the physicality of men even as it dramatises the limitations, sometimes tragic, more often poignant, of the physical. Though male spectators identify with boxers no boxer behaves like a 'normal' man when he is in the ring and no combination of blows is 'natural'. All is style.

Muhammad Ali vs. Sonny Liston, Miami Beach, February 1964.
Copyright: Hulton Deutsch Collection Ltd.

Muhammad Ali, December 1964. Stanley Weston Collection.
Courtesy: The Ring Magazine.

Every talent must unfold in fighting.
So Nietzsche speaks of the Hellenic past, the history of the 'contest' – athletic, and otherwise – by which Greek youths were educated into Greek citizenry. Without the ferocity of competition, without, even, 'envy, jealousy, and ambition' in the contest, the Hellenic city, like the Hellenic man, degenerated. If death is a risk, death is also the prize – for the winning athlete.

In the boxing ring, even in our greatly humanised times, death is always a possibility – which is why some of us prefer to watch films or tapes of fights already past, already defined as history. Or, in some instances, art. (Though to prepare for writing this mosaic-like essay I saw tapes of two infamous 'death' fights of recent times: the Lupe Pintor-Johnny Owen bantamweight match of 1982, and the Ray Mancini-Duk Koo-Kim light-weight match of the same year. In both instances the boxers died as a consequence of their astonishing resilience and apparent indefatigability – their 'heart', as it's known in boxing circles.) Most of the time, however, death in the ring is extremely unlikely; a statistically rare possibility like your possible death tomorrow morning in an automobile accident or in next month's headlined airline disaster or in a freak accident involving a fall on the stairs or in the bathtub, a skull fracture, subarachnoid haemorrhage. Spectators at 'death' fights often claim afterward that what happened simply seemed to happen – unpredictably, in a sense accidentally. Only in retrospect does death appear to have been inevitable.

If a boxing match is a story it is an always wayward story, one in which anything can happen. And in a matter of seconds. Split seconds! (Muhammad Ali boasted that he could throw a punch faster than the eye could follow, and he may have been right.) In no other sport can so much take place in so brief a period of time, and so irrevocably.

Because a boxing match is a story without words, this doesn't mean that it has no text or no language, that it is somehow 'brute', 'primitive', 'inarticulate', only that the text is improvised in action; the language a dialogue between the boxers of the most refined sort (one might say, as much neurological as psychological: a dialogue of split-second reflexes) in a joint response to the mysterious will of the audience which is always that the fight be a worthy one so that the crude paraphernalia of the setting – ring, lights, ropes, stained canvas, the staring onlookers themselves – be erased, forgotten. (As in the theatre or the church, settings are erased by way, ideally, of transcendent action.) Ringside announcers give to the wordless spectacle a narrative unity, yet boxing as performance is more clearly akin to dance or music than narrative.

To turn from an ordinary preliminary match to a 'Fight of the Century' like those between Joe Louis and Billy Con, Joe Frazier and Muhammad Ali, Marvin Hagler and Thomas Hearns is to turn from listening or half-listening to a guitar being idly plucked to hearing Bach's *Well-Tempered Clavier* perfectly executed, and that too is part of the story's mystery: so much happens so swiftly and with such heart-stopping subtlety you cannot absorb it except to know that something profound is happening and it is happening in a place beyond words.

Boxing's claim is that it is superior to life in that it is, ideally, superior to all accident. It contains nothing that is not fully willed.

The boxer meets an opponent who is a dream-distortion of himself in the sense that his weakness, his capacity to fail and to be seriously hurt, his intellectual miscalculations – all can be interpreted as strengths belonging to the Other; the parameters of his private being are nothing less than boundless assertions of the Other's self. This is dream, or nightmare: my strengths are not fully my own, but my opponent's triumph. He is my shadow-self, not my (mere) shadow. The boxing match as 'serious, complete, and of a certain magnitude' – to refer to Aristotle's definition of tragedy – is an event that necessarily subsumes both boxers, as any ceremony subsumes its participants. (Which is why one can say, for instance, that the greatest fight of Muhammad Ali's career was one of the few fights Ali lost – the first heroic match with Frazier.)

The old boxing adage – a truism surely untrue – that you cannot be knocked out if you see the blow coming, and if you *will* yourself not to be knocked out, has its subtler, more daunting significance: nothing that happens to the boxer in the ring, including death – 'his' death – is not of his own will or failure of will. The suggestion is of a world model in which we are humanly responsible not only for our own acts but for those performed against us.

Which is why, though springing from life, boxing is not a metaphor for life but a unique, closed, self-referential world, obliquely akin to those severe religions in which the individual is both 'free' and 'determined' – in one sense possessed of a will tantamount to God's, in another totally helpless. The Puritan sensibility would have understood a mouth filling with blood, an eye popped out of its socket – fit punishment for an instant's negligence.

A boxing trainer's most difficult task is said to be to persuade a young boxer to get up and continue fighting after he has been knocked down. And if the boxer has been knocked down by a blow he hadn't seen coming – which is usually the case – how can he hope to protect himself from being knocked down again and again? The invisible blow is after all – invisible.

'Normal' behaviour in the ring would be unbearable to watch, deeply shameful: for 'normal' beings share with all living creatures the instinct to persevere, as Spinoza said, in their own being. The boxer must somehow learn, by what effort of will non-boxers surely cannot guess, to inhibit his own instinct for survival; he must learn to exert his 'will' over his merely human and animal impulses, not only to flee pain but to flee the unknown. In psychic terms this sounds like magic. Levitation. Sanity turned inside out, 'madness' revealed as a higher and more pragmatic form of sanity.

The fighters in the ring are time-bound – surely nothing is so excruciatingly long as a fiercely contested three-minute round – but the fight itself is timeless. In a sense it becomes all fights, as the boxers are all boxers. By way of films, tapes, and photographs, it quickly becomes history for us, even, at times, art. Time, like the possibility of death, is the invisible adversary of which the boxers – and the referee, the seconds, the spectators – are keenly aware. When a boxer is 'knocked out' it does not mean, as it's commonly thought, that he has been knocked unconscious, or even incapacitated; it means rather more poetically that he has been knocked out of Time. (The referee's dramatic count of ten constitutes a metaphysical parenthesis of a kind through which the fallen boxer must penetrate if he hopes to continue in Time.) There are in a sense two dimensions of Time abruptly operant: while the standing boxer is *in time*, the fallen boxer is *out of time.* Counted out, he is counted 'dead' – in symbolic mimicry of the sport's ancient tradition in which he would very likely be dead. (Though, as we may recall, the canny Romans reserved for themselves as spectators the death blow itself: the triumphant gladiator was obliged to wait for a directive from outside the arena before he finished off his opponent.)

If boxing is a sport it is the most tragic of all sports because more than any human activity it consumes the very excellence it displays – its drama is this very consumption. To expend oneself in fighting the greatest fight of one's life is to begin by necessity the downward turn that next time may be a plunge, an abrupt fall into the abyss. *I am the greatest,* says Muhammad Ali. *I am the greatest* says, Marvellous Marvin Hagler. "You always think you're going to win," Jack Dempsey wryly observes in his old age, "otherwise you couldn't fight at all". The punishment – to the body, the brain, the spirit – a man must endure to become even a moderately good boxer is inconceivable to most of us whose idea of personal risk is largely ego-related or emotional. But the punishment as it begins to show in even a young and vigorous boxer is closely gauged by his rivals, who are waiting for him to slip. (After junior welterweight champion Aaron Pryor won a lacklustre fight last year a younger boxer in his weight division, interviewed at ringside, said with a smile: "My mouth is watering". And there was 29 year-old Billy Costello's bold statement – "If I can't beat an old man [of 33] then I should retire" – shortly before his bout with Alexis Arguello, in which he was knocked out in an early round.)

In the ring, boxers inhabit a curious sort of 'slow' time – amateurs never box beyond three rounds, and for most amateurs those nine minutes are exhausting – while outside the ring they inhabit an alarmingly accelerated time. A 23 year-old boxer is no longer young in the sense in which a 23 year-old man is young; a 35 year-old is frankly old. (Which is why Muhammad Ali made a tragic mistake in continuing his career after he had lost his title for the second time – to come out of retirement, aged 38, to fight Larry Holmes; and why Holmes made a similar mistake, years later, in needlessly exposing himself to injury, as well as professional embarrassment, by meeting with the light-heavyweight champion Michael Spinks. The victory of the 37 year-old Jersey Joe Walcott over the 30 year-old Ezzard Charles, for the heavyweight title in 1951, is *sui generis*. And Archie Moore is *sui generis*...) All athletes age rapidly but none so rapidly and so visibly as the boxer.

So it is, the experience of watching great fighters of the past is radically different from having seen them perform when they were reigning champions. Jack Johnson, Jack Dempsey, Joe Louis, Sugar Ray Robinson, Rocky Marciano, Muhammad Ali, Joe Frazier – as spectators we know not only how a fight but how a career ends. The trajectory not merely of ten or fifteen rounds but that of an entire life...

Everything that man esteems
Endures a moment or a day.
Love's pleasure drives his love away,
The painter's brush consumes his dreams:
The herald's cry, the soldier's tread
Exhaust his glory and his might:
Whatever flames upon the night
Man's own resinous heart has fed.
– William Butler Yeats,
from *The Resurrection*

Jack Dempsey and manager Jack Kearns, c. 1920s.
Courtesy: The Ring Magazine.

Sonny Liston, 20 July 1962. Stanley Weston Collection.
Courtesy: The Ring Magazine.

Actress Clara Bow, posing on Malibu Beach, January 1927.

A fairy-tale proposition: the heavyweight champion is the most dangerous man on earth: the most feared, the most manly. His proper mate is very likely the fairy-tale princess whom the mirrors declare the fairest woman on earth.

Boxing is a purely masculine activity and it inhabits a purely masculine world. Which is not to suggest that most men are defined by it: clearly, most men are not. And though there are female boxers – a fact that seems to surprise, alarm, amuse – women's role in the sport has always been extremely marginal. (At the time of this writing the most famous American woman boxer is the black champion Lady Tyger Trimiar with her shaved head and theatrical tiger-striped attire). At boxing matches women's role is limited to that of card girl and occasional National Anthem singer: stereotypical functions usually performed in stereotypically zestful feminine ways – for women have no natural place in the spectacle otherwise. The card girls in their bathing suits and spike heels, glamour girls of the 1950s, complement the boxers in their trunks and gym shoes but are not to be taken seriously: their public exhibition of themselves involves no risk and is purely decorative. Boxing is for men, and is about men, and *is* men. A celebration of the lost religion of masculinity all the more trenchant for its being lost.

In this world, strength of a certain kind – matched of course with intelligence and tirelessly developed skills – determines masculinity. Just as a boxer is his body, a man's masculinity is his use of his body. But it is also his triumph over another's use of his body. The Opponent is always male, the Opponent is the rival for one's own masculinity, most fully and combatively realised. Sugar Ray Leonard speaks of coming out of retirement to fight one man, Marvin Hagler: "I want Hagler. I need that man". Thomas Hearns, decisively beaten by Hagler, speaks of having been obsessed with him: "I want the rematch badly [...] there hasn't been a minute or an hour in any day that I haven't thought about it." Hence women's characteristic repugnance for boxing *per se* coupled with an intense interest in and curiosity about men's fascination with it. Men fighting men to determine worth (i.e. masculinity) excludes women as completely as the female experience of childbirth excludes men. And is there, perhaps, some connection?

In any case, raw aggression is thought to be the peculiar province of men, as nurturing is the peculiar province of women. (The female boxer violates this stereotype and cannot be taken seriously – she is parody, she is cartoon, she is monstrous. Had she an ideology, she is likely to be a feminist.) The psychologist Erik Erikson discovered that, while little girls playing with blocks generally create pleasant interior spaces and attractive entrances, little boys are inclined to pile up the blocks as high as they can and then watch them fall down: "The contemplation of ruins," Erikson observes, "is a masculine speciality". No matter the mesmerising grace and beauty of a great boxing match, it is the catastrophic finale for which everyone waits, and hopes: the blocks piled as high as they can possibly be piled, then brought spectacularly down. Women, watching a boxing match, are likely to identify with the losing, or hurt, boxer; men are likely to identify with the winning boxer. There is a point at which male spectators are able to identify with the fight itself as, it might be said, a Platonic experience abstracted from its particulars; if they have favoured one boxer over another, and that boxer is losing, they can shift their loyalty to the winner – or, rather, 'loyalty' shifts, apart from conscious volition. In that way the ritual of fighting is always honoured. The high worth of combat is always affirmed.

Boxing's very vocabulary suggests a patriarchal world taken over by adolescents. This world is young. Its focus is youth. Its focus is of course *macho* – *machismo* raised beyond parody. To enter the claustrophobic world of professional boxing even as a spectator is to enter what appears to be a distillation of the masculine world, empty now of women, its fantasies, hopes, and stratagems magnified as in a distorting mirror, or dream.

Here, we find ourselves through the looking-glass. Values are reversed, evaginated: a boxer is valued not for his humanity but for being a 'killer', a 'mauler', a 'hit-man', an 'animal', for being 'savage', 'merciless', 'devastating', 'ferocious', 'vicious', 'murderous'. Opponents are not merely defeated as in a game but are 'decked', 'stiffed', 'starched', 'iced', 'destroyed', 'annihilated'. Even the veteran sportswriters of so respectable a publication as *The Ring* are likely to be pitiless toward a boxer who has been beaten. Much of the appeal of Roberto Durán for intellectual boxing *aficionados* no less than for those whom one might suppose his natural constituency was that he seemed truly to want to kill his opponents: in his prime he was the 'baby-faced assassin' with 'dead eyes' and 'deadpan' expression who once said, having knocked out an opponent named Ray Lampkin, that he hadn't trained for the fight – next time he would kill the man. (According to legend Durán once felled a horse with a single blow.) Sonny Liston was another champion lauded for his menace, so different in spirit from Floyd Patterson as to seem to belong to another sub-species; to watch Liston overcome Patterson in tapes of their fights in the early 1960s is to watch the defeat of 'civilisation' by something so elemental and primitive it cannot be named. Masculinity in these terms is strictly hierarchical – two men cannot occupy the same space at the same time.

It was once said by José Torres that the *machismo* of boxing is a condition of poverty. But it is not, surely, a condition uniquely of poverty. Or even of adolescence. I think of it as the obverse of the feminine, the denial of the feminine-in-man that has its ambiguous attractions for all men, however 'civilised'. It is a remnant of another, earlier era when the physical being was primary and the warrior's masculinity its highest expression.

ATHLETA · BRITANNICUS,
99

Charles Rossi, *The British Pugilist*, 1828. Petworth House (Sussex), The National Trust.
Courtesy: The Courtauld Institute of Art.

Pugilism, Painters and National Identity in Early Nineteenth-Century England

Marcia Pointon

"By this time they had stripped, and presented a strong contrast in appearance. If Neate was like Ajax, 'with Atlantean shoulders, fit to bear' the pugilistic reputation of all Bristol, Hickman might be compared to Diomed, light vigorous, elastic, and his back glistened in the sun, as he moved about, like a panther's hide. There was now a dead pause – attention was awe-struck. Who at that moment, big with a great event, did not draw his breath short – did not feel his heart throb? All was ready. They tossed up for the sun, and the Gasman won. They were led up to the scratch – shook hands, and went at it."
– W. Hazlitt, 'The Fight', first published in *The New Monthly Magazine*, (February 1822)

In his celebrated essay, 'The Fight', William Hazlitt (1778-1830) describes travelling by coach to a boxing match in Newbury; he evokes the anticipation and thrill of the fight in language combining vernacular terms with ideas about masculine beauty grounded in the educated gentleman's engagement with Classical culture. The attraction of the fight to Hazlitt lay in no small degree in the populist nature of an event where men of all classes mingled, where it was possible to gaze upon highly developed masculine musculature, and where comparisons between the physical characteristics of boxers could be made. Hazlitt was unusual only in his capacity to translate his experience into a gripping narrative for those members of a literate urban audience not fortunate enough to get to Newbury. This essay examines the context of Hazlitt's narrative, exploring the connections between boxing and the elite world of the Royal Academy – its members, students and patrons – in early nineteenth-century England.

On 19 June 1808 at 12.30pm the Royal Academician, Joseph Farington, visited his friend Dr Anthony Carlisle, and found "a room filled with company at breakfast". After the repast Carlisle (shortly to be elected Professor of Anatomy at the Royal Academy and, in 1821, to receive a knighthood as Surgeon Extraordinary to the Prince Regent) showed the company into his front drawing room where: "We found Gregson, the Pugilist stripped naked to be exhibited to us on acct of the fineness of his form – he is six feet two inches high – all admired the beauty of his proportions from the knee or rather from the waist upwards including his arms & small head – The bone of his leg it was Sd is too short & His toes are not long enough & there is something of heaviness abt the thighs, knees & legs – but on the whole He was allowed to be the finest figure the persons present had seen He was placed in many attitudes."

The pugilist told Farington about his Lancashire origins and his recent fight with Gulley (who gained respectability as MP for Pontefract and colliery proprietor), then the company made a collection of five shillings each and the whole party was invited to meet Gregson at Lord Elgin's later that month "to compare His form with some of the antique figures". Farington concludes his diary entry in his customary fashion with a list of those present. On this occasion they included the painters West, Northcote, Daniell, Shee, Howard and Westmacott.[1] The meeting at Lord Elgin's naturally attracted more attention because of the sensational idea of posing the boxer nude among the recently imported fragments of the Parthenon frieze (now in the British Museum). Of even greater news value was a further meeting, also at Lord Elgin's, on 29 July when four pugilists staged a sparring match.

The Royal Academicians whom Farington records as present at Carlisle's house were among the most favoured and promising members of the London artistic establishment at the time. When Gregson, the pugilist, posed "in many attitudes" in the courtyard of Lord Elgin's residence in Piccadilly the company was more numerous and even more distinguished. It included most of the Academicians who had attended Carlisle's display but also Sir George Beaumont (amateur artist, collector and patron of Turner, Constable and Wilkie); Sir William Beechey (portraitist of the Royal family); Robert Smirke (the most promising young British architect of his day and future designer of the British Museum); Thomas Lawrence (Treasurer of the Royal Academy, who was to be knighted by the Prince Regent in 1815 and to become President of the Royal Academy in 1820); John Hoppner (portrait painter to the Prince of Wales); Charles Rossi (whose sculpture *The British Pugilist* of 1828 was purchased by Lord Egremont); and finally, one of the most highly regarded landscape painters of the period, Augustus Wall Callcott (knighted in 1837).

On 29 July 1808, when the sparring match between Gulley, Belcher, Dutch Sam and Gentleman Jackson took place, the company was very much the same with the addition of two sculptors: John Flaxman and Joseph Nollekens; and Charles Bell, surgeon and author of a tract on physiognomy, *Essays on the Anatomy of Expression in Painting* (1806). Farington gives the impression of a relatively sober affair with Dutch Sam's figure (five foot six inches, nine stone and seven and a half pounds) being much admired by Rossi on account of its symmetry, an admiration which must have inspired his heroic sculpture. A rather different account is given by Charles Bell: "He [Lord Elgin] proposed a great treat to his friends. He entertained an ingenious notion that, by exposing the natural figures of some of our modern athletes in contrast with the marbles, the perfection of the antique would be felt, and that we should see that the sculptors of the best time of Greece did not deviate from nature [...] but no sooner was the bulky form of Jackson, no longer young, opposed to the fine elastic figure of the champion of all England, than a cry arose, and 'the ring' pressed forward; and ancient art and the works of Phidias were forgotten."[2]

According to William Whitley, Bell had heard of the meeting at Lord Elgin's on 30 June and "was not pleased," so Lord Elgin invited him to a second exhibition of the same nature presumably so that he could judge for himself. Bell clearly had no knowledge of Carlisle's prior exhibition otherwise he would not have referred to Lord Elgin's "ingenious notion". In view of the turn of events later that year it might have been as well for Bell had he known of Carlisle's precedent and endeavoured to disguise his own disapproval. The necessity of canvassing energetically for membership or office within the Royal Academy was a fact of life in London artistic society in the early nineteenth century.[3] Undoubtedly Carlisle's success in establishing a fashionable way of combining sporting, anatomical and artistic interests contributed to the overwhelming vote of 25 to four in his favour in December of the same year when he was in competition with Charles Bell for the Professorship of Anatomy at the Royal Academy.

For the early nineteenth-century English gentleman, boxing epitomised heroic and patriotic masculinity while also allowing a transgressive relationship to 'low life' customs and practices. Rossi's sculpture of 1828 is not just any muscular figure but *The 'British' Pugilist*. In 1832 Eugene Delacroix was to remark that he found in Moroccan towns and villages "men of the consular type, Catos and Brutuses [...] The Antique has nothing more beautiful."[4] Cultivated Englishmen in the early years of the century searching for a modern equivalent to antique nobility found the same heroic qualities in British pugilists. In *Boxiana: Sketches of Ancient and Modern Pugilism* (1812) one of the most celebrated writers on boxing, Pierce Egan, reminded his readers of the Greco-Roman origins of the sport while asserting that "the manly art of Boxing, has infused that true heroic courage, blended with humanity into the hearts of Britons, which have made them so renowned, terrific and triumphant, in all parts of the world. We feel no hesitation," states Egan, "in declaring that it is wholly – BRITISH".[5] Typically, his description of the Game Chicken – a celebrated pugilist who died in 1800 and who was immortalised by Egan – depends heavily on standards of comparison between Greek heroes and modern day pugilists which must derive from the sort of exhibition that impressed Farington at Carlisle's and Lord Elgin's in 1808. In style Egan's prose also evokes Winckelmann, Lessing and other well-known eighteenth-century writers on antique sculpture: "It might be said of the Game Chicken that he was not only a favourite, but a pupil of the [...] Deity [Nature] and who, in giving him a fine athletic form, strength, wind and agility, had finely tempered those rare requisites with the most manly courage and sublime feeling; and, *if* ever greatness of soul raised the character of man, or humanity alone resplendent in the breast of a human being – a purer claim to those inestimable qualities were never witnessed, than that of Henry Pearce."

Winckelmann had stated in his extremely influential *On the limitation of the Painting and Sculpture of the Greeks* (1755) that the excellence of Greek art was due to the availability of fine models in a genial climate: "The gymnasia, where, sheltered by public modesty, the youths exercised themselves naked, were the schools of art. These the philosopher frequented, as well as the artist. Socrates for the instruction of a Charmides, Autolycus, Lysis; Phidias for the improvement of his art by their beauty. Here he studied the elasticity of the muscles, the ever varying motions of the frame, the outlines of fair forms, or the contour left by a young wrestler on the sand. Here beautiful nakedness appeared with such liveliness of expression, such truth and variety of situations, such a noble air of the body, as it would be ridiculous to look for in any hired model of our academies."[6]

It followed, therefore, that England would never establish the long-desired national school of history painting or heroic sculpture unless the climatic disadvantage could be overcome. Charles Bell remarked that the deficiencies of anatomical drawing in this country were hardly surprising given the fact that men of heroic physique were not to be observed walking around in the nude providing inspiration and the means of study to young artists. The most aspiring artists could hope for in 1806 was an academy model "probably some hired artisan, with his muscles unequally developed by the labour of his trade, pale and shivering, and offering none of those fine carnations which more constant exposure gives to the body, as we see in the face, nor having that elegant freedom of limb, which youth, under a genial climate and the various exercises of the gymnasium acquired."[7]

By the time Dickens published *Dombey and Son* (1846-8) the idea that there might be found in the British pugilist a descendant of those men of Olympian beauty described by Winckelmann but not normally seen in nineteenth-century England must have been familiar to an audience not in any way confined to Royal Academicians. Pierce Egan had established an inflated literary style for writing about boxing and Dickens was thus able to be deeply ironic in describing The Game Chicken, the pugilistic companion of Florence Dombey's admirer, as "quite the Apollo of Mr. Toots' Pantheon". Dickens was undoubtedly drawing attention to the decline of the sport in the middle years of the century, yet the fact that he compares this person (who "wore a bright, red fireman's coat" when steering Mr. Toots' six-oared cutter down the Thames and "concealed the perpetual black eye with which he was afflicted beneath a green shade") with the God of music and poetry, youth and beauty, suggests that he had in mind an idea of the heroic physique of the pugilist that was still widely accepted.

For Farington and his friends, the glory of Gregson, Gulley and Belcher was their physique and if that could be studied and measured at close quarters in a natural state so much the better. For Ruskin, a generation later, discipline and moral strength were qualities associated with boxing but nudity was quite another matter. Believing that artists should study "the souls of men in their bodies, not their bodies alone," Ruskin made a violent attack on one of his contemporaries, William Mulready, whose fine life studies he described as "more degraded and bestial than the worst grotesques of the Byzantine or even the Indian image makers". Ruskin was deeply suspicious of nude statuary and the life class and yet boxing received his approval in *Modern Painters* (1860) as a sport which, unlike field sports, did not waste "time, land, and energy of soul".[8] It would never have occurred to Ruskin to acknowledge an implicit connection between nudity and boxing. Similarly, Thomas Hughes' 'muscular Christians' maintained the "old chivalrous and Christian belief, that a man's body is given him to be trained and brought into subjection, and then used for the protection of the weak, the advancement of all righteous causes, and the subduing of the earth which God has given to the children of men".[9] The neo-classical attitude to the nude which was covertly hedonistic and by which Farington and his friends were influenced had, by the middle of the century, become divorced from ideals of sport in the minds of writers like Ruskin and Hughes. For the Victorians, Winckelmann and his world were well and truly dead and, although the association between pugilism and the art of antiquity lingered to be exploited in an ironic fashion by Dickens, boxing now belonged either to the boys of Rugby school at one extreme or to a criminal underworld at the other.[10]

Farington and his friends did not limit their interest in pugilists to the discreet confines of their own residences. Robert Smirke and Thomas Lawrence watched the contest between Cribb and Tom Molineux in pouring rain at East Grinstead on 10 September 1810 along with 20,000 other spectators, having dissuaded the 72-year-old President of the Academy, Sir Benjamin West, from accompanying them.[11] However, they do not appear to have themselves participated in the sport. The younger generation of artists did exactly that.

William Mulready (1786-1863) and his friends John Varley, John Linnell and George Dawe were all in their twenties at the time of Lord Elgin's exhibition. Already their interests were directed towards a new form of naturalistic landscape painting in and around the area of the Kensington Gravel Pits and brick kilns.[12] Their preoccupation with a semi-urban landscape quite alien from the Italianate landscape tradition – tolerated within the Academy since Richard Wilson (1724-82) had made this lowly form of art respectable – immediately establishes a gulf between them and the older generation of artists who met at Carlisle's and Lord Elgin's. The Varley brothers were friends of Blake and while Linnell certainly aspired to academic success he was never one of the academic establishment and is often now remembered chiefly as the father-in-law of the highly non-conformist Samuel Palmer. Also Mulready and Dawe spent much of their time in 1805-8 with William Godwin and his circle of radically minded friends. However, to identify changes in aspiration among artists in the early nineteenth century is a difficult task. Mulready's *Pancrastinae* suggests an interest in boxers not dissimilar from Rossi's concern with a masculine heroic form based on antique models, and yet there is a world of difference between Rossi's *British Pugilist* and Mulready's *The Fight Interrupted* of 1816, an image of a playground quarrel between boys (Victoria and Albert Museum).

Mulready and his young friends would scarcely have expected an invitation to join Lord Elgin and his friends in viewing Gregson nude among the marbles. But they did not lack the means of studying the physique, attitudes and movements of pugilists first hand. Mulready was himself well known among his friends as a powerful pugilist. Indeed his son, Paul, told Albert Varley (John Varley's eldest son) when he enquired about ill-feelings among the extremely quarrelsome members of the Mulready family, that he could forgive every wrong his father had done towards them except his failure to reveal one of the first principles of boxing: that one should never keep the fist tightly clenched or the muscles become strained. That failure he would never forgive as long as he lived.[13]

The celebrated pugilist Mendoza was Mulready's teacher and is said to have found the artist the best pupil he ever had. An entertaining anecdote concerning the two men is related by Mulready's biographer. Late in Mendoza's life, after a considerable lapse of time in their acquaintance, Mulready met him at the stage door of Drury Lane Theatre. Following the usual exchange of greetings, Mulready was asked by his erstwhile boxing master what he was doing. "Well," said Mulready, who by that time was well known, "I've been painting pictures". "Ah!" cried the champion, with an apologetic sigh, "we must all do something !"[14]

Mulready's biography also recounts innumerable stories about Royal Academy students 'setting to' with their tongues and fists against the bargees who frequented the riverside tavern, 'The Fox under the Hill'. It was said that Mulready, at the sight of any row in the street "would stay any conversation, and quit any company to study the changes of a fight. He would dodge about the lookers-on for scientific points of view, and with head advanced and set lips, followed the combat, watched the champions as they went round and round, attended each attack with ardour, and each retreat with expectation."

John Linnell was only five feet five inches high. He strained himself trying to keep pace with Mulready's pugilistic skills and "never completely

THE SECOND CONTEST BETWEEN CRIB & MOLINEUX, SEPT.R 28:1811.
Published by Geo. Smeeton, Dec.r 17. 1812.

Anonymous engraving after William Mulready, *The Second Contest between Cribb and Molineux*, 28 September 1811, from Pierce Egan's 'Boxiana', 1812.

recovered". He cannot, however, have been wholly unsuccessful as a boxer since in 1850 he is reported to have still had in his possession a boxing glove stained with the blood of his former opponent George Dawe.[15] Varley's house was described by Linnell's biographer as "a regular school of boxing" and Linnell himself referred to the Royal Academy during the early years of the century as "quite a boxing school for artists".

On at least one occasion a match all but took place on the august premises of the Royal Academy itself. Linnell tells the story: "I acquired much physical as well as mental development from my intercourse with Mulready who taught me the use of the gloves at which he was first rate. I never knew him to be engaged in a serious contest with fists though he was very near it once at the RA. One of the porters who had been a pugilist was drunk and very abusive and threatened some students. Mulready took up their defence and offered to fight the porter who very wisely declined the contest and succumbed [...] The porter was called Little Sam to distinguish him from the other porter Sam-Strowger, who was a tall man and the usual model in the life academy. Little Sam was a stout paunchy man about forty, a low bred man and often drunk. Mulready had pulled off his coat and I as a second with a lot of students were going out of the Hall for the square at Somerset House (a rather bad place for a fall, because all rough stone) when Little Sam gave in [...]"[16]

Pierce Egan would certainly have approved the settling of a dispute of honour by means of the gloves. The happy outcome of the quarrel between the Royal Academy students and Little Sam would have evidenced his assertions concerning the superiority of the British with their boxing to the other European nations who allegedly settled all their quarrels with the stiletto or the rapier.[17] Egan probably knew Mulready as a fellow Irishman through mutual ringside acquaintance. Mulready was commissioned to execute nineteen out of 22 engraved illustrations to Boxiana as well as contributing a portrait of Egan.[18] The other three were the work of the Cruikshank brothers who subsequently co-operated with Egan on the *Boxing Mirror*, the *Sportsman's Gazette* (1813) and *Life in London* (1821).[19] It could have been these illustrations which influenced Gericault in 1818 when executing his lithograph *Combat de Boxe*.

The attention which the eighteen-year-old artist paid to physiognomy in *Boxiana* and the way in which he painstakingly recorded facial expression (even in the case of posthumous portraits) testifies to his own ability as an artist. His solemn portraits also reflect the author's oft-advertised view of the nobility and magnanimity of the best pugilists. It is symptomatic of the changing attitudes to the sport, of the alienation from the idea of antique grandeur, that Egan's later works were illustrated not by Mulready (who, as well as being interested in physiognomy, was also celebrated for his life drawings) but by George Cruikshank, who was skilled in representing crowds. Gradually the audience takes over. In *London* (published in 1872, the drawings executed in 1869) Gustave Doré is fascinated more by the spectators – who are but cursorily treated in Mulready's illustration of the second contest between Cribb and Molineux in 1811 – than by the fight itself.

The taste for pugilism displayed by Farington's friends did on occasions benefit the younger group of artists, but their resultant productions were markedly different. In 1810 George Dawe took advantage of Anthony Carlisle's discovery in a hospital in Liverpool of a black sailor who possessed in Farington's words "the character and perfection of many of the antique statues" and whose arm, when suspended, "appeared like that of the Antinous" and, when contracted, "like the Farnese Hercules" – Lawrence made an oil study of the man and Dawe paid him two guineas a week to pose for him.[20] The following year Dawe won a premium at the British Institution (established in 1806 as a rival exhibition body to the Academy) for his painting *A Negro overpowering a Buffalo*. The picture is now lost but such a subject probably did not reflect a slavish devotion to the antique but rather a new-found Godwinian concern with liberty combined with notions of superior natural strength of the sort incorporated seven years later into a black male figure symbolising hope at the apex of the composition in Géricault's *The Raft of the Medusa* (Musée du Louvre).

The younger generation of artists looked to pugilism from an empirical viewpoint. Their concern was with actuality not with the ideal. Physiognomy interested them as much as physique and they related what they experienced not to nostalgia for the lost excellencies of the antique world but to the aspirations and idiosyncrasies of their own society. The encounters with pugilists arranged by Carlisle and Lord Elgin in 1808 were part of a homosocial pattern that was class-specific and mediated through aesthetic discourse. They also offered the occasion for a comparative racial typology implicit in Carlisle's 'discovery' in Liverpool and in the interest shown in black boxers. It would be interesting to know whether the black male figure that forms part of Westmacott's monument to Charles James Fox (Westminster Abbey) was modelled from a boxer. Certainly such models were available. *Boxiana* lists, for example, Bill Richmond "a man of colour and native of America" and the frequently portrayed Molineux was black. But Rossi's model was white and he never tried his hand again at anything like *The British Pugilist* after 1828. These artists wanted the classical principles of art tested against the model. For Mulready, on the other hand, and as far as one can tell for George Dawe also, boxing was not only an enjoyable pastime and the means of studying heroic physiques but also offered the artist insight into human psychology and experience.

A macabre but interesting example of the professional relationships between artists and pugilists provides a fitting conclusion to a tale which begins with an attempt by aristocrats and gentlemen to resurrect the world that Winckelmann had evoked. In December 1823 all London was buzzing with the news of the trial for murder at Hertford Assizes of the trainer and boxing promoter John Thurtell (the Mr Turtle of Hazlitt's 'The Fight'), and two other men, William Probert and Joseph Hunt. The unprecedented interest was due, it has been suggested, to the increasing role of the newspapers as reporters of criminal proceedings and the connection of Thurtell with the world of the Fancy and, in a lesser way, with that of the theatre.[21] Egan attended the trial and, having interviewed the condemned prisoner whose calm self-possession impressed everyone, wrote a booklet early in 1824.[22] Mulready was also among those attracted to the trial and, infected by the desperate haste for up-to-date news bulletins which characterised the affair, as soon as the verdict was announced dispatched an account of the trial and the deportment of the accused to his patron, Sir John Swinburne, in Northumberland. Mulready believed that Swinburne would be unable to tolerate the inevitable delay in receiving the account published in the *Examiner*.[23] The artist describes to Sir John not the ex-pugilist's physique or appearance but his

William Mulready, *Portrait of John Thurtell*.
Courtesy: The Board of Trustees of The Victoria & Albert Museum.

bearing and his manner, a description which echoes the drawings Mulready executed of the prisoner: "There is one thing upon which I unfortunately cannot agree with anybody, the feelings expressed by the countenances and actions of the prisoners. I dare not venture to begin a detailed description of all that I thought I saw, but I must say that Thurtell appeared to me to be ever, with the exception of a very few moments, on the watch, assiduously on the watch and ready to seize upon any little slip in the evidence of the witnesses against him or any trifling contradiction or appearance of contradiction amongst them: but he never had a single chance and it was extremely painful to me to see towards the close of the evidence for the prosecution, the agony and death of his watchfulness and the 'gathering up of himself' to hear the worst."[24]

Thurtell was condemned to death and executed on 9 January 1824. His body was consigned to the surgeons and, plaster casts having been taken, it was used by the students at Sass's art school in their attempts to master anatomy. Some time later, William Mulready received the following communication: "My friend the surgeon has recently received the skeleton of the unfortunate Thurtell and I am informed as fine a one as was ever seen. The inspection of it will be freely granted to you."[25] It was hoped in some quarters that the execution of Thurtell might at least provoke reflection, if not terror, among his former associates. However, as the reporter in the *Examiner* remarked: "Though they were aware that Thurtell's first plunge into crime was occasioned by his predilection for prizefighting and other similar savage amusements, many of them were speculating, at the very moment before his death, whether he had heard of the recent fight which took place near Worcester."[26]

This is a revised version of an essay that was first published in the *Gazette des Beaux-Arts*, October 1978.

**I would like to thank David Mellor for remembering it, Gilane Tawadros for liking it, and David Chandler and Tania Guha for editing it.
MP**

1 *The Farington Diary*, 19 June 1808, (Windsor, MS Royal Library). Ed. K. Garlick and K. Cave, *The Farington Diary*, (Yale University Press, 1984). An index is in preparation at the Mellon Centre for Studies in British Art.
2 Sir Charles Bell, *The Anatomy and Philosophy of Expression as connected with the Fine Arts*, (London, G. Bell & Sons, 1890), seventh edition revised, pp.10-11. First published as Sir Charles Bell, *Essays on the Anatomy of Expression in Painting*, (London, Longmans & Co., 1806).
3 For primary sources on this problem see contemporary diaries and letters e.g. *The Farington Diary*; Ed. W.B. Pope,*The Diary of Benjamin Robert Haydon*, (Cambridge, Mass., Harvard University Press, 1963); Ed. R.B. Beckett, *John Constable's Correspondence*, (Ipswich, Suffolk Records Society, 1962-75).
4 Ed. Andre Joubin, *Correspondance Generale d'Eugene Delacroix*, (Paris, 1935, 29 Feb. 1832), vol. i, p.319.
5 Pierce Egan, *Boxiana: Sketches of Ancient and Modern Pugilism*, (London, Sherwood, Neely and Jones, 1812). Facsimile ed. D. Prestidge introd. (Leicester, Vance Harvey Publishing, 1971), p.14. Egan was celebrated for his authorship of *Life in London*; or *The Day and Night Scenes of Jerry Hawthorne Esq., and His Elegant Friend Corinthian Tom...*, (London, Sherwood, Neely and Jones, 1821).
6 English translation by J.H. Fuseli in 1765; D.Irwin ed. *Winckelmann, Writings on Art*, (London, Phaidon, 1972), p.64. This selection also contains passages from Winckelmann's *History of Ancient Art* (1764) in which his influential climatic theories were elaborated. For a recent discussion of Winckelmann in relation to theories of masculinity, see A. Potts, *Flesh and the Ideal*, (New Haven and London, Yale University Press, 1944).
7 Sir Charles Bell, op. cit., p.10.
8 J. Ruskin, 'Val d'Arno', *The Works of John Ruskin*, (Library Edition, XXIII, 1874), p. 18; *Modern Painters*, V, op. cit., 1860, VIII, p.34a.
9 Thomas Hughes, *Tom Brown at Oxford*, first published 1861, ch. XI.
10 For a discussion of the latter subject see K. Chesney, *The Victorian Underworld*, (Harmondsworth, Penguin Books, 1970).
11 *The Farington Diary*, 22 December 1810.
12 For conditions in Kensington at this time see P. Malcolmson, 'Getting a living in the Slums of Victorian Kensington', *London Journal*, 1975, 1, No.1. For examples of the work of the gravel pit painters see London, Colnaghi, *A Loan Exhibition of Drawings, Watercolours, and Paintings by John Linnell and his Circle*, (10 January – 2 February 1973).
13 A.T. Story, *James Holmes and John Varley*, (London, Richard Bentley and Sons, 1894), pp. 238-9.
14 F.G. Stephens, *Memorials of William Mulready*, (London, Bell & Daldy, 1807), pp. 74-5.
15 A.T. Story, *The Life of John Linnell*, (London, Richard Bentley & Son, 1892), i, pp.33-4.
16 J. Linnell, *Autobiographical Notes*, MS, The Linnell Trust. The story is told in abbreviated form in Story, op. cit. p.33.
17 That the association between British pugilism and national honour survives is evinced by an incident in Bosnia reported in *The Times* (3 August 1995) in which allegedly a British amateur boxer, Corporal Neil Coull, serving with the UN forces, was challenged to fight at a Muslim roadblock and, knocking out his opponent in thirty seconds, opened an aid route to a Canadian convoy.
18 Unlocated, undated MS list of portraits, London, National Art Library, Victoria and Albert Museum, 86 NN 1.
19 A.M. Cohn, *George Cruikshank: A Catalogue Raisonné...*, (London, from the Office of 'The Bookman's Journal', 1924), pp.260-3.
20 *The Farington Diary*, 18 August 1810.
21 C. Reid, *Bucks and Bruisers, Pierce Egan and Regency England*, (London, Routledge and Kegan Paul, 1971), p.105.
22 P. Egan, *Recollections of John Thurtell*, (London, Knight & Lacey, 1824).
23 *The Examiner*, No. 832, 12 January 1824.
24 William Mulready to Sir John Swinburne, 11 January 1824, MS Northumberland County Record Office. Sir John's neighbour, Sir John Hussey Delaval of Seaton Delaval was also a keen boxing enthusiast and instrumental in arranging fights. See Delaval MSS, 2/DE.43. Northumberland County Record Office.
25 Undated letter from M. Gilbertson, MS. London, National Art Library, Victoria and Albert Museum, 86 NN 1.
26 *The Examiner*, No. 832, 12 January 1824.

SEPTEMBER
25 Cents
The RING
Who Stands
Best Chance
Against Marciano?
Official World Ratings
La Starza
I Make He-Men
Out of Weaklings!

Joe Louis and Murray Goodman, Publicity Director of the International Boxing Club, October 1953.
Courtesy: The Ring Magazine.

There were technical determinants as well as others which were and are harder to place. Why the Magic Eye, for instance, which was coterminous with Joe Louis' career? Why, too, those anthropomorphic action shots of the 1950s: Kid Gavilan, for instance, as a rubber rhomboid after a right cross to the jaw?

A Picture Prologue

The relationship between boxing and photography began restrainedly enough in the 1920s. By the 1950s, though, it had become a scandal. Old-timer Sam Andre, writing in *The Ring* in 1955, remarked on the disorder which characterised boxing: "[...] today the weighing-in ceremonies for a championship fight are a fantastic madhouse, topped only by the super madhouse called the winner's dressing room. It gets as much coverage as the President taking oath."

Andre, a photographer for the New York *American*, was a veteran. When Madison Square Garden opened in 1925 his colleagues in the business were Izzy Kaplan of the New York *Daily Mirror* and Hank Olin of the *Daily News*. Each had a 4 x 5 Graflex with a 12-inch lens, which they used in available light. The trio took pictures from balconies – previously installed for circus lighting – overhanging the mezzanine, from where the ring canvas served as a backdrop: "[...] a knockdown was the best bet for a good picture as the action slowed up enough to conform with the slow speed in which the camera had to be operated."

What preoccupied Andre in 1955 was the coming of chaos to what had once been an orderly world. Disorder was a topic then, for the growth of televised boxing in the 1940s and 1950s had thoroughly disrupted the framework. Andre held the Erneman chiefly responsible for photography's fateful moment. The Erneman was a German camera with a 1.9 lens, marketed in the 1930s as "the fastest made". It also functioned in available light, but was, according to Andre, "a tough camera to use in that the focus had to be right on target. If the lens was set for say ten feet distance and the shutter was snapped when the boxers were at either nine or eleven feet, the picture would be out of focus, and could not be enlarged to any great extent." To cope with the camera's focusing problems, photographers had to get to the ringside, which

'The Challenger Goes Down', *The Ring*, September 1937, p.6. "In the group on this page [left] we see Jimmy Braddock landing the right uppercut to the chin of the challenger, and Joe Louis goes down with a bang but gets right up. From top to bottom we follow the knockdown:
1, Louis, forcing the fight throughout the first round, cornered the champion against the ropes and was on the verge of crashing his left when -
2, Braddock, in desperation, let loose a powerful right-hand uppercut as Louis was coming forward. 3, Joe, taken by surprise, tried to jump into a clinch, but – 4, The punch landed with full force and sent the Bomber to the canvas, with Jimmy almost toppling over him. 5, Referee Tommy Thomas orders the champion to a neutral corner. Note how the champ is racing from his fallen victim. 6, But Louis gets to his feet with alacrity while Braddock is still on his way to the corner. Though there was no count made by the referee, *The Ring* Editor's timepiece showed a count of two."
Courtesy: The Ring Magazine.

'As Magic Eye Caught Knock-out' *The Ring*, September 1937, p.7. "How Joe Louis' right registered on Braddock's jaw is clearly shown in this Magic Eye sequence of pictures in the eighth round at Comiskey Park, Chicago. 1- Louis' right crashes against Braddock's chin with the full force of the shoulders behind the punch. 2, The champion starts to drop to the canvas. 3, Braddock, in severe pain, doubles up as he sinks and Louis, eyeing him closely, stands over him, watching his rival's tumble. 4, Braddock strikes the ground and finds himself toppling over. He is semi-conscious.
5, Referee Thomas orders Louis to the farthest neutral corner while the champion's head drops over Braddock's arms. 6, And a new champion is crowned as the referee counts out the helpless figure of the fighting Irishman."
Courtesy: The Ring Magazine.

meant a place in 'the sacred working press row'.[3] He even remembered the moment: "Jimmy Powers started it by getting Hank Olin a seat next to his. When I mentioned it to my sports editor, the late Ed Frayne, I was given a seat too." Once the breach had been made all and sundry poured through.

The old press hierarchy, with the photographers on their balconies and the scribes safely in their sacred seats, had been replaced by a free-for-all: "To get a clear shot of the action, a photographer in the first row must lay on his stomach on the ring apron and get his camera under the ropes. Since the photo-syndicates and some of the newspapers have at least two photographers working from the first row, the crowding in each corner makes it almost impossible for two men to work with reasonable efficiency."

Additional technical developments had also been a contributing factor in de-structuring the profession. The Erneman's use had faded "when the strobe light came into being. With this speed light now in use, it is no longer necessary to have a special camera and lens or even a high speed film. The light itself makes the picture and with the many experienced news photographers using it, outstanding fight pictures are being made." They were his colleagues, after all.

Andre's values were those of boxing itself: regard for hierarchy, respect for person and place as manifest in the use of proper names and admiration for professionalism. His parable, told as a short history, shows those values in jeopardy. The battle against his concept of chaos was well on the way to being lost in 1955.[1]

The Magic Eye

Andre mentioned the Erneman, which was a common tool of the trade but not the Magic Eye which was a specialist instrument. In 1935, it seems, International News had acquired or developed what they called a Magic Eye Camera, able to take fifteen pictures per second. It became possible to register boxing's decisive moments in detail. In September 1935, fifteen of these instants were published in vertical series in *The Ring*. They were of Joe Louis' stoppage of Primo Carnera in the 6th round of their meeting in July: 'The Historic Sixth. Flashes Not To Be Forgotten'. This was the first appearance of Magic Eye pictures which came to be associated with Louis' fights throughout the rest of the 1930s. Louis seems to have been specially selected for the experiment for the Max Baer vs. Jim Braddock world title fight, which took place around the same time, was conventionally recorded for *The Ring*, and the results published in the August issue. The usual Erneman way was to show the fight as a series of significant tableaux beyond the ropes.

Ringside photographs in the 1930s connoted and expressed the event. Magic Eye pictures offered forensic access to the moment. An onlooker could now follow the trajectory of the blow and this was especially relevant in Louis' fights because of his reputation for short, quick punching. Henceforth it was possible to take a studious or 'scientific' interest in fighting and the Magic Eye came to symbolise that quality. A major fight report in *The Ring* would thus be prefaced by, say, two pages of ringside pictures, standing for the event as a history, followed by one or two Magic Eye series, adding a closely observed, analytic element.

Ringside pictures protected the myth of boxing as heroic, violent and sudden even if a fight was uneventful. By contrast and in addition, the Magic Eye laid claim to objectivity. (Series of Magic Eye pictures resemble Muybridge's studies of the human figure in motion). Thus the myth was qualified and at the same time preserved.

The Magic Eye is closely connected with Louis' career, as reported in *The Ring*. Carnera in 1935 marked the beginning of its use, and Tami Mauriello – whom he defeated in November 1946 – the end. It was used on other occasions, but not often: for instance Barney Ross vs. Henry Armstrong, in August 1938, for the welterweight championship which ran under the heading 'What Barney Didn't Do'.

Charisma vs. Colour

Louis tantalised and disturbed commentators. Traditionally, the lower weights, up to light-heavyweight, had provided 'science' to which the heavies added 'colour'. Louis, by contrast, was all 'science' and no 'colour'. It was, too, a particularly austere science. In an article of May 1935, Nat Fleischer, editor of *The Ring* explained the difference: "There is nothing of the flashing colourful stylist about him, nothing of the swift stab and getaway, dazzling, feinting, dancing footwork with which an agile mitt-handler sometimes draws admiring tribute to his

The Challenger Goes Down

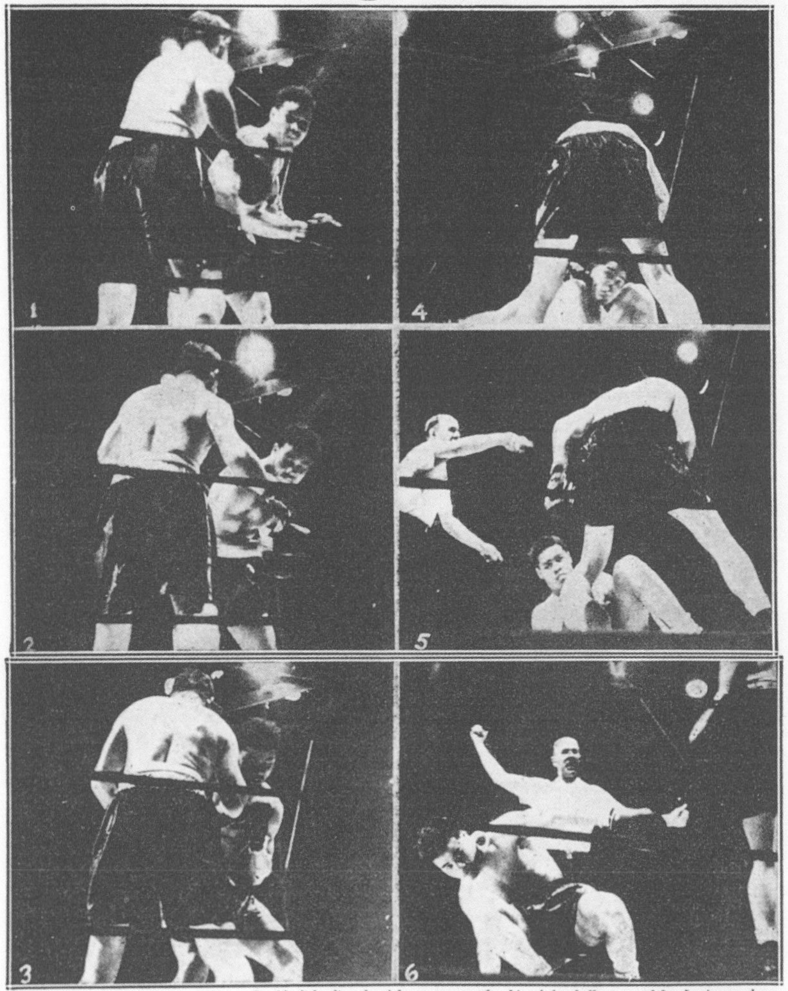

In the group on this page we see Jimmy Braddock landing the right uppercut to the chin of the challenger, and Joe Louis goes down with a bang but gets right up. From top to bottom we follow the knockdown: 1, Louis, forcing the fight throughout the first round, cornered the champion against the ropes and was on the verge of crashing his left when— 2, Braddock, in desperation, let loose a powerful right-hand uppercut as Louis was coming forward. 3, Joe, taken by surprise, tried to jump into a clinch, but— 4, The punch landed with full force and sent the Bomber to the canvas, with Jimmy almost toppling over him. 5, Referee Tommy Thomas orders the champion to a neutral corner. Note how the champ is racing from his fallen victim. 6, But Louis gets to his feet with alacrity while Braddock is still on his way to the corner. Though there was no count made by the referee, THE RING *Editor's timepiece showed a count of two.*

As Magic Eye Caught Knockout

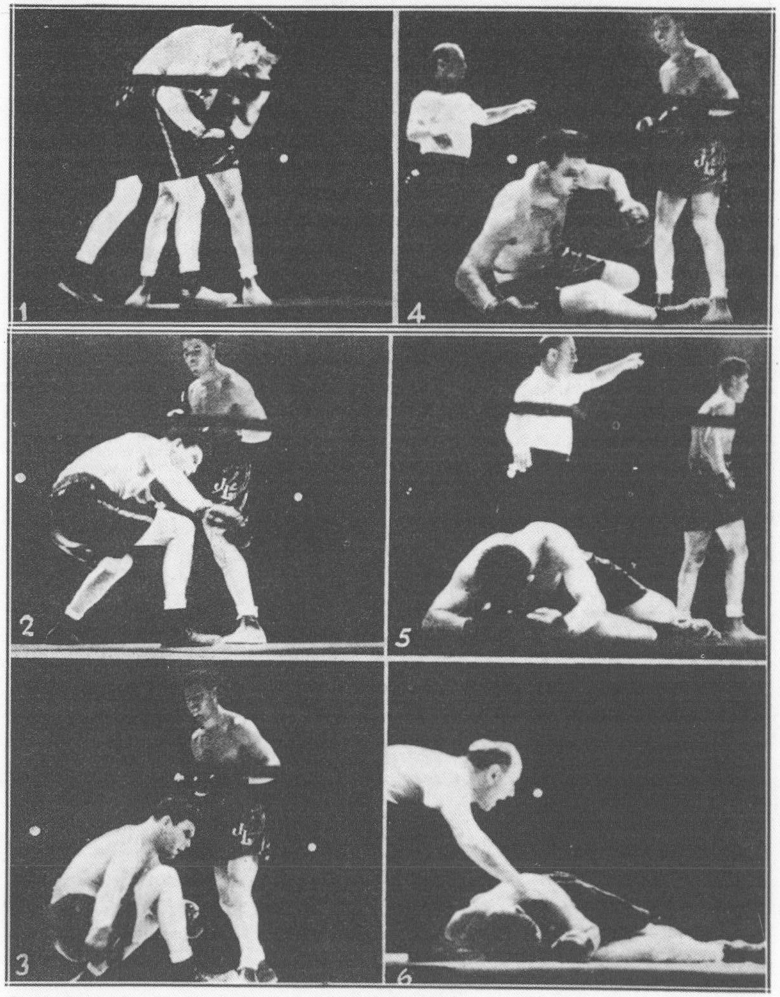

How Joe Louis' right registered on Braddock's jaw is clearly shown in this Magic Eye sequence of pictures in the eighth round at Comiskey Park, Chicago. 1, Louis' right crashes against Braddock's chin with the full force of the shoulders behind the punch. 2, The champion starts to drop to the canvas. 3, Braddock, in severe pain, doubles up as he sinks and Louis, eyeing him closely, stands over him, watching his rival's tumble. 4, Braddock strikes the ground and finds himself toppling over. He is semi-conscious. 5, Referee Thomas orders Louis to the farthest neutral corner while the champion's head drops over Braddock's arms. 6, And a new champion is crowned as the referee counts out the helpless figure of the fighting Irishman.

'The Historic Sixth!, Carnera vs. Louis. *The Ring*, September 1935, p. 8. "Here is what the camera's magic eye recorded in the round that ended Carnera's fistic career. From top to bottom, first row: 1, Louis preparing to crash that looping right to the jaw. 2, Primo senses the danger. 3, Crash! Right on the jaw! 4, The blow spins Primo around. 5, He is on his way down. Middle row: 6, Going! Going! 7, Gone! Sprawled on all fours. 8, Primo falls to canvas again after he has gotten on his knees. 9, Primo begins to rise. 10, The Game Italian struggles to his knees. Right: 11, He can barely get to his feet. 12, Bewildered, like a cornered animal, he faces his foe. 13, Mouth agape, he spars off. 14, Joe closes in, right hand cocked, ready for the coup de grace. 15, Another smash to the head and down Primo goes for a second count."
Courtesy: The Ring Magazine.

'The Downfall of a Game, Fighting Contender', Louis vs. Godoy, *The Ring*, September 1940, pp.10-11.
Courtesy: The Ring Magazine.

The HISTORIC SIXTH!

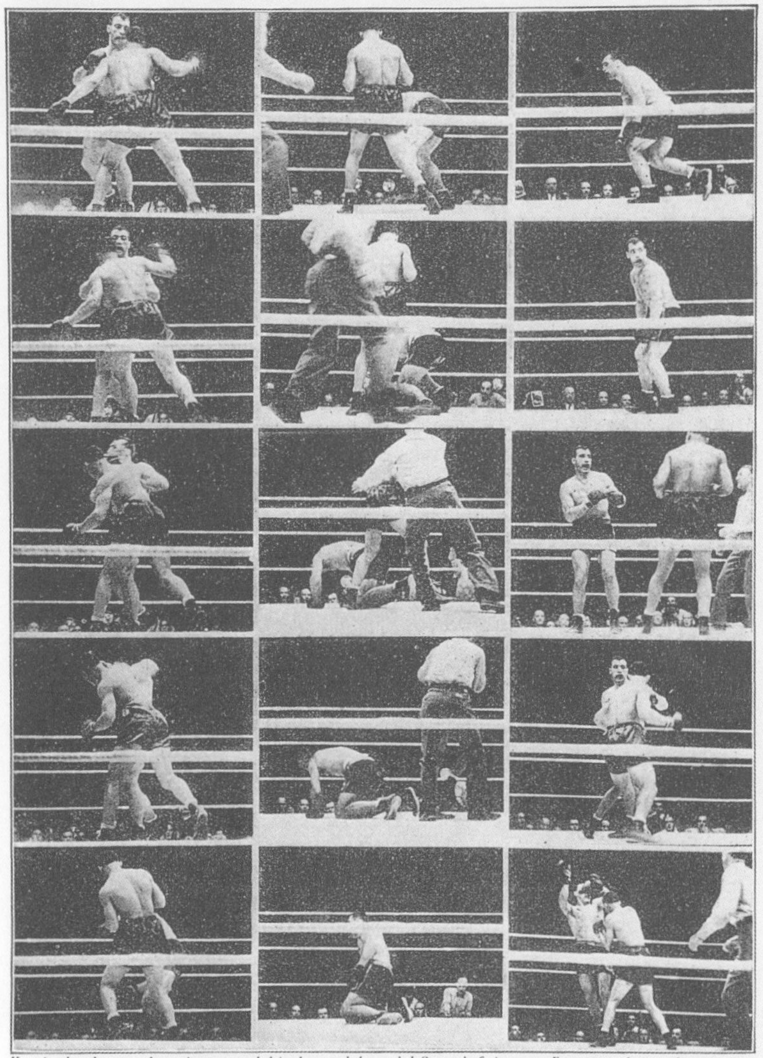

Here is what the camera's magic eye recorded in the round that ended Carnera's fistic career. From top to bottom, first row: 1—Louis preparing to crash that looping right to the jaw. 2—Primo senses the danger. 3—Crash! Right on the jaw! 4—The blow spins Primo around. 5—He is on his way down. Middle row: 6—Going! Going! 7—Gone! Sprawled on all fours. 8—Primo falls to canvas again after he has gotten on his knees. 9—Primo begins to rise. 10—The Game Italian struggles to his knees. Right: 11—He can barely get to his feet. 12—Bewildered, like a cornered animal, he faces his foe. 13—Mouth agape, he spars off. 14—Joe closes in, right hand cocked, ready for the coup de grace. 15—Another smash to the head and down Primo goes for a second count.

The Downfall of a Game, Fighting Contender

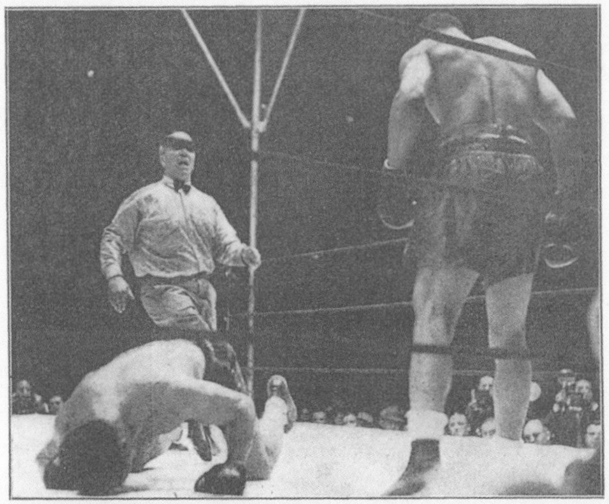

The second knockdown in the eighth round. Godoy falls on all fours and the referee rushes forth for the count. Arturo's head struck the floor with a thud as he fell to the canvas.

Godoy, game as they come, starts to rise as Billy Cavanagh orders Louis to a neutral corner. Dazed, weary, blood gushing from a deep wound under the eye, Arturo tries desperately to get to his feet, and before the count got started, he collapsed.

The referee wasted no time. As Godoy fell forward again, Cavanagh waved his hands indicating that he had stopped the fight. He mercifully saved the Chilean from further punishment.

The referee rushes to the aid of the defeated challenger. He raises him from the canvas and then—

Godoy, on his feet, realizes the meaning of the referee's interference, and immediately goes into action. He rushes forth to resume the battle, while referee and seconds restrain him. Note Louis eyeing the defeated gladiator as Joe calmly gets to his corner.

cleverness from ringside reporters and patrons." Fleischer tried again in June in his article 'Boxing's Poker Face': "He is colourless, so far as the spectacular is concerned, but what he lacks in that he makes up for in hitting power [...]". In September Fleischer wrote of the Louis v. Carnera fight, that Louis boxed "with machine-like precision. Every move was a picture". In addition, Fleischer noted in June, he had "no vices" and his features when fighting were "absolutely expressionless". Looking back in June 1939, by which time Louis was well-established as world champion, Daniel M. Daniel reflected on Louis' 'colour' problem: "The Black-Roxborough [managerial] combination has not sold Joe Louis to the American public as a colourful fighter, as a dramatic champion, as a man loaded with human interest. This failure traces to the type of material with which they have to work."

Despite lacking 'colour', Louis attracted intense interest and huge audiences (60,000 in the fight with Carnera, which was the largest since Sharkey vs. Dempsey). In September 1935 Daniel M. Daniel credited him with the salvation of boxing: "[...] there is only one man who is responsible for this new lease of life to a sport that was rapidly going to smash."

How could such an unostentatious persona fascinate the fight world? "Louis refuses to smile. He refuses to talk. He seems to have been drilled in silence."[2] There were attempts on the part of the press to identify and explain him. Because his family originated in Alabama he was touted as the Alabama Assassin. Then, in honour of his home town, he was the Brown Bomber of Detroit, before simply becoming the Brown Bomber. As befitted a former car-worker in Detroit, he boxed "with machine-like precision".[3] In a retrospective article in *The Ring* in September 1946, Daniel M. Daniel referred to his "photographic mind [...] a cerebellum which takes motion pictures, and which can unroll those pictures whenever he wants it to. When he fights a man, that motion picture machine in the back ofhis noggin keeps taking films. Once taken, these films are analysed by the Louis sub-conscious." His interpreters drew on up-to-date, visual imagery, reserving the anachronistic and anecdotal for his opponents. His nickname associated him less with grenadiers than with that threat from the air which had troubled the collective imagination since the Great War. If he embodied the virtues and the dangers of a war-machine, his image was completed by the Magic Eye which brought with it an idea of reconnaissance, of battlefield analysis. Magic Eye pictures amounted, in his case, to a view from the control room.

Fans attended his fights less in the hope of the kind of upsets which occurred at other times, than as witnesses to the champion's unprecedented abilities, although he was catastrophically defeated by Max Schmeling in 1936.[4] Above all he was known for return matches, during which earlier errors were quickly corrected. For instance, the second fight with Schmeling, in 1938, ended devastatingly in the first round.[5] More than anything he exemplified control to a public preoccupied by the ill-fortunes of the Depression.

The Cleansing of America

Louis entered the American story when boxing, which provided the raw material for its epic, was in a state of disrepute. This particular bout of disrepute, following the retirement of Gene Tunney in 1928, was long-

Former World Heavyweight Champion Max Schmeling's first post-war comeback fight against Werner Vollmer, 28 September 1948, Frankfurt. Courtesy: The Ring Magazine.

standing and acute enough to have gathered a symbolic dimension bearing on the Depression. The post-Tunney champions were neither unsympathetic nor ineffectual. Their fault lay elsewhere; they were, or could be taken to be, acquiescent in a culture where acquiescence could be fatal. Louis, by contrast, coped with chance, and re-instated an image of certainty almost as soon as he emerged in 1935.

Max Baer was the most sublimely representative of all the pre-Louis personifications and responsible for any amount of fancy and hysterical writing. He defeated Carnera for the title in 1934 and then on 14 June 1935 was himself defeated by Jim Braddock, who at eight to one was expected to make no impression. Louis finally took the title from Braddock in 1937. Baer, while champion was an unrepentant hedonist: "Can you imagine me playing solitaire in New York with the Hollywood, the Paradise, the Casino de Paris and other swell joints just around the corner."[6] The solitaire player in question was Jim Jeffries, one of the great champions from long ago, who had played solitaire during intervals of training. Baer tempted fate: "[...] how he loves the spotlight, the lure of music, the dance, the Venus offerings laid at the championship shrine by innumerable lovely ladies."[7] Fate caught up with him, and after being KO'ed in the fourth by Louis in November 1935 he owned up to Eddie Geiger of the Chicago *American*: "Wine, women and song, cigarettes and the lack of sleep put me where I am tonight, not Joe Louis. I was susceptible to flattery, and I have paid for my playboy folly."[8]

Like any boxer from the West more presentable than a gorilla, Baer was "another Lochinvar".[9] They called him Gorgeous Max and Max of the Golden West, and in honour of his place of origin the Livermore Larruper, Lah-dee-dah and Lothario. In defeat he was the Great Lover and "The arrogant Baer, the cynical, clowning, care-free, love-crazy playboy of Alameda, California".[10]

Baer represented misrule. He deliberately tempted that malign fate which had laid waste to the American economy. Not only did he gamble, but sometimes failed to train thus trusting again to chance. He seemed to prefer appearance to substance, choosing to fight in exhibitions rather than title bouts. He also made efforts to get into pictures.

Braddock, although far more worthy than Baer, was in some respects more disquieting to contemporaries. Much defeated he had virtually retired until "reduced to accepting money from relief agencies".[11] "Investments, made with hard-earned ring purses, went blooey," and the story had it that he turned up at Madison Square Garden one day to ask his manager Joe Gould for a loan of $35 to pay the milkman.[12] Gould put him to fighting again, probably as a trial horse, but in the process he overcame Art Lasky, John Henry Lewis and Corn Griffin to earn a shot at the title. Braddock's story, described by Nat Fleischer as "an Horatio Alger cycle", established him as Jersey's Cinderella Man and as an exemplification of the Depression made good; yet he was acting in Louis' shadow, and his history as a hobo, stevedore and janitor as well as a failed investor attached him to the Depression.

Louis defeated Carnera in 1935, and Carnera, too, symbolised uncertainty. Carnera, a.k.a. Da Preem, was a suspect champion "lavishly press-agented when he made his debut in the US and his famous 'sucker' tour, bowling over set-ups from coast to coast, is still good for a laugh wherever talking fighting fans grow

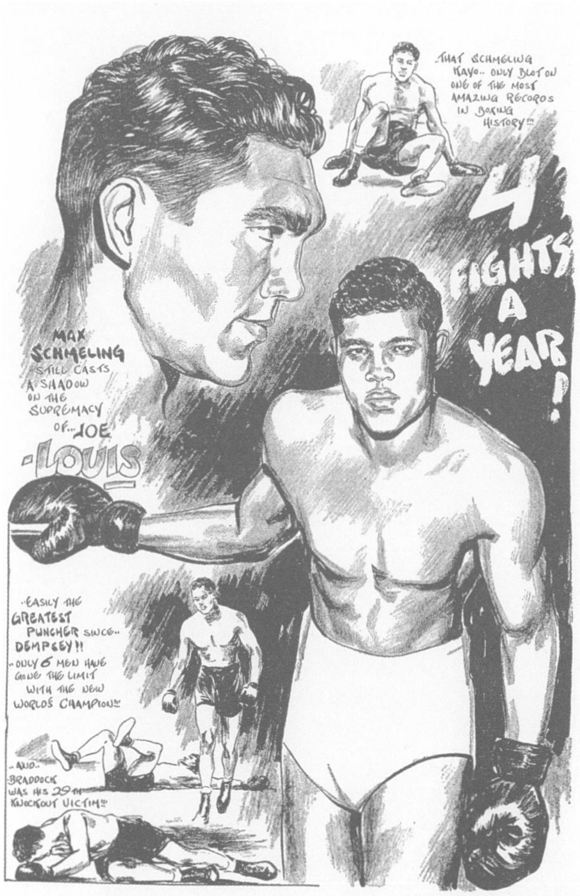

Max Schmeling vs. Joe Louis, illustration from *The Ring*, September 1937, p.19. Courtesy: The Ring Magazine.

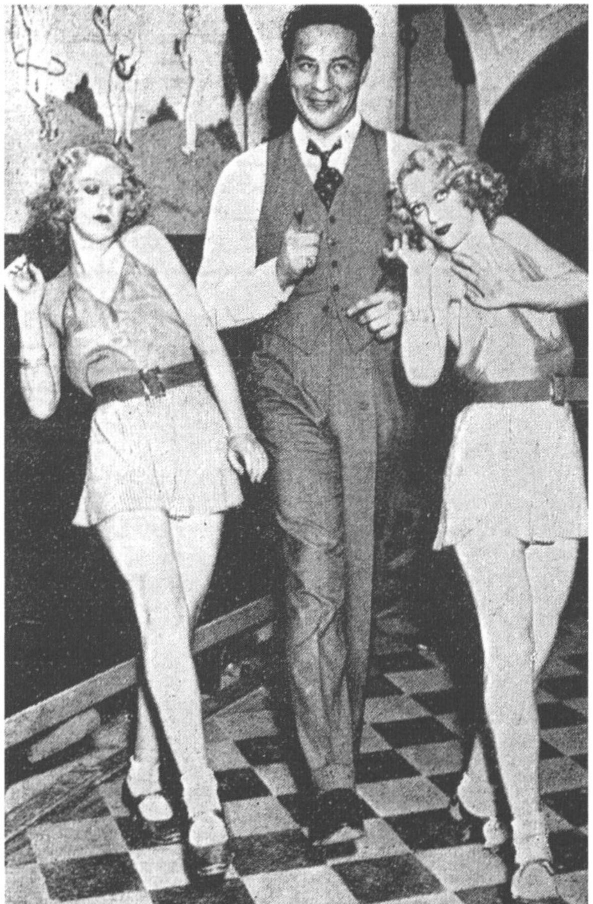

'Max Baer, the Playboy, in a characteristic mood.' *The Ring*, September 1935, p.18. Courtesy: The Ring Magazine.

Rocky Marciano vs. Joe Louis, 26 October 1951.
Courtesy: The Ring Magazine.

reminiscent."[13] It was rumoured even that in 1933 he had KO'ed Jack Sharkey for the championship with "a phantom punch", and when he fought for the title had more managers than any other heavyweight in history. These included Bill Duffy, "reported to be in the business of disseminating alcoholic beverages" in the Prohibition era, and Ownie Madden "exiled from New York by Mayor Fiorello la Guardia."[14] Jack Sharkey's defeat of Carnera on 12 October 1931, in their first meeting, was acclaimed by the fans, who were already suspicious. Sharkey himself, 'the Former Gob' (gob = sailor), was the first heavyweight champion to lose the title at the first defence. Mob involvement may not have been decisive, but suspicion undermined confidence.

Louis finally established his full significance against Max Schmeling, known as the Black Uhlan, for he was an unusually dark-skinned German, and sometimes as the Dempsey from Germany and the Socker from Swastikaland. Germans, quite naturally, thought of Schmeling as representing Germany, as did New York's Jews, who boycotted his first meeting with Louis in 1936 to the great detriment of the gate. To complicate the picture Schmeling had in Joe Jacobs the most Jewish of all boxing managers, who was photographed in Hamburg (Schmeling v. Dudas) Heil Hitlering while smoking a cigar. Jacobs specialised in casting doubt on decisions against his boxers, and coined the phrase "We wuz robbed" when Schmeling went down controversially and on points to Jack Sharkey at the Garden Bowl in 1932.[15] Herr Max was ten years older than Louis and had a record which established him as Fortune's fighter. He had been elected champion in 1930 after a fight in which his opponent, the ubiquitous Jack Sharkey (a Lithuanian named in honour of an Irishman), had been disqualified for a low blow in the fourth. In January 1931 he was dethroned, again by committee, for refusing a return with Sharkey. Instead he chose to meet WL 'Young' Stribling in Cleveland (himself killed in a motorcycle accident in 1933). He was the fighter *par excellence* of the post-Tunney interregnum. Thus his demolition of Louis in August 1936 by a KO in the tenth was a catastrophe, representing the triumph less of Germany than of uncertainty. Louis' atonement in 1938, not boycotted by Jewish fans, was absolute, for it ended in the first round. Ring writers thought that this victory signified "the complete collapse of the Aryan theory",[16] but Schmeling's real significance was as a representative of the old order in boxing and never as a man from the master race. Besides he had been KO'ed by Max Baer, the Nightclub Champion and Luxuriant Luxurist, on 8 June 1937. Jacobs, game to the end, claimed "a gimmick" in Louis' glove: fabric wrapped around a lead strip.

Equilibrium

Louis represented reliability. On the other side of the scale stood Baer, Carnera, Braddock and Schmeling, as personifications of everything that fortune had to offer, for good and ill. It was less a case, however, of total repression than of constraint and licensing. As long as he was there, boxing's phantasmagorical side could be entertained and held in check; and this dualism is expressed in, for example, those reports in *The Ring* where sets of ringside compositions picture the fight as idea and myth in relation to the objectivism of a series from the Magic Eye.

In this respect one of Louis' greatest achievements was the presentation of Two-Ton Tony Galento, a challenger knocked out in the fourth in August 1939. Galento elicited one of Louis' few phrases of note: "What for that fat little man call me a bum?" He came to notice from Orange, New Jersey by means of a series of fights against doubtful opposition. Known to the scribes as the Newark Night Stick, he owned a beer tavern and was his own best customer. Where the imperturbable Louis was a poor source of copy, Galento obliged: "[...] Galento has the wallop, but defence means a wooden railing surrounding a ball park to Jersey's heroic hippo." He also participated, with Lou Nova, in what was thought to be "probably the dirtiest fight since Cain and Abel".[17] Like Baer he incited writers to lese-majesty, but during Louis' reign that hardly mattered; for with Louis there the centre could be seen to be secure.

Molech and the Sluggers[18]

Louis signed off, not very convincingly, against Jersey Joe Walcott on 5 December 1947. Sid Feder, writing for *The Ring*, was aghast: "The customers booed Louis at the finish – the first time in his life. Just why the gallery bugs should climb on Joe, who has been in a class by himself as a sportsman and champion, is about as clear as pea soup, inasmuch as Joe had nothing to do with the officials' votes."[19]

EVERLAST

His retirement brought an interregnum, which as always meant trouble in boxing. Eliminators might produce a champion of sorts, but when the line of succession was broken there could be no real legitimacy. Nor were any of the candidates representatives in the manner of 1935. Jersey Joe Walcott, b. Arnold Cream, had been dubbed after the great Barbadian lightweight of the 1920s, Joe Walcott, and *The Ring* tried to present him as The Brown Braddock, which amounted to very faint praise.[20]

The public imagination had also moved on since 1935. Post-war it was animated by new imagery, identified by Nat Fleischer in 1946 in an article on the re-emergence of the middleweight: "Rocky is a thunderous fighter whose haymakers have been compared to forked lightning and the atomic bomb; and his vicious, slashing, relentless manner of milling evoked comparison of Graziano with the great Stanley Ketchel."[21]

Feder's 'gallery bugs', also known as the fans, came to prominence post-war. Pre-war there had been fans too of course, and as "the masses" they had never been fond of Gene Tunney, for instance.[22] By 1951 their influence was all important. In an article, 'Slugging, Today's Hallmark of Quality', Johnny Salak regretted a falling off: "In an age when the ability to slug is a fighter's hallmark of quality, so far as the fans are concerned, it may seem strange to the younger element that there was a time when the scientific boxer reigned supreme and was applauded by followers of the game."[23] Despite *The Ring's* best efforts to recall Stanley Ketchel *et al* "the younger element" now lived for the moment, and the cynosure hardly needed even to be a champion. Rocky Graziano, "the personal saint of all the neighbourhood kids", epitomised this new order.

The Ring responded defensively to the new ethos of the slam-bang brawl with a Hall of Fame, or pantheon of boxing, established in 1954. By then, however, television – which in turn stood for a new mind set, fixated on the moment – had turned boxing into a spectacular rather than epic affair. Photographers and their editors had persevered with identity, stressing full-figure formats until around 1950, but began soon after to compose pages from expressive fragments: Gavilan's jaw, for instance, under acute lateral pressure, if possible haloed by droplets of sweat caught in the light. These fragments of the 1950s proposed intensities of suffering which overrode issues of science and identity. The greatest slugfests of the 1950s (Robinson v. Fullmer is a good example) were used up as they were enacted, to be commemorated in a return, and yet another return. Where the ideal onlooker of 1935 was a forensic expert, historian and connoisseur, that of 1955 was a vicarious victim, engrossed by stress and pain, or by 'thrills' as they were known in the business.

Although the impatient imagination of Feder's 'gallery bugs', primed by atomic imagery, pre-dated the onset of television, it was television which took the blame, making Jeremiahs of boxing's commentators. Boxing was the first major art form to undergo destabilisation by TV, for local boxing venues closed down in relationship to the rise of television fights. It had been different pre-war: "Summer and winter, a dozen or more swat parlours were functioning weekly within a 25-mile radius of Times Square." As the 'swat parlours' closed so boxing ceased to recruit from the Jewish, Irish and Italian neighbourhoods from which it had traditionally drawn. Thus closed a phase in American immigrant history, and the

'The Kid's Last Fight', Kid Gavilan vs. Carmen Basilio of Canastota, NY, *The Ring Magazine*, December 1953, p.15. Courtesy: The Ring Magazine.

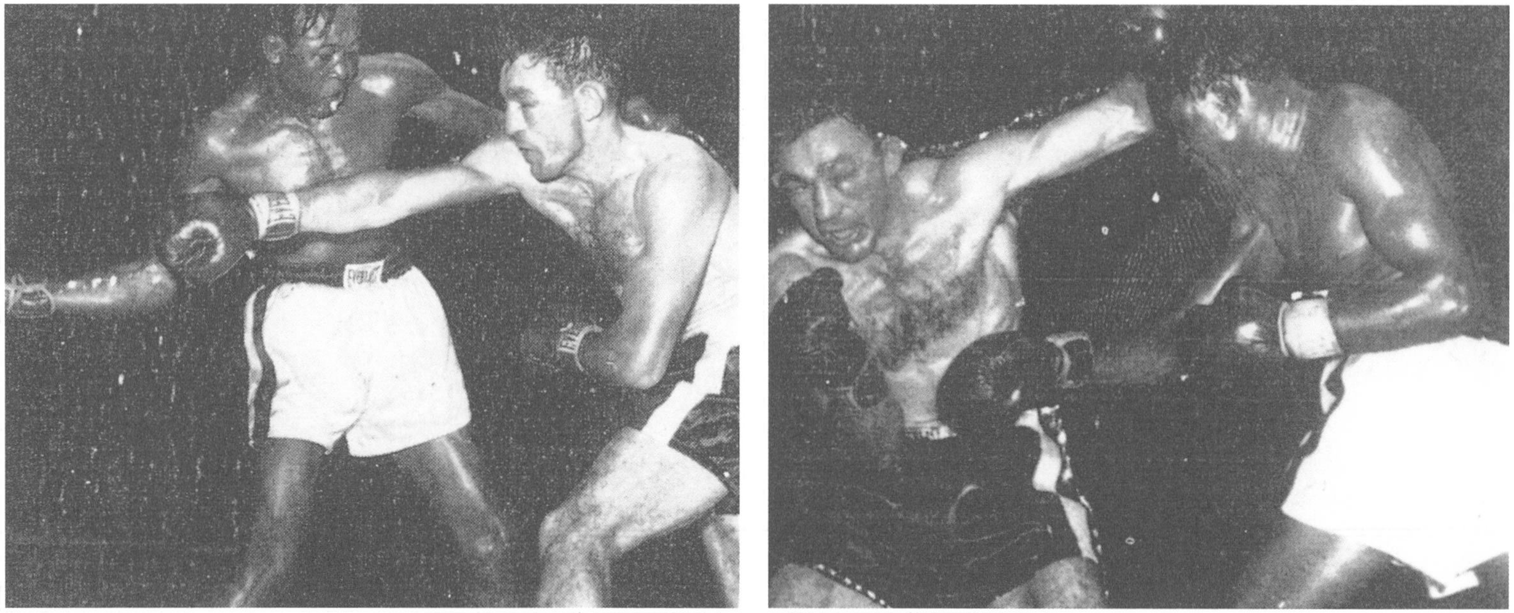

scribes were all too aware of its passing, for it meant that their recall of the Star Casino, the Empire A.C., etc. ceased to be relevant.[24]

Television was characterised as a Molech (see note 18) with an appetite for raw, untutored talent. In 1955 Nat Loubet wrote: "The insatiable requirements for talent built up by the constant scheduling of televised fights has caused many a promising youngster to be fed into the destructive hopper." Or it was defined as a sub-set of boxing, comparable to wrestling which had fallen well into disrepute by 1951. Jim Londos reckoned that it had "reached a silly stage [...] All this marcelled hair and fancy bathrobes and effeminate gear is so much phooey as far as I am concerned."[25]

Real boxing enjoyed its moment of truth on 11 February 1953, when the largest television audience to date saw Kid Gavilan "explode the Chuck Davey myth in Chicago Stadium". Davey was described by Jack Hand of *The Ring* as "the Golden Boy of the collegiate ranks"; he was also a TV boxer who had, to his detriment, entered the rankings.[26]

Boxing was reported by old men with long memories: Fleischer was as old as Methuselah; Al Buck, who regretted television's "slam-bang brawls" of the mid-50s, had reported his first championship battle in 1926 (Dempsey vs. Tunney); Jersey Jones, responsible for television coverage in *The Ring,* had interviewed Joe Jeannette in 1919 for the old New York *Globe*. They were, in effect, the first modernist critics in any medium to encounter the postmodern public in all its ruinous irresponsible invisibility.[27] Like their bookish contemporaries, Joyce, Pound and Eliot, they both believed in and hoped for the re-integration of the past into the present. Fleischer made the case in 1956, by which time his cause was all but lost: "Legends are the backbone of sports. In boxing there would be little to write about the romance of pugilism if it weren't for the legends that have been handed down over the years."[28]

Feder's "pea soup", the Graziano phenomenon, Londos' "phooey", and Andre's "madhouse" scenes of 1955 all bore witness to a state of affairs into which the past (Fleischer's "legends") could no longer be integrated. The masses, or fans, abetted by television – sponsored by Gillette and Pabst beers especially – had at last inherited the cultural earth and broken free from that benign tutelage of the kind exemplified by Fleischer and *The Ring.* It was the first fatal encounter between a modernist elite and the postmodern public, at last confident and protected enough to admit that it cared rather more about Graziano's "neckties"[29] than it did about the Ketchel successsion.[30]

All references are to *The Ring*, unless otherwise stated. *The Ring*, established by Nat Fleischer in February 1922, was originally a monthly magazine of boxing and wrestling, but as wrestling bouts degenerated into charades during the 1940s coverage diminished. In 1910 Fleischer began as a sports reporter for the old New York *Press*, before becoming sports editor of the *Morning Sun*. In 1962 Budd Schulberg described him as "The venerable historian and keeper of the records."

1 All quotes in this first section are from Sam Andre, 'Press Photographer', (October 1955) pp.30-31.

2 Harvey Thorne, 'Baer and Carnera Show Nature's Errors' (September 1935) pp.18-19.

3 Nat Fleischer, 'Better Get Those White Hopes Ready' (September 1935) pp.2-3.

4 Ed van Every, 'Louis' Meteoric Rise' (September 1937) pp.3-5. Jack Blackburn, Louis' trainer, attributed the Schmeling victory to Louis' recent marriage, and to the fact that "Lakewood [the training camp] was too warm and there was too much Coney Island trimmings there".

5 Daniel M. Daniel, 'Nine Warn Against Second Louis Fights' (September 1946) pp.2-3.

6 Ed Smith, '"I'll be Different", Baer Tells Ed Smith - and the World' (March 1935), pp.2-3.

7 Arthur T Lumley, who managed John L. Sullivan 40 years ago, 'How Champions Pass from the Picture' (March 1935) pp.20-22.

8 Nat Fleischer, 'Up the Ladder for Max; Down the Chute for Max' (December 1935) pp.2-5.

9 Carl Morris, the Sequilpa Giant and Irish-Cherokee White Hope of the Johnson era (post-1910) was, for example, "the large Lochinvar who came out of the West".

10 Nat Fleischer, 'Braddock's Amazing Feat Sets Fistic Mark' (August 1935) pp.2-3. Fleischer deplored the behaviour of Baer, who "sneered superciliously" as he lost to Braddock.

11 Daniel M. Daniel, 'Baer-Braddock Match Packs Human Drama' (July 1935) pp.2-3.

12 George T. Tickell, 'Dame Fortune Smiles on Braddock' (July 1935) pp.12-15.

13 George T. Tickell, 'Ballyhoo in Fisticuffs' (February 1935) pp.20-21.

14 Dan Daniel, ' Did Carnera K.O. Sharkey with Phantom Punch?' (March 1957) pp.10-11.

15 Ted Carroll, 'Golden Days of Boxing' (February 1947) p.30.

16 Ted Carroll, 'A Great Champion Arrives' (September 1938) pp.18-19.

17 Sid Feder, '"Psycholerizing" Wins Fights Too' (September 1949) p.7. "The only reason they didn't bite each other was because their rubber mouthpieces wouldn't let them." Feder was probably too engrossed by boxing's language for his own good as a *Ring* writer: "They were saying before that one 'that Max didn't have the chance of a bottle of beer at a temperance meeting against Louis'[...]": 'What now for Joe Louis?' (December 1946) p.12.

18 Molech (Leviticus 18.21), a pagan idol to which children were sacrificed, seems to have prefigured television's relation to boxing.

19 Sid Feder, 'Pride and Gold Delay Bomber's Retirement' (February 1948) pp.2-3.

20 Irving Rudd, 'The fighter and the Man' (August 1946) pp.28-29.

21 Nat Fleischer, 'Middleweights Regain Fistic Spotlight' (August 1946) pp.9-13.

22 Arthur T. Lumley, 'How Champions Pass from the Picture' (March 1935) pp.20-22: "Fighting, with Gene, was purely a business proposition [...] he was never popular with the masses." Nat Fleischer's *Gene Tunney, The Enigma of the Prize Ring* had recently been published.

23 Johnny Salak, 'Slugging, Today's Hallmark of Quality' (October 1951) pp.19-20.

24 The television debate flourished in the mid-50s: eg Nat Loubet, 'Rough on Ryff' (May 1955) pp.4-5, and Jersey Jones 'No Acorns, No Oaks' (June 1995) pp.8-9.

25 Daniel M. Daniel, 'T.V. Vexing Issue' (June 1951) p.3. Jim Londos, retired to San Diego, continued: "The pity of it is that many of the men going in for the daffy stuff are really good wrestlers. Gorgeous George, for one, is a capable performer." Joyce Carol Oates' *On Boxing* (New York, 1994) p.189, cites Gorgeous George as an Ali precursor. Wrestlers were pioneers inasmuch as they were the first to circumvent a mediating, supervisory elite and to relate directly to the public.

26 Jack Hand, 'T.V. Fight Circuit' (November 1955) pp.22-23. The Chuck Davey story is also re-told as a moral fable, by Bud Schulberg in an essay of 1977, 'Where Have You Gone, Holly Mims?', republished in *Sparring with Hemingway*, 1995.

27 During the 1930s Jack Johnson wrote for *The Ring*, as did Philadelphia Jack O'Brien, undefeated light-heavyweight champion from the Golden Age. O'Brien was born Joseph F. Hagan in the City of Brotherly Love (Philadelphia) famous for home-town decisions. Joe Jeannette (b.Jennette) was, with Johnson, Sam Langford and Sam McVey, one of the famous Ebony Four, reduced to fighting each other, often in France, during the White Hope era. Jeannette introduced Carpentier to boxing, and fought Langford fourteen or fifteen times. The rise of Louis in 1935 renewed interest in that era: Willie Lewis, 'Negro Courage Recalled' (June 1935) pp.8-10.

28 Nat Fleischer, 'The Langford Legend' (April 1956) pp.10-11. Langford had just died.

29 Irving Rudd, 'The Fighter and the Man' (August 1946) pp.26-29: "It is not unusual to see Graziano, who abhors neckties, appear in the ring when being introduced at Madison Square Garden, in peg pants, sharpie sandals, a garish bright-colored sports jacket or sweater, and tousled black hair, rarely combed." Such humanising circumstantial reporting only began to emerge in the post-war period. Jake LaMotta had a perforated eardrum and bred Dobermanns.

30 Daniel M. Daniel, 'Ketchel Versus Papke. Socking Series Saga' (December 1946) pp.23-25. Ketchel had four fights with Billy Papke (1908-9), recalled by the Graziano-Zale series. Ketchel (b. Stanislaus Kiecal in Grand Rapids, Michigan on 14 September 1886) was killed by a dope-crazed farm-hand at Conway, Mo., 15 October 1910.

James Coleman's *Box (Ahhareturnabout)*

Jean Fisher

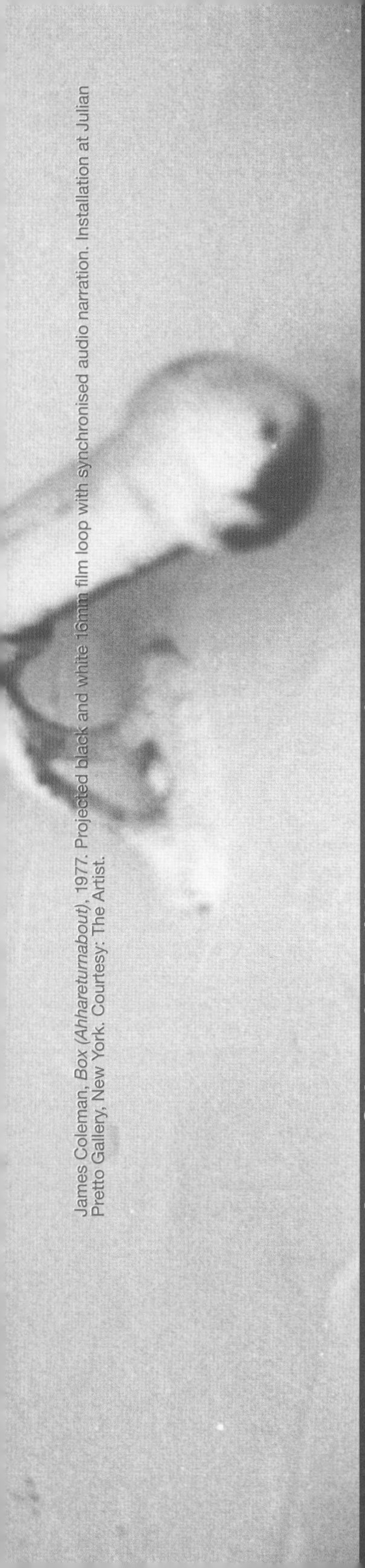

James Coleman, *Box (Ahhareturnabout)*, 1977. Projected black and white 16mm film loop with synchronised audio narration. Installation at Julian Pretto Gallery, New York. Courtesy: The Artist.

"Tunney was running away. Gene landed a left to the jaw, Jack hooked him to the jaw and put a right to the body when on the ropes. Gene danced away however…"

In September 1927, the American boxer Jack Dempsey met the world heavyweight champion, Irishman Gene Tunney, for a return bout. Dempsey, who had held the world title since 1919, had lost it to Tunney the previous year, in 1926. The return bout, however, resulted in a hung verdict, becoming one of the great legends of boxing folklore.

James Coleman took this historical scenario as the ostensible subject matter of *Box (Ahhareturnabout)*, 1977, a black and white 16mm continuous film loop with synchronised voice-over, to be projected in a manner which would evoke the public transmission of such a sports spectacle, one such possibility being a television over the bar in a pub. *Box* presents us with grainy fragments from original footage of the two boxers circling each other round the ring, the images intermittently interrupted by passages of black film leader. The voice-over, projecting Tunney's imagined interior thoughts during the fight, is one of the most extraordinary soundtracks to accompany a work of visual art. This acoustic space, composed of disjointed words and phrases orchestrated with a low pulse, whose frequency is reminiscent of a slightly accelerated heart-beat, together with expressive, non-verbal, bodily or guttural utterances (grunts, sighs, laboured breathing), captures us in an erotically emotional register, enclosing us as if we were in the mind and body of the boxer. The work's play on circularity – its pulsating, structural endlessness, the movement of the boxers round the ring and Tunney's circling thoughts – induces a near-hypnotic state of attention.

Tunney's interior monologue, as elliptical as that of dream or reverie, refuses our desire for linear narrative coherence; rather, it propels us into a labyrinth of associations whose threads weave together several possibilities of meaning. Fragmented utterances concerning the immediate task of the fight, oblique references to Anglo-Irish colonial relations, Ireland's nationalistic myths, anguished thoughts of public immortality and private death are nevertheless so deeply imbricated that to attempt to unravel them would be rather a futile task.

Box is a 'dramatised recitation', adressing itself to listening not reading, perhaps, somewhat subversively, alluding to an oral storytelling tradition. This is in part due to its employment of phonetic puns; but it is also the result of its emphasis on the qualities of the voice itself to carry meaning, relying as much on what Roland Barthes called 'the grain of the voice' (the subjective inflection in the act of enunciation) as on those expressive gestures which are signifiers of 'character' in orthodox theatre. However, composed of heterogeneous, abbreviated and seemingly disconnected words and mental images, the text is saturated not with any determinable 'meaning' but with 'sense' – indeed, its effect is *sensual* in its uncommon ability to play on the rhythmic chords of the viewer's mind and imagination beyond the merely visual. Neither poetry nor prose narrative, this dialogical monologue may perhaps be analogous to Paul Willemen's description of 'inner speech': it negotiates the heterogeneous and contradictory impulses operating at the juncture of unconscious and preconscious-conscious processes and, as such, like the ego, far from signalling a pure and unmediated selfhood, is itself a "discursive process determined by the social and psychological histories that combine to produce that particular individual in that time and place."[1]

Box is not, of course, 'about' boxing in any literal sense; and yet the fact that it refers to a specific historical contest and known boxers is of crucial importance to the work's conceptual apparatus. *Box* is nonetheless about *conflict:* both between the work of art and its institutions and of the identity of the self in its historical and psycho-social relations with the symbolic order. As such, *Box*, nearly twenty years on, remains highly pertinent to contemporary aesthetic discourse.

Like much art practice at the time, Coleman's work of the late 1960s and early 1970s was recent heir to a critique of the formalist aesthetics dominated by the US. Here the modernist art object was conceived as the bearer of an autonomous, universal and ahistorical truth, in relation to which cultural memory, narrative, the non-visual and the rhetorical were irrelevant distractions to be purged[2] – a monopolistic value judgement which exposes the extent to which modernist visual aesthetics is bound to western imperialist thought. Crucially, in this modernist schema, the viewer is cast in the role of a passive receiver of a transcendental truth, a position increasingly untenable with the shift from structuralist to post-structuralist theories of the role of language in the construction of subjectivity, as well as, in art, the influence of temporal, interactive, audience-implicated 'neo-Dadaist' provocations like those of the loosely affiliated Fluxus groups. Taking on board a more Wittgensteinian approach to language – that meaning was in the use – artists of Post-Minimalist and Conceptual tendencies had begun to de-emphasise the role of authorship in favour of a more critical attention to spectatorship and the nature of the object itself.

Moreover, within the high modernist canon, visuality is granted a privileged status as the domain of objectivity and truth, which has to be seen as a disavowal both of the complex semantic field by which art recognises itself historically and of those rather ineffable but equally affective aspects of a work: its rhythm, spatial and tactile qualities. The affectivity of a work is undoubtedly a combination of all these factors as they work on the more unconscious processes of reminiscence and desire. That these possess both a collective and an individual inflection means that the field of meanings set up by the maker are not equivalent to the field of interpretations constructed by the viewer, such that the significations of a work of art can never be fixed or pre-determined.

Coleman's work of the early 1970s assumed the analytic *modus operandi* of the time, but rather than draw on linguistic or philosophical models, it pursued an enquiry of the relations between perception, memory and anticipation, maintaining a position squarely in the domain of visual art and a critique of visual traditions, introducing a time-based structure that temporalised vision.[3] This work is, however, less concerned with phenomenological questions of the spectator's reception of art than with the processes of interpretation and the role of representation in identity formation, concerns that were to lead quickly to an incorporation of social and historical dimensions into the artist's formal explorations of the perceptual apparatus. What emerged in the mid-70s, through works like *Box*, was a multi-layering and cross-cutting of visual and verbal references, increasingly elaborated through (more often than not) a critical or parodic use of familiar narrative forms, whether they be popular narrative genres like television soaps, pulp novels and photo-romans, or Irish literature and storytelling.

At one level, Coleman was drawn to the Tunney-Dempsey fight as a scenario which played out a modern, popular expression of the ancient 'hero' myth. The boxer of the early twentieth century, like the contemporary Latin American footballer, emerges, through his uncommon talents, from the ranks of the socially deprived to gain the highest public affirmation, functioning at this point as a national icon and individual role model. Should the hero transgress public expectations, however, he is, in Oedipal fashion, 'cast out' of the group (a painful exile, as witnessed by the recent fate of Maradona and OJ Simpson). Its significance here is as myth, a particular narrative form of language that allegorises the socialisation of the (male) self according to a persistent stereotype. Language, however, is a social institution that 'comes from the dead'; it pre-exists the individual's entry into the world and predicates his entry into the symbolic order as a

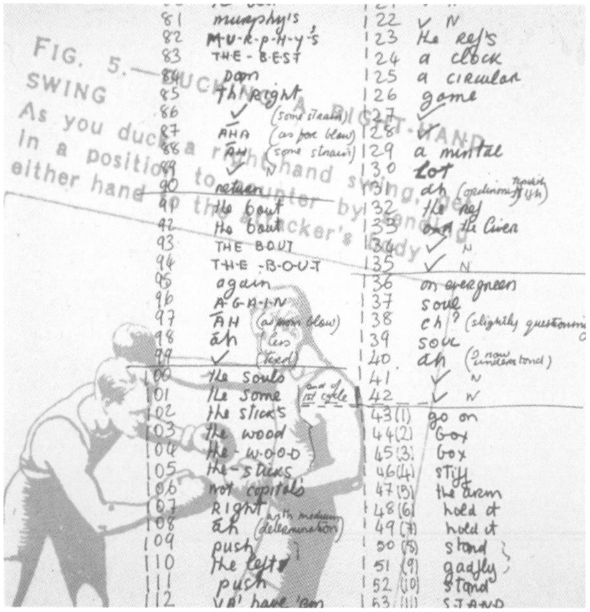

James Coleman, part of the script for the voice-over to *Box* (*Ahhareturnabout*), 1977. Courtesy of the Lisson Gallery, London.

functional subject. Coleman speculates on how far one's sense of reality is conditioned (and stultified) by such commodified images of subjectivity (projected above all through television), in which interpretation is an already given (the 'prediction' and the secret of the 'elixir of life' that surface in Coleman's more recent narrations, the key to which is invariably held by a figure of the symbolic order).[4]

The other side of this question, and one that gains greater prominence in the artist's projection works of the 1990s, such as *Background* (1992-93), *Lapsus Exposure* (1993), and *I N I T I A L S* (1994), is to what extent lived experience or individuated usages of language – *parole* in linguistic terms – can be called into play as a resistance to socially institutionalised interpretations of reality. *Box,* however, imagines that, if Tunney's private sense of selfhood is too fully imbricated with his public, heroic role then, in having to defend his title – being simultaneously 'champ' and 'not-champ' – he is in the untenable position of having to fight with a mortal body to maintain his immortality: an anxiety transmitted to the viewer through the visceral nature of the work. Caught in the endless repetition of *Box*, Tunney's physical and mental struggle to maintain self-coherence against disintegration has no satisfying narrative closure, no redemptive release. Interpretative language, the elixir of eternal life, like Plato's *pharmakon*, is both poison and medicine depending on how it is used, offering either a tragic vampiric arrest or a transformation of life as lived.

This thought slips into another function of the hero, that of the national icon, and in this register *Box* translates as a critique in allegorical form of myths of identity promoted by the nation-state in its efforts to construct and police a homogeneous and unified nationhood. Such myths are idealisations of assumed national characteristics – a communally held idea of the past, aims and aspirations – and their propagandist use acts to suppress what does not fit with the national agenda. Where this displaces history and mutates into a kind of sentimental nostalgia for what is no more than a phantasm, a society's ability to deal with the realities of the present becomes crippled and it runs the risk of cultural stagnation – the vampiric inertia, or endless, futile struggle to sustain a fictional past, projected through Tunney in *Box*.

Coleman's work displays a profound distrust of essentialist identities. Drawing on the artist's own local context, it frequently alludes to the continuing dominance of an outdated folkloric-literary construct of what constitutes 'Irish' culture, against which the realities of subsequent generations of Irish artists must fight for legitimation. The work insists, however, that if such cultural stereotypes cannot easily be overcome, they can – because they are not inherent traits but representational constructs – be repossessed and reinvested with other meanings. Coleman's work is thus salutary in any discussion of cultural identity and difference since it demonstrates the sterility of commodified and ahistorical signs of ethnicity which stunt the self's ability to trust the truth of its own experience. The work's insistence on building into itself the spectator's physical and mental awareness is one of its many ways of asserting that interpretation is not a given but a matter of negotiating one's own psycho-social history with the immanence of present experience through and against social institutions like formal language. If it is through the latter that the social creates stereotypic deformations of self, then it is by reinscribing these social institutions through historical consciousness that the self can narrate itself anew and transform its reality.

Finely tuned in both verbal and visual registers, Coleman's work understands the processes and uses of language and capitalises on the disjunction in sense that occur between the vernacular or personalised utterance and the institution of language.
It creates zones of ambivalence, opening a way to layerings or slippages of meaning, and thus to little resistances. *Box* is indeed concerned with the politics of representation – with representation *as* a political act – where the self is in a perpetual struggle to decipher its own 'truth' against the seductive pressures of those institutional forces that seek to impose others' fictions.

"Jack rushing drove a right and left to the jaw and Gene landed a light right and left to the head and body. Dempsey boxed in and put a left and right to the body just as the bell went…"
- Irish Independent,
Dublin, 23 September 1927

1 Paul Willemen, 'Cinematic Discourse: The Problem of Inner Speech', *Screen* 22, 1981, p.89.
2 For an excellent analysis of Coleman's work see Benjamin Buchloh, 'Memory Lessons and History Tableaux: James Coleman's Archaeology of Spectacle', *James Coleman: Projected Images: 1972-1994*, Dia Center for the Arts, 1994.
3 Ibid, p.53.
4 Jean Fisher, 'Concerning James Coleman's Recent Work', Dia Center for the Arts, op. cit.

West
Books
PL5000 - PR6021
PR602
CURRENT
PERIODICALS

Skin Tight

Glenn Ligon

I was eight years-old in 1968 when James Brown released *Say It Loud, I'm Black and I'm Proud*. The single went to number one on the rhythm and blues charts and number ten on the pop charts. In his autobiography, Brown says that the song is "obsolete now" and was "obsolete, but needed" when it was recorded, but he made it so that children could grow up with a sense of pride. I remember the thrill I got when I first heard the record on the little black plastic transistor radio I carried to school with me every day. Although the rhetoric of the black power movement hadn't quite made it to the public housing project in the Bronx where my family lived, I knew the song expressed something new and subversive. I was well aware of the issues of race, having attended a predominantly white elementary school in a wealthy neighbourhood in Manhattan since I was six years-old. The song became the anthem of my own burgeoning black consciousness movement, although when I was around my white classmates I could only manage to whisper the response to James' *Say It Loud*, fearful and ashamed of its strident nationalism.

One year before the release of *Say It Loud* Muhammad Ali refused induction into the US Army, on the grounds of his religious beliefs. In a statement issued at the time, Ali said: "I am proud of the title World Heavyweight Champion, which I won in the ring in Miami on 25 February 1964. The holder of it should at all times have the courage of his convictions and carry out those convictions, not only in the ring but throughout all phases of his life." Ali was immediately stripped of his title, his passport was confiscated and he was not allowed to fight for three years.

Although I knew nothing about boxing and wasn't interested in the sport, I knew about Ali and was fascinated by him. A Korean American friend said that when he was a kid he was also fascinated by Ali because he represented what he had been told was a very, very dangerous thing to be in America: a person who spoke his mind. Fiercely skilled in the ring and verbally adept, Ali was a scirocco that blew through the nation, embodying a 'New Negro' that was beginning to take the helm from traditional civil rights and religious leaders. Ali was also stunningly handsome. One sportswriter wrote that he "glowed, sort of a strange colour". His physical beauty penetrated to a region of my mind just beginning to be aware of my desire for the bodies of other men and seeing his image on TV or in the print media invariably caused me to skip a breath.

More recently Ali's words and his body became the centre of my installation *Skin Tight*, which employs the form of the punch bag as a means to investigate how black men have used boxing to confront issues of black American identity. The work deals with the construction of masculinity in relation to questions of violence, the commodification of black subjects, sexuality and resistance.

Joyce Carol Oates has remarked that although you *play* other sports, you don't *play* boxing. I believe she is correct in suggesting that boxing is where battles are fought far larger than the immediate spectacle of two fighters in the ring. Here in America, and throughout the world, people of colour have faced cultural and political struggles. Boxing is one of the most important and most visible arenas in which these struggles have been played out.

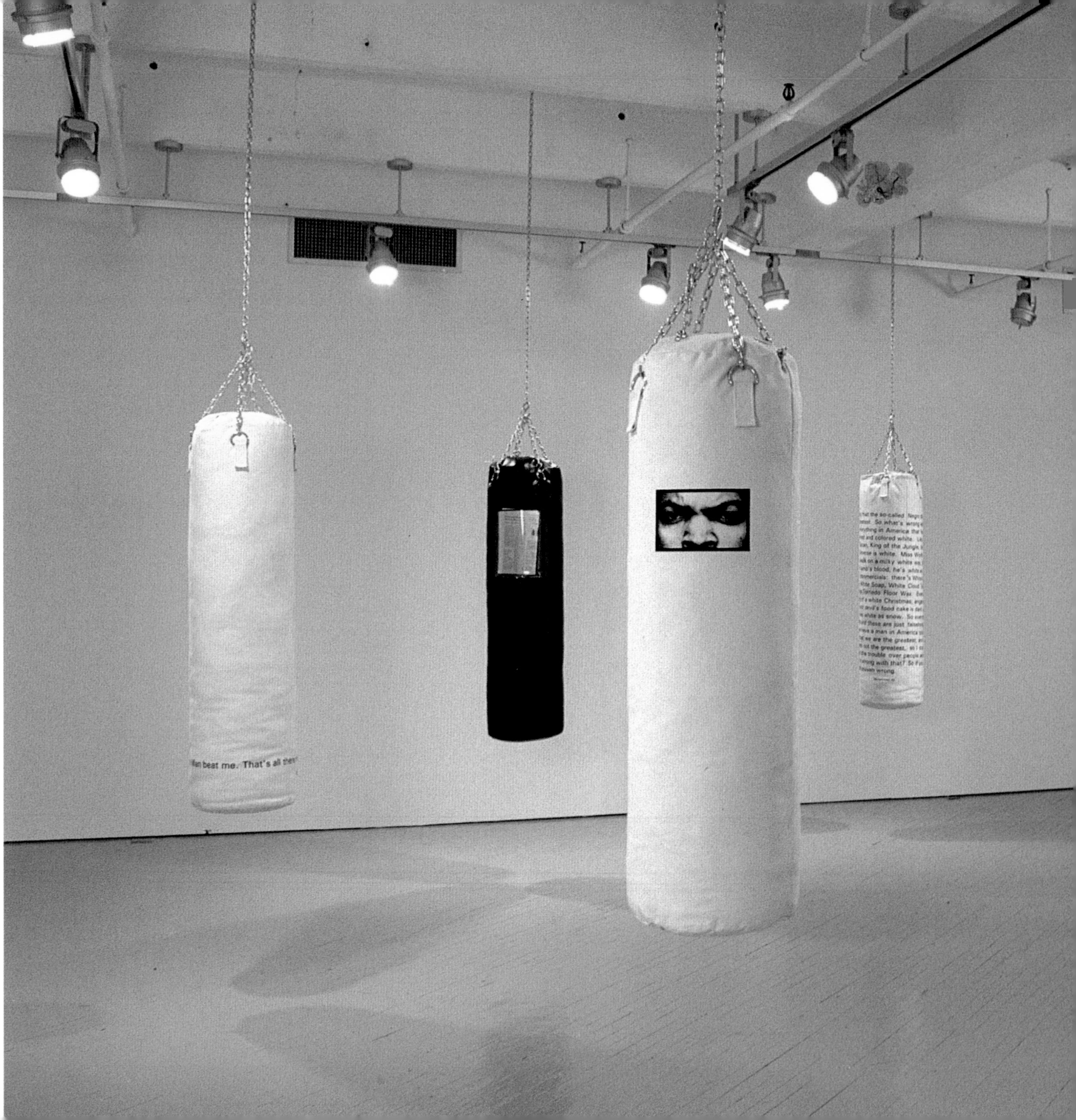

Previous page: Glenn Ligon, *Skin Tight*, Installation view at MIT. Copyright: Charles Mayer, 1995. Courtesy: The Artist.

Glenn Ligon, *Skin Tight*, Installation at The Fabric Workshop, April 1995. Courtesy: The Artist.

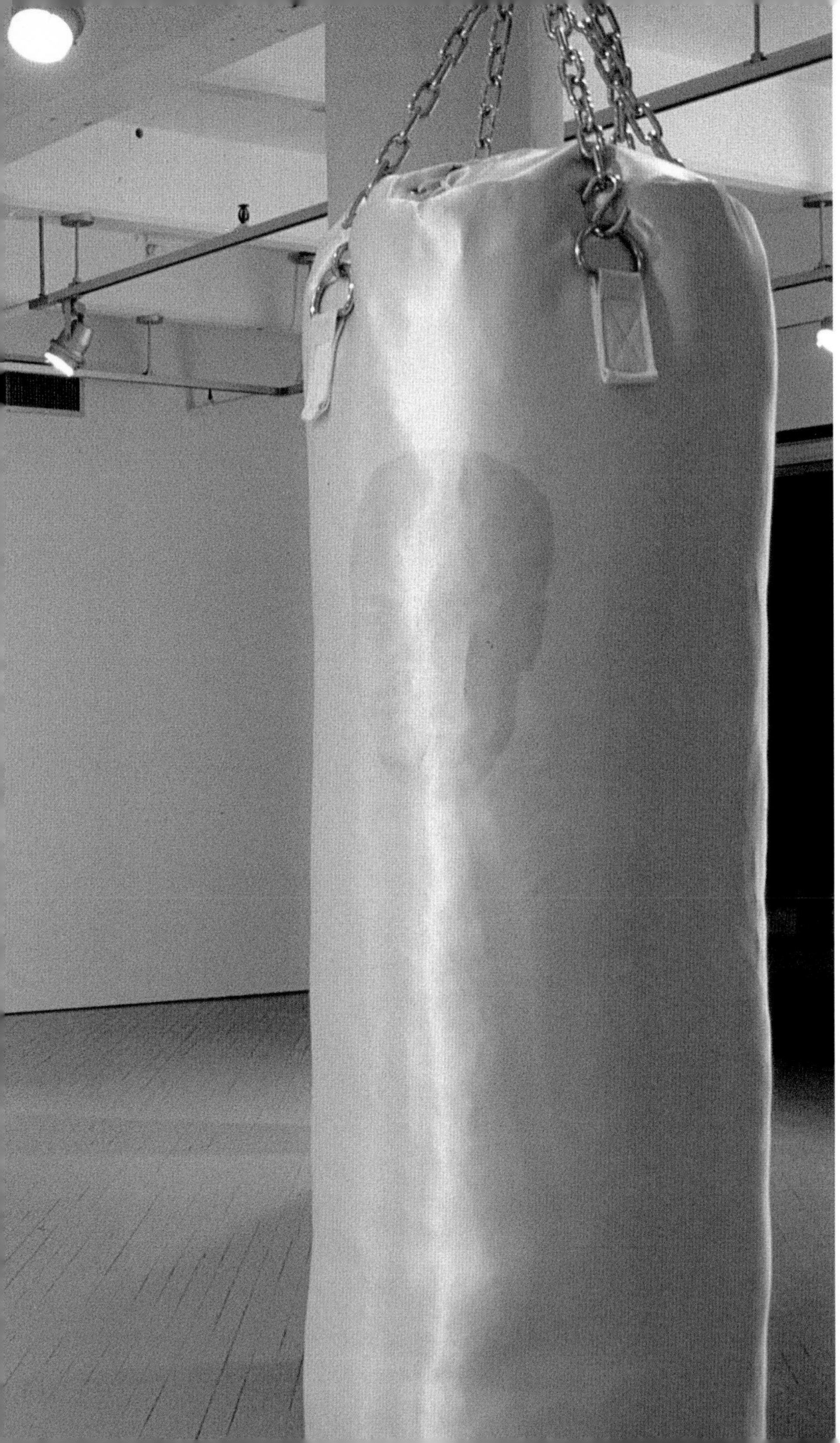

Glenn Ligon, *Skin Tight: Ice Cube's Eyes*, 1995. Black pigment on natural canvas. 51 x 14 x 15 inches. Ed. 7. Courtesy: Max Protetch Gallery and The Artist.

Glenn Ligon, *Skin Tight*, Installation view at MIT. Copyright: Charles Mayer, 1995. Courtesy: The Artist.

Glenn Ligon, *Skin Tight: Leon Spinks Quote*, 1995. Black pigment on natural canvas. 51 x 14 x 15 inches. Ed. 7.
Courtesy: Max Protetch Gallery and The Artist.

Glenn Ligon, *Skin Tight: Photo Pocket*, 1995. Black vinyl and clear acetate. 58 x 13 x 14 inches. Ed. 7.
Courtesy: Max Protetch Gallery and The Artist.

Glenn Ligon, *Skin Tight: Muhammad Ali's Head*, 1995. Black pigment on natural canvas. 53 x 13 x 15 inches. Ed. 7.
Courtesy: Max Protetch Gallery and The Artist.

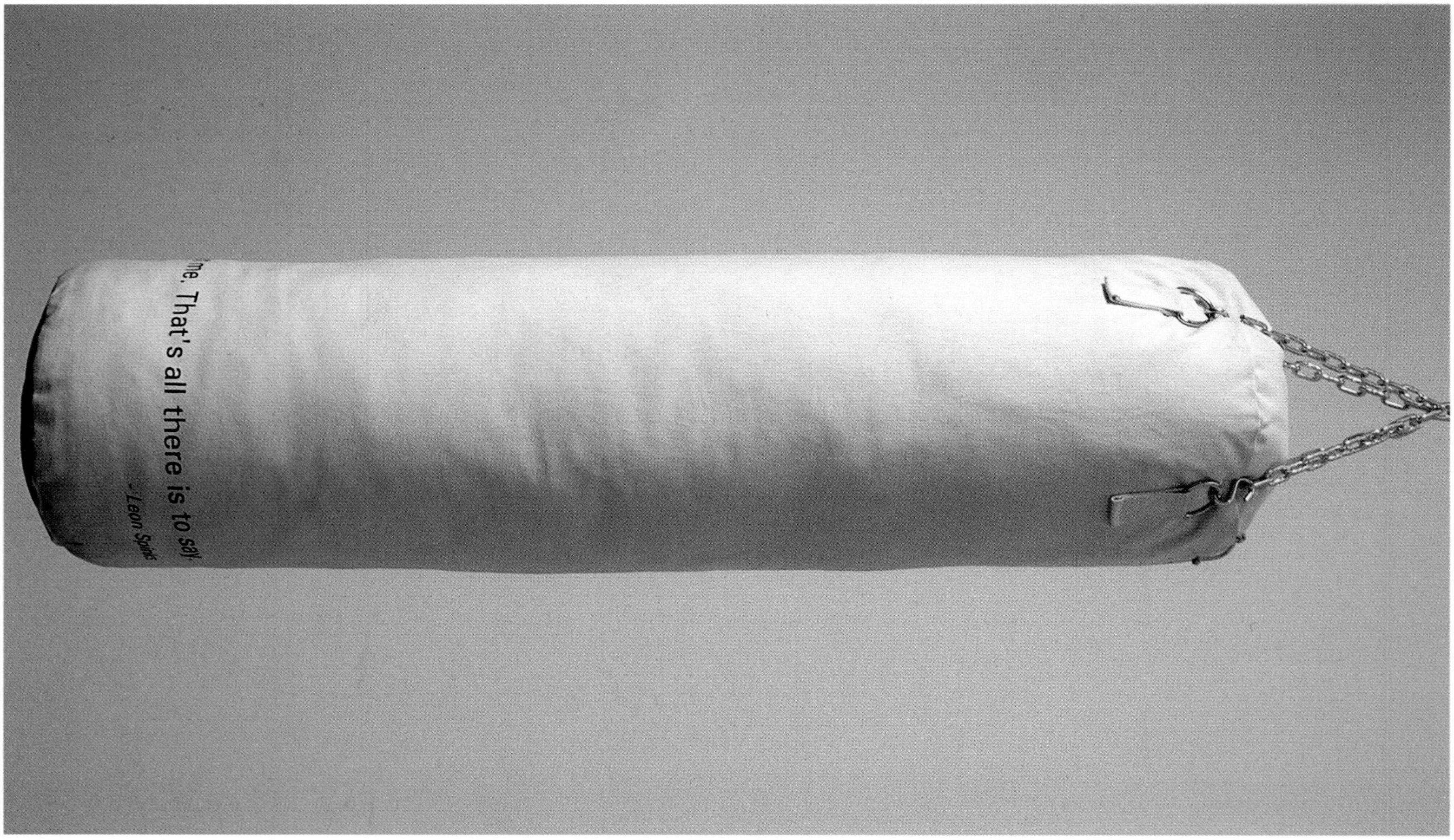

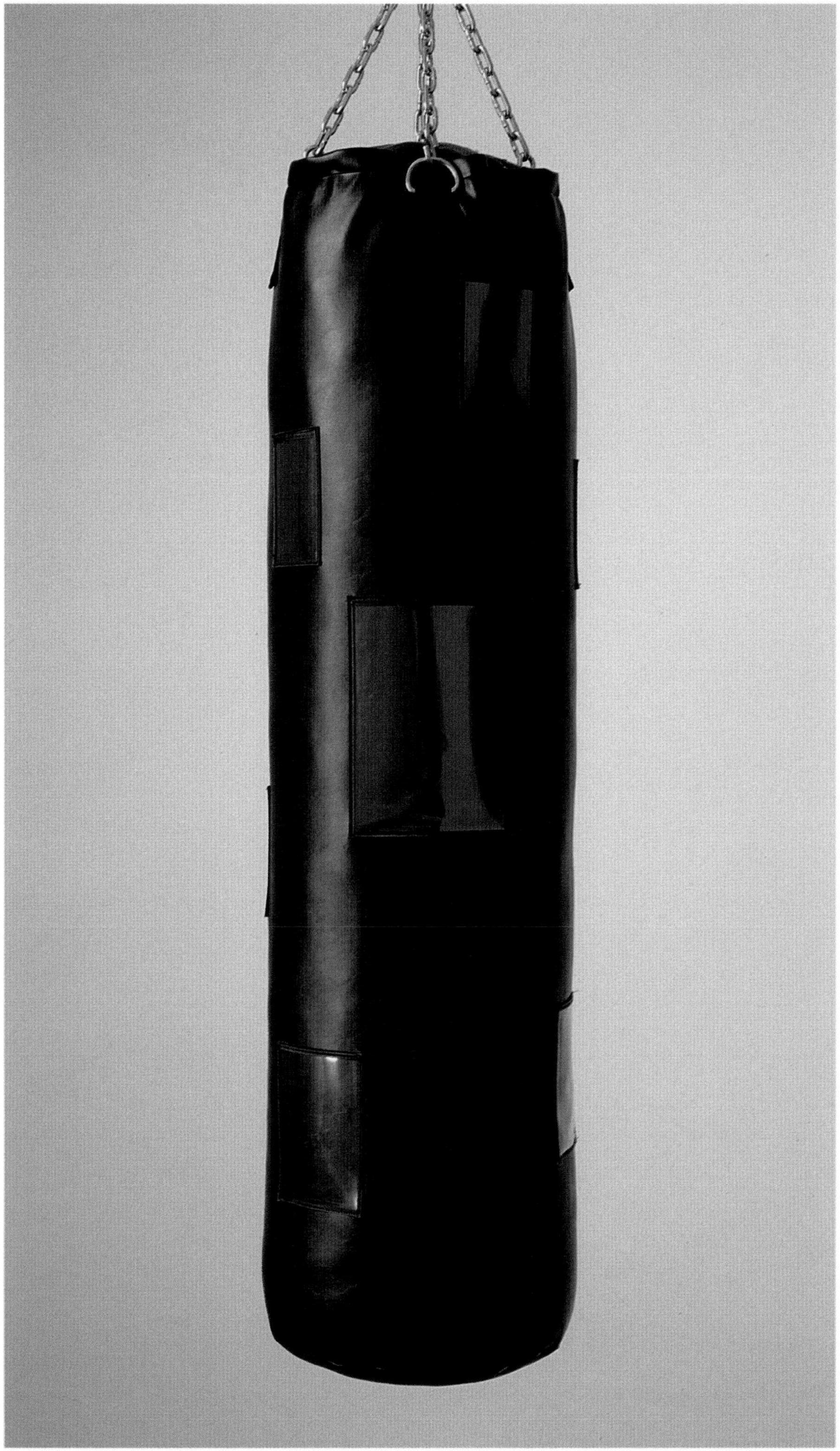
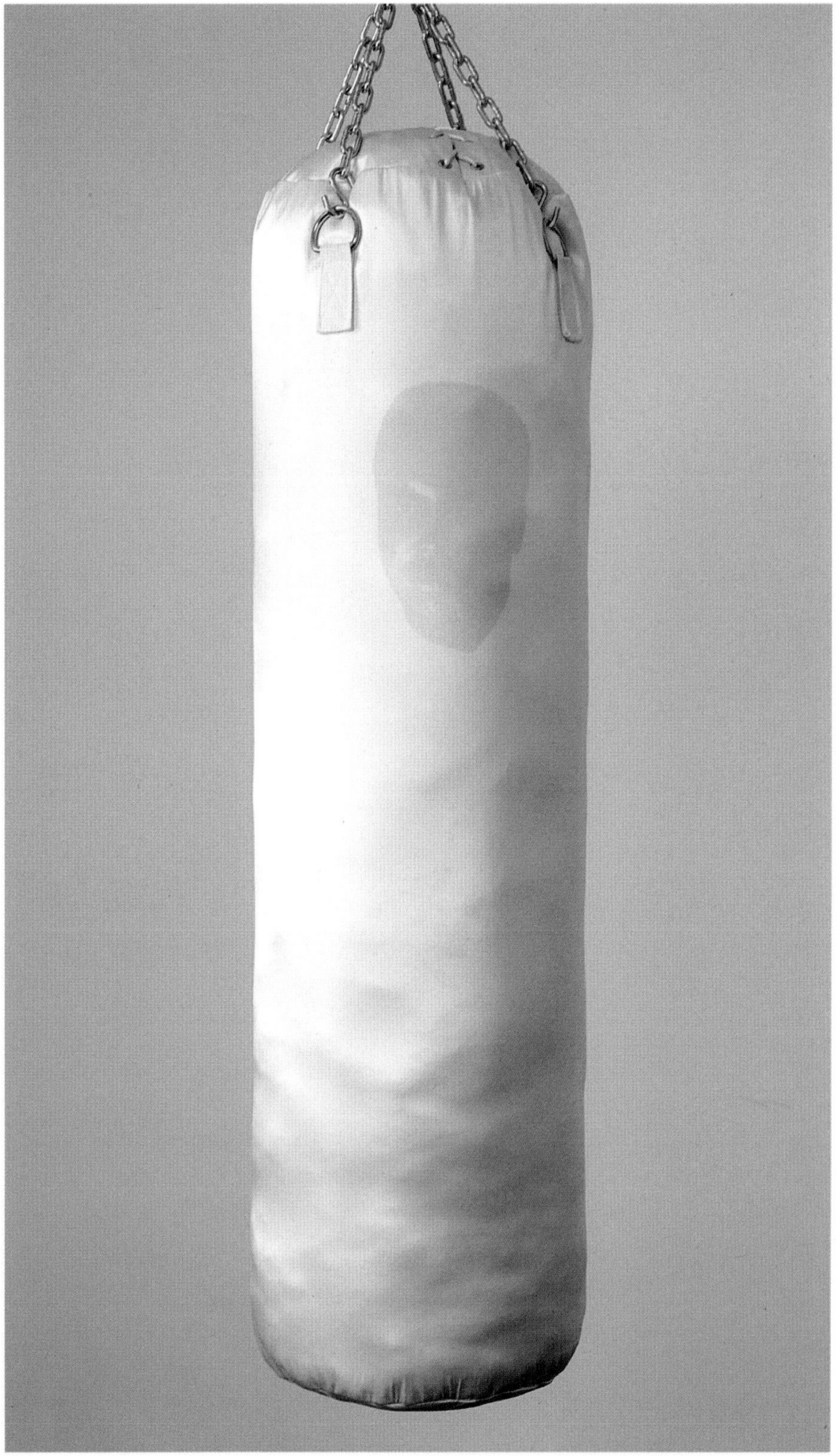

THUGLIFE®
U.S.A.

Glenn Ligon, *Skin Tight: Thug Life II*, 1995. Yellow ink on black vinyl. 60 x 13 x 14 inches. Ed. 7.
Courtesy: Max Protetch Gallery and The Artist.

Glenn Ligon, *Skin Tight: Muhammad Ali Text*, 1995. Black pigment on natural canvas. 59 x 13 x 14 inches. Ed. 7.
Courtesy: Max Protetch Gallery and The Artist.

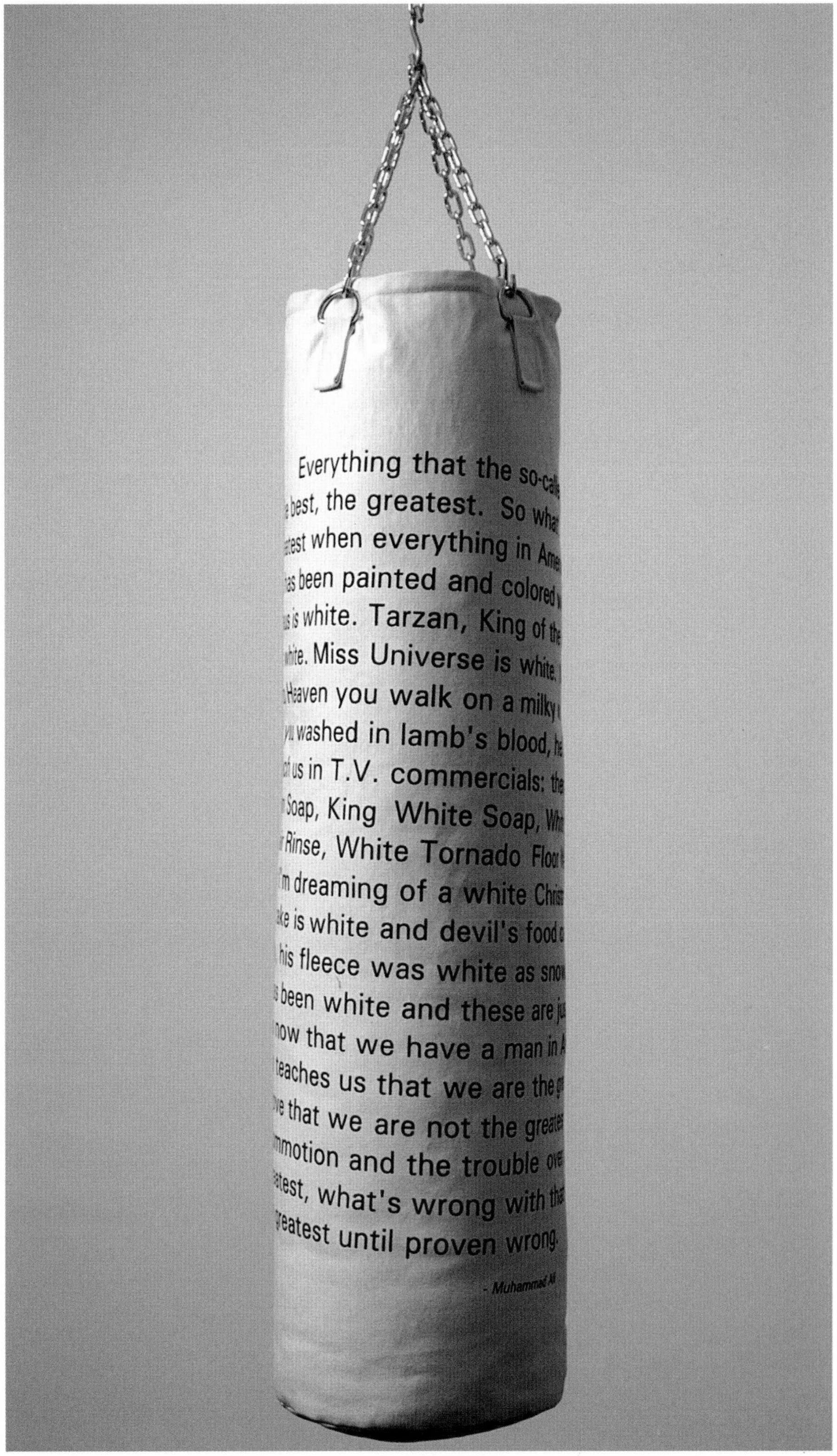
Everything that the
the greatest. So
when everything in
been painted and
white. Tarzan, King of
Miss Universe is
Heaven you walk on a
washed in lamb's blood,
us in T.V. commercials:
Soap, King White Soap,
Rinse, White Tornado
dreaming of a white
is white and devil's food
his fleece was white as
been white and these are
that we have a man in
teaches us that we are the
that we are not the
and the trouble
what's wrong with
greatest until proven wrong.
- Muhammad Ali

that's all there is

Glenn Ligon, *Skin Tight*, Installation at The Fabric Workshop, April 1995.
Courtesy: The Artist.

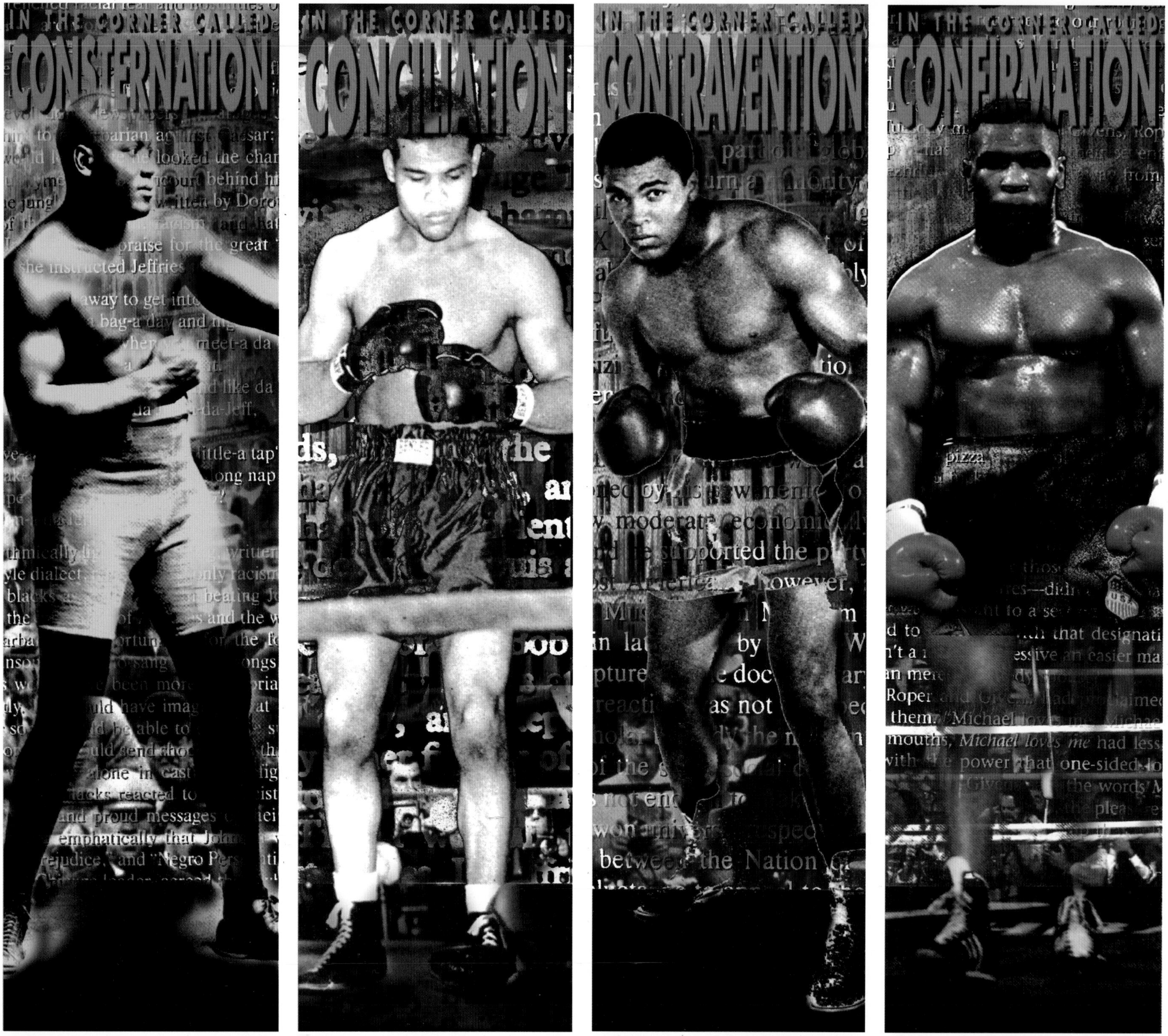
IN THE CORNER CALLED
CONSTERNATION
IN THE CORNER CALLED
CONCILIATION
IN THE CORNER CALLED
CONTRAVENTION
IN THE CORNER CALLED
CONFIRMATION

Four Corners, A Contest of Opposites

Keith Piper

Keith Piper, *Four Corners, A Contest of Opposites*, 1995. Commissioned by the Institute of International Visual Arts for the touring exhibition *Boxer*, curated by John Gill and organised by Walsall Museum and Art Gallery. Courtesy: The Artist.

I The genesis of the involvement of black men in the arena of prizefighting embodies a complex set of markers which have fixed and influenced wider social readings of the black boxer ever since. In *Narrative of the Life of Frederick Douglas,*[1] the American ex-slave, activist and historical commentator recounts the widespread practice of slave owners pitting their 'finest physical specimens' against one another for the glory of the plantation and sizeable wagers.

In a sense this prefigures the wider development of boxing. From its very beginning the 'prizefight' has been invariably an affair sponsored by a social and economic elite but contested by individuals from the very bottom of the social spectrum. The relationship between the prizefighting slave and the slave master was merely the most extreme expression of what has developed into an ongoing legacy of disempowerment and control endured by boxers at the hands of their economic sponsors and controllers. The slave owner has been joined and superseded by the capitalist entrepreneur, the criminal syndicate, the media mogul and most recently the big fight promoter as the virtual owner of the boxer's body. As Mike Marqusee points out in his essay *Sport or Stereotype: From Role Model to Muhammad Ali,* "Boxing today appears highly individualistic but [...] boxers have less power over their bodies and careers than almost any other sports people. Even successful boxers [...] are bound like serfs to promoters, managers and satellite TV companies."[2]

In fact a significant dual burden has always rested upon the shoulders of the prizefighter. As slave or serf he was always forced to carry the symbolic prestige of his sponsor, be that promoter or plantation owner. At the same time, he would often exist within the view of his peers as somehow representative of their interests and aspirations. His struggles within the boxing ring were seen to provide a metaphoric foil for their daily struggle for survival. Although in most instances the prestige and privilege conferred upon the successful prizefighter would inevitably distance him from the social setting out of which he emerged, disenfranchised communities from the slave plantation to the Brownsvilles of the late twentieth century, have felt themselves empowered by the successes of their prizefighting sons and brothers.

As the profile and visibility of the boxer increases, so inevitably does the scale of the symbolic constituency which he is seen to represent. The boxing ring has often been elevated to the status of an arena across which wider narratives of identity, visibility, race and nation have been played out. As Jeffrey T. Sammons points out in his book *Beyond the Ring*: "Since prizefighting has been characterised by some as a true test of skill, courage, intelligence and manhood, boxing champions have traditionally stood as symbols of national and racial superiority."[3]

It is against this highly charged backdrop that the black boxer has been forced to negotiate an often tentative path between agendas set and demands imposed upon the black body by the dominant social order to whom his paymasters belong, and the symbolic aspirations of that black portion of the fight audience to whom he carried special significance.

For the earliest of black boxers who managed to secure some measure of visibility, the deadening weight of white supremacist anxieties would all too often prove more than a match for their athletic prowess within the ring. In his book *Tom Molineaux: Career of an American Negro Boxer in England and Ireland, 1809-18,*[4] historian Paul Magriel describes the 'blackout' on the part of the American press during which they ignored the massive impact which two former slaves, Bill Richmond and Tom Molineaux, were having on the fledgling British fight scene. The epic confrontations of 1801-1811 between Molineaux and British champion Tom Cribb, immortalised in contemporary etchings such as *Boxeurs*[5] by Theodore Gericault, were widely perceived in racial and nationalistic terms, and the subsequent triumph of the Englishman was seen as a victory of whiteness.[6] America would not be ready for such a heavyweight spectacle for another 80 years.

The spectacle finally came with a 61-round contest between Peter Jackson, a West Indian-born Australian, and so-called Gentleman Jim Corbett on 21 May 1891. Although Corbett managed to hold Jackson to a draw, the prospect of a credible black challenger to the heavyweight crown proved too potent during a period of wider re-entrenchment of white political and economic power. As a result Jackson was pointedly refused a rematch with either Corbett, or the other great white heavyweight of the period, John L. Sullivan.

Mike Tyson, London, 21 July 1989.
Courtesy: The Ring Magazine.

A sense therefore arises that uniquely among the boxing categories, the heavyweight division has, at particular political moments, carried the burden of wider political agendas. This has at times led to its widespread perception as an exclusively white preserve despite the excellence of many black contenders. The roots of the 'heavyweight' phenomenon lie in the significance conferred on and global visibility afforded to heavyweight champions. Historian Jeffrey T. Sammons makes an interesting point about the reasons why, at the turn of the century, black boxers in lighter divisions such as George Dixon and Joe Walcott, were allowed access to title fights while heavyweights such as Peter Jackson found themselves excluded. "Dixon, Gans and Walcott all fought in the lighter weight classifications, and though their battles against whites may have been disturbing to many whites, their size was a mitigating factor; they do not symbolise the nation or their race, since the biggest fighting men have always had that burden."[7]

We can therefore begin to understand why in the twentieth century, once the avalanche of black contenders for the heavyweight crown became irrepressible, the images of individual fighters who achieved visibility within this arena have come inevitably to sit at the core of prevailing discourses around race, sexuality, political orientation and the dichotomy between the good and the bad negro.

It is within this contest of symbols that I would argue four twentieth-century heavyweight prizefighters have emerged as key players. Each has, within his own epoch, enjoyed the status of being the most visible black male on the planet. Each has, albeit in very different ways, been moulded by and at the same time has profoundly shaped prevailing debates surrounding perceptions of black masculinity. These prizefighters were Jack Johnson, Joe Louis, Muhammad Ali and Mike Tyson.

II

In his article *Sport and Stereotype*, Mike Marqusee discusses the differences between Jack Johnson and Joe Louis under the heading 'Uncle Toms and bad Niggers'.[8] While I would shy away from such a potentially pejorative appraisal of Joe Louis' role (the Uncle Tom of the title), this dichotomy provides us with an interesting starting point. The black fighter is forced to negotiate a precarious line between, on the one hand, the prescriptions of the white status quo, the boxing promotions industry, the press and to an extent, apologist portions of the black middle class; on the other hand, the aspirations of black audiences yearning for an empowering antidote to their powerlessness. The myriad, complex and in certain instances contradictory ways in which each of these four fighters have been placed, or have sought to place themselves, in relation to these shifting demands and agendas will form the basis of this text. I will employ what I accept is a rather simplistic contrast between the good and bad negro. The fighters who have to an extent conformed to the prevailing codes of acceptable black behaviour as prescribed by the white power structure, and those who have operated in opposition to those prescribed codes. I will argue that while Jack Johnson and Muhammad Ali waged a symbolic war on the imposed and prescribed norms of the day, Joe Louis, and more controversially, Mike Tyson, have – albeit in very different ways – conformed to and reinforced the dominant messages about the nature of black masculinity.

The symbolic contests of opposition waged by Jack Johnson and Muhammad Ali share similarities only at the most immediate level of aesthetics. Both fighters exhibited an eloquent arrogance, both inside and outside the ring, that was deliberately galling to those who shared the consensus that sportsmen, and black sportsmen in particular, should assume an air of modesty about their prowess and achievements.

Jack Johnson's ring craft inflamed a whole set of white supremacist anxieties, not only by presenting the spectre of a black male physically humiliating white opponents, but also (and far worse) by Johnson's visible enjoyment of that process made blatantly obvious by his constant gleeful grin. Against the backdrop of a heavyweight division at that time crammed with colourless contenders, Johnson's newsworthy bravado initially succeeded in tearing a fissure in the so-called 'colour barrier' – something which had so effectively denied Peter Jackson a title shot. After the retirement of Jim Jefferies in 1905, the popularity of prizefighting took a nose dive. Jack Johnson was finally allowed a title shot against the then champion, German-Canadian Tommy Burns in a calculated bid to restore public interest in prizefighting. Jeffrey T. Sammons describes contemporaneous attitudes in the following terms: "Should Tommy Burns, who was a lacklustre, unpopular foreigner, lose, boxing would gain, for a black champion would bring back interest and money to the game, his reign would surely be temporary, and his ultimate defeat would symbolically reaffirm white racial supremacy."[9]

In other words, it was primarily Johnson's bravado which rendered him attractive to the financial controllers of the fight industry – albeit as a marketable menace. It was only when Johnson refused to follow the script and dispatched a series of 'white hopes' that the clamour grew for the former champion Jim Jefferies to return to the ring so that the 'natural order of things' be restored. In Jefferies own words, he was returning in response to: "That portion of the white race that has been looking to me to defend its athletic superiority."[10]

On 4 July 1910, Johnson humiliated Jefferies through fifteen rounds, punctuating each blow with the words: "Package being delivered Mister Jeff". The film recording this ritual humiliation proved so galling to white supremacists and anti-boxing activists that it lead to a complete ban on fight films which remained in place for years.

Visibility and the power of film and television was also key to the case of Muhammad Ali. From the moment he emerged into the professional fight industry as Cassius Clay, the Louisville Lip lived up to his billing by berating his opposition with a torrent of verbal abuse and bragging which was to prove highly marketable. This potential was quickly recognised and the young Clay found himself sponsored by a consortium of white Louisville businessmen. As early as 1963, Clay fully recognised the importance of his brash persona as a means of rendering himself visible and thereby circumventing the racist limitations routinely enforced upon the black body: "Where would I be next week, if I didn't know how to shout and holler and make the public take notice? I'd be poor and I'd probably be down in my home

Joe Louis, c. 1934.
Courtesy: The Ring Magazine.

town, washing windows or running an elevator and saying 'yes suh' and 'no suh' and knowing my place."[11]

Both Johnson and Ali employed vocal and gestural bravado as a way to entice the white establishment into giving them a high profile. In both cases, once their visibility was firmly established, it was used to promote and deliver agendas which that same establishment would find unacceptable in the extreme.

This however is where the similarities end. The content of Johnson's and Ali's transgressive acts can be seen as diametrically opposed. Jack Johnson rose to visibility during a period when the white hegemony was violently fortifying its position. The notorious US Supreme Court *Plessy v. Fergson* ruling of 1896 had institutionalised segregation and sought to fix blacks within a separate and unequal category. The white supremacist hierarchy saw its God given role as being to forcefully exclude the 'other', and the black 'other' in particular, from the privileged domains over which it exercised control. These included the 'actual' domains of political and economic power, judicial authority, the right to suppress through force of arms, access to systems of knowledge and learning and the 'symbolic' domains of recreation, culture and above all, sex.

Writers from Eldridge Cleaver to Frantz Fanon have explored the often brutal contest of terrain played out around access to the bodies of white women. It was a contest into which Jack Johnson enrolled as a key player. In Randy Roberts' book, *Papa Jack* (1929), we are told that: "He would celebrate every major victory in his career in the arms of one or more white females."[12] Jeffrey T. Sammons appraises the impact of Johnson's very public and visible transgression into the white supremacists' exclusive domain in the following terms: "Eventually this affinity for white women, which met with overwhelming public resentment and hostility, combined with Johnson's ring prowess and antics to make him the most controversial and perhaps the most courageous boxer of all time."[13]

Following his historic defeat of Sonny Liston in February 1964, the recently renamed Cassius X declared: "I don't try to move into white neighbourhoods. I don't want to marry a white woman [...] I'm a good boy. I never have done anything wrong. I have never been to jail [...] I don't join any integration marches [...] I don't pay attention to all those white women who wink at me."[14] At first sight, the statement would have reassured and comforted any white supremacist still smarting from the nightmare of the miscegenation that was Jack Johnson. However, upon closer inspection one begins to trace the markers of a transgressive position every bit as terrifying to the white establishment as Jack Johnson's had been 60 years before. By the early 1960s, the Civil Rights Movement's efforts had set in motion a transformation of the political landscape that would initiate the slow process of compelling the liberal establishment to grant a measure of enfranchisement to a small number of 'good negroes'. Implicit was an assumption that every negro dreamed of access to the domain of white privilege. In 1964 Cassius stated, "I believe in Allah," signalling the complete overturning of these assumptions. It was the gradual maturation of a process began in 1959 when the young Clay first heard Elijah Muhammad speak in Chicago, and was further strengthened in 1962 when, along with his brother Rudolph, Cassius met Malcolm X at a Detroit mosque. Although Malcolm derided boxing as 'exploitative', he also recognised its key significance in the contest being played out around the visibility of a black opposition to the cultural hegemony of mainstream white America. In his autobiography, Malcolm describes the significance of Ali's 1965 contest with the devout Christian, Floyd Patterson: "This fight is the truth [...] It's the Cross and the Crescent fighting in a prize ring [...] for the first time. It's a modern Crusade [...] a Christian and a Muslim facing each other with television to beam it off Telstar for the whole world to see."[15]

To Malcolm, Islam represented a rejection of Western ideology. He also recognised that Ali's victory over Patterson was made all the more significant by the massive visibility which technology was beginning to afford. This provides a fascinating reversal of white supremacists' anxieties concerning the film of Jack Johnson's victory over Jim Jeffries. All concerned recognised the power of visual symbol and of language. Within this, a recurring contest was played out around the power to name. The insistence of Patterson in 1965, Ernie Terrell in 1967 and Joe Frazier in 1971 on calling Ali by his pre-Muslim name 'Clay', not only sought to undermine Ali's contest of language, but also emphasised each of these fighters' personal affiliation with the views of the white establishment. In each case, Ali's response – echoing a technique used by Jack Johnson before him – was to punctuate each blow with the question, "What's my name?"

So terrifying was the visibility of Ali's transgressive act that, as in the case of Johnson, the full weight of the legal establishment swung into action against him. In Jack Johnson's case the 'White Slave Traffic' or Mann Act of 1910 was brought to bear, using his travels with a white woman called Belle Schreiber as a pretext for forcing him into exile. In Ali's case, the government and military mobilised against him for refusing to 'serve' in the Vietnam war. Ali was stripped of his title and unable to pursue his career from 1967 to 1971.

If Jack Johnson and Muhammad Ali incurred the wrath of the establishment through their highly visible transgression of society's imposed codes, Joe Louis and to an extent Mike Tyson, conformed to those codes and yet suffered similar fates.

Joe Louis was the first black boxer to attain world-wide popularity after the 25-year-long 'colour bar' enforced in the wake of Jack Johnson's war of transgression. From the outset Louis was groomed by his handlers, initially black managers John Roxborough and Julian Black, to present an image which would allay white American fears about the nature of black males in general, and black prizefighters in particular. With Johnson no doubt in mind, Louis was firmly instructed to "never have his picture taken alongside a white woman" and always "keep a 'dead pan' in front of the cameras."[16] Here, once again, we find an acknowledgement and understanding of the power that image and the mass media carry – in this instance, as a means to navigate a safe path through a dangerous and troubled racial landscape. Even in terms of his moniker, The Brown Bomber, Louis' 'packaging' sought to diffuse the disturbing overtones which a connection with 'blackness' could bring.

Louis would find himself the symbolic champion of the white establishment's most progressive elements as well as the darling and standard bearer of black communities across the country. For a seemingly apolitical fighter, Louis was often cast within the most politically charged prizefighting contests. The Italian fighter, Primo Carnera, came to be closely associated, at least in the eyes of the American press, with Italian Fascist leader

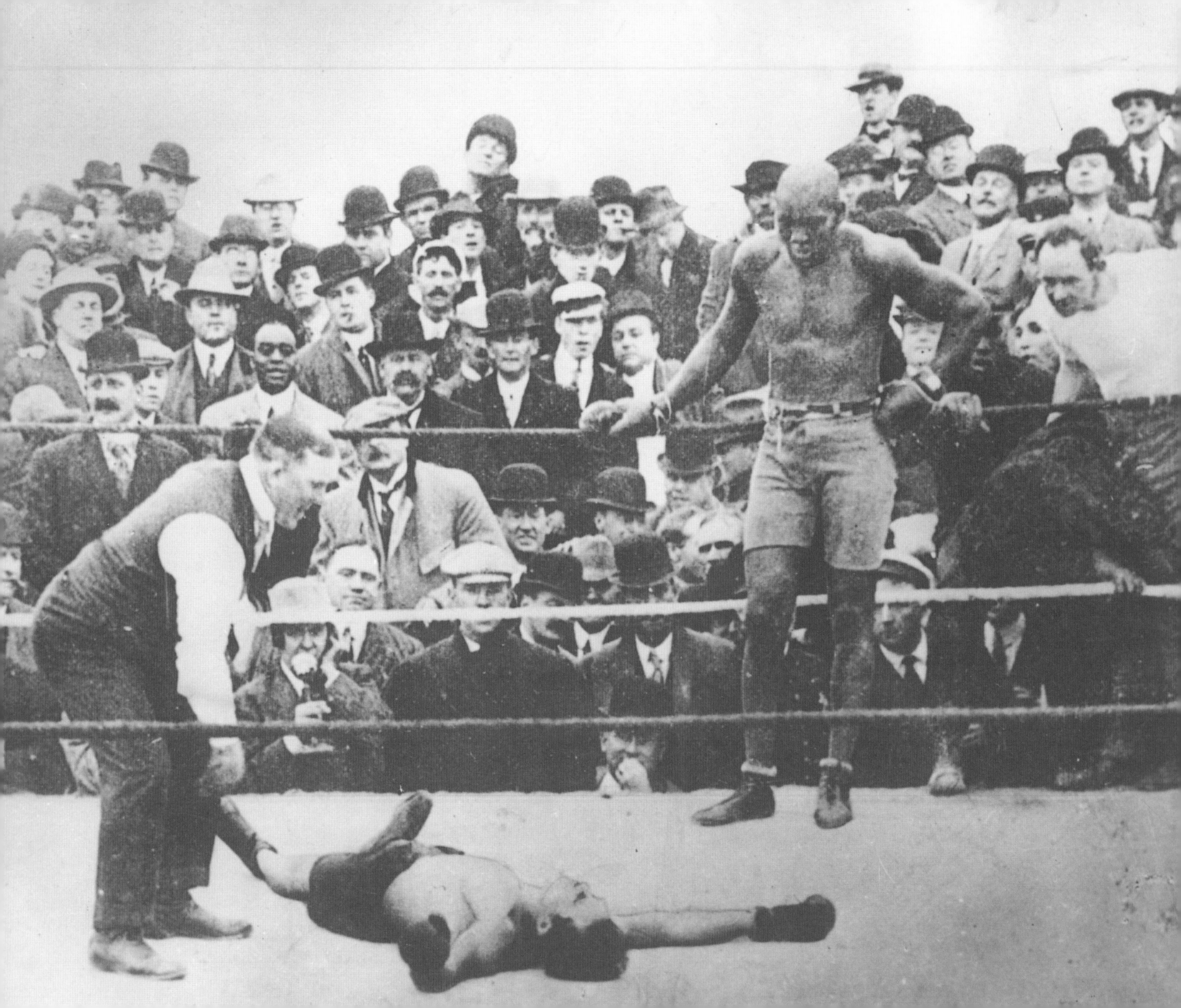

Knock-out of Stanley Ketchel by Jack Johnson in the 12th round, 16 October 1909.
Courtesy: Calif Colma, The Ring Magazine.

Benito Mussolini, who enthused about boxing as an "exquisitely fascist means of self-expression."[17] Mussolini's invasion of Abyssinia in 1934 led to the Carnera-Louis confrontation of the following year being seen as a symbolic re-enactment of the war between Italy and the small African nation.

The rise to visibility of Max Schmeling, a German fighter closely associated with the Nazi regime, was to generate an even more fevered war of symbols. In fact the Jewish fighter Max Baer, who met and defeated Schmeling in 1933, declared that: "Every punch in the eye I give Schmeling is one for Adolf Hitler."[18] When against the odds, Louis was defeated in the twelfth round by Schmeling on 22 June 1936, it was read by white supremacists, not only as a victory for Germany or Nazism over America, but as positive proof of the black race's inferiority. George Spandau was to declare that the fight symbolised: "White honesty over black brutality and lack of discipline [...] Through the German Schmeling the white race, Europe and White America, defeated the black race."[19]

Therefore, the second Louis-Schmeling confrontation on 22 June 1938 took on the symbolic connotations of an epic international conflict. Awareness of the Nazi menace had begun to permeate popular consciousness in the US and Louis suddenly found himself recast as the standard bearer for the nation in a fight being billed as "democracy versus fascism, pacifism versus militarism, and ultimately good versus evil."[20] In the event Louis destroyed Schmeling in 124 historic seconds and provided prizefighting with one of its most powerful and enduring symbolic moments.

Unlike Ali, Louis had elected to serve and become a 'credit to his race' in terms which America could understand and endorse. The establishment was able to co-opt him as their hero, both inside the boxing ring and as a morale boosting 'physical instructor' in the nation's armed forces. Nonetheless, none of these distinctions deterred the same state from mercilessly hounding Louis for back taxes through the later years of his life. As a consequence he was reduced to wrestling for money and working as a doorman in a Las Vegas casino.

At first sight, it may appear difficult to locate Iron Mike Tyson within a scenario which any type of establishment would find reassuring. At the age of fifteen, Tyson was mistakenly rumoured to be the nephew of the late Sonny Liston.[21] It was an easy mistake to make. Both Liston and Tyson had at one time been the very personification of the urban nightmare, the black epitome of criminality and chaos aptly described in the film *CB4* as "the nigger waiting for you in the dark". Liston was an ex-convict with a record of nineteen arrests. He had carried his terrifying physical persona undiluted into the boxing arena to become what Maurice Berude would describe as the "stereotypical nightmare of the bad nigger, the juvenile delinquent grown up."[22]

At the age of twelve, Tyson was sent to Spofford Detention Centre in the Bronx for armed robbery. The narrative of his progression to the upstate Tyron School for Boys where we are told he found redemption under the tutelage of Cus D'Amato has been elevated to the status of legend. Nevertheless, like Liston, Tyson would continue to cultivate his terrifying persona as an unmediated street hooligan deep into his professional career. In a telling statement following his defeat of Jesse Ferguson in February 1986, Tyson declared the following with considerable relish: "In the fourth round, I saw an opening for the uppercut. I always try to catch them on the tip of the nose because I try to push the bone into the brain."[23]

Beyond Tyson's apparently faithful replaying of Sonny Liston's 'bad nigger' theme, lurks an even darker scenario which would appear to link him to the 'black menace' that was Jack Johnson. It is a scenario that unfolds in the realm of sexual practice. Tyson is seen to transgress contemporary notions of acceptable conduct in a way which would seem to parallel Johnson's transgression of the separatist and segregationist orthodoxies of his day. However, it has become clear through accounts in books such as Jose Torres's *Fire & Fear* and Phil Bergers's *Blood Season,* as well as from the growing number of accounts by Tyson's victims, that unlike Jack Johnson, Tyson's sexuality hinged on violence and a disregard for consent. Tyson's incarceration in the Indiana Youth Centre for the brutal rape of Desiree Washington in an Indianapolis hotel room in July 1991, seemed, in retrospect, an inevitable consequence of such behaviour.

However, I would contest the argument which views Tyson's behaviour as 'transgressive' in the sense in which Johnson's and Ali's behaviour incurred the wrath of an establishment desperate to deny them visibility.

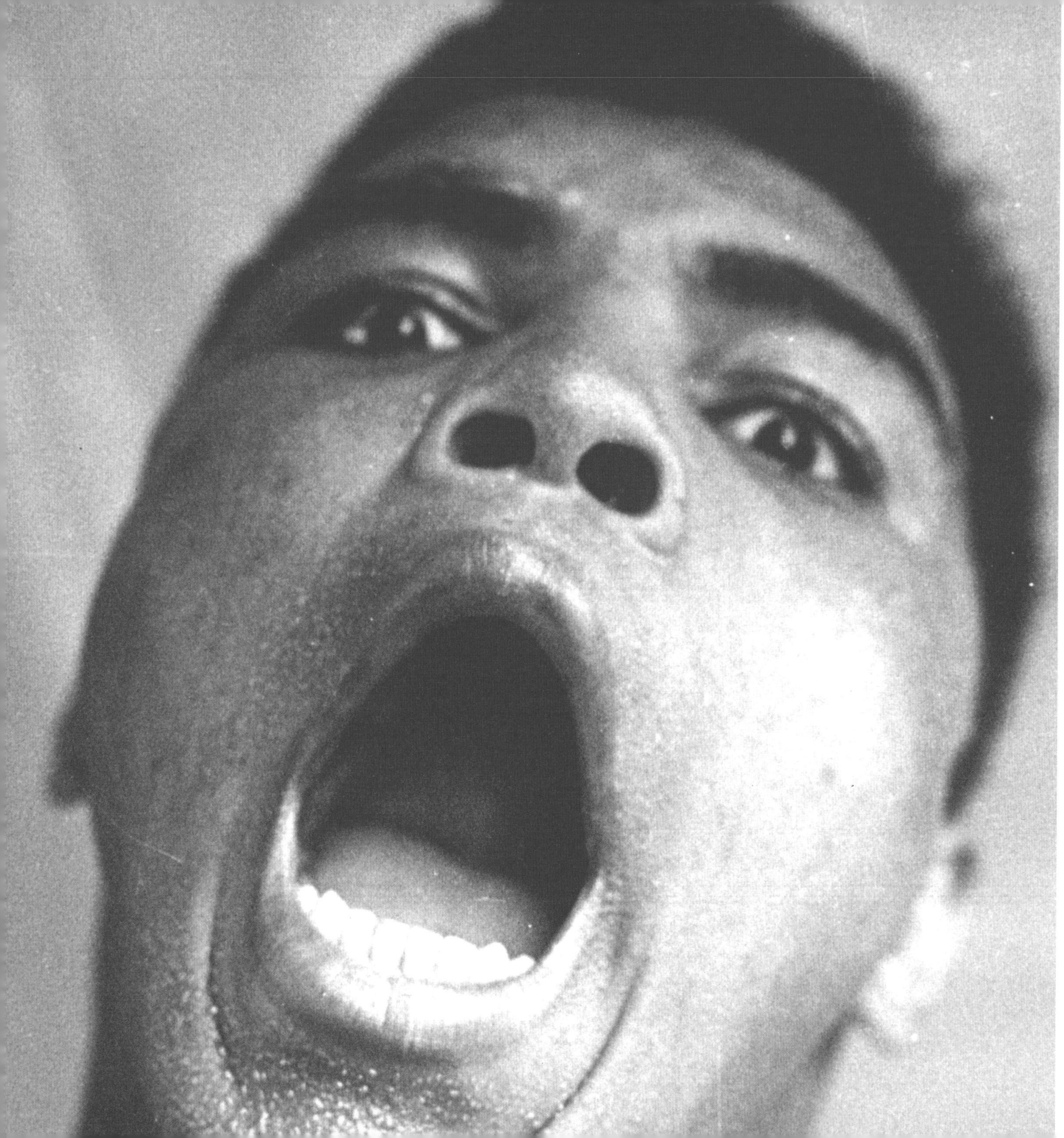

Muhammed Ali, 17 February 1964.
Copyright: Hulton Deutsch Collection Ltd.

The Tyson narrative instead centres on the parading and restating of a number of grand themes, of which his imprisonment is but one, which the press have made public thus reinforcing notions about white paternalism and a black masculinity out of control.

The well rehearsed Tyson narrative pivots on the child born in 1966 and left to grow wild by a dysfunctional contemporary black family. In the 'little fairy boy' version of this saga, we are presented with a softly spoken and timid child who only connects his inner rage once a local thug pulls the head off one of his pigeons. Thus traumatised a pre-pubescent monster is unleashed to prey upon the inhabitants of a war-zone neighbourhood. Inevitable incarceration leads to a series of watershed encounters with the stabilising power of white paternalism. First, there is the tough but fair ex-prizefighter Bobby Stewart, who, recognising Tyson's raw potential, introduces him to the legendary Cus D'Amato who runs a boxing programme in Catskill, upstate New York. Terms such as 'Svengali'[24] are used liberally when describing D'Amato. He had in the past rescued a young Floyd Patterson from a similar Brooklyn war-zone and moulded him into the modest, clean living young heavyweight champion of the late 1950s. Now aged 75, Cus viewed Tyson as his final opportunity to repeat the accomplishment and bask in the prizefighting limelight once more. In Reg Gutteridge's book *For Whom the Bell Tolls*, a chapter titled 'The Taming of Tyson' quotes D'Amato's partner Camille Ewald on the civilising process: "Mike was a very rebellious and angry young man. Rude, even. He was deeply suspicious and we had to win his trust." [Gutteridge continues] "But slowly, like a sculptor working on a masterpiece, Cus chipped away at him until he earned first of all his respect, then his loyalty, and ultimately his love."[25]

To complete this blissful scene, trainers with dependable names like Teddy Atlas and the experienced promotions team, Bill Cayton and Jim Jacobs, steered the reformed young fighter towards immortality. Within this narrative, the death of Cus D'Amato in November 1985 signals a watershed. Although a year later Tyson is smoothly guided to a contest with Trevor Berbick in which he becomes the youngest fighter in history to lift the heavyweight crown, the cracks are already beginning to show. Robbed of his 'father figure', we are told that Tyson is adrift. Increasingly he is drawn into the orbits of influence of what comes to be characterised as a terrifying black trilogy: the boxing promoter Don King, the young actress Robin Givens and her mother, Ruth Roper.

Despite a career in promotion which dates back to the historic Ali-Foreman 'Rumble in the Jungle' of 1974, it is difficult to find a complimentary appraisal of Don King's influence in any mainstream boxing article. James Dalrymple's account is typical: "Like some dark, crooning Nemesis, he came to Tyson when he was down and beaten and bewildered, took him in his arms and whispered to him that it was time finally to leave the white man's domain for good and join the brothers."[26]

Robin Givens and Ruth Roper are similarly demonised by a press incredulous at the motives of this "well-brought up young woman from New Rochelle [...] a Sarah Lawrence graduate" in her dealings with the semi-literate Tyson.[27] Once again Dalrymple presents an account which reads like bad soap opera: "Givens – aided by her rapacious mother, Ruth Roper – bled him dry in under a year of ferocious spending. She reeled him in with sexual promises for months, finally married him, exposed him on network television as a drug addict and wife beater and looted his bank account of an estimated $10 million in cash."[28] Tyson's subsequent defeat in the ring, manic depression and imprisonment for rape complete this American odyssey.

In a heavyweight division that almost exclusively comprises black Americans, the old themes of race and nation which shaped readings of Johnson, Louis and Ali are largely absent in the Tyson saga. Tyson's narrative is instead expressed in the uniquely late twentieth century terms of individual redemption and condemnation. It attempts to convince us of the possibility of meteoric rise, which it portrays as the All American Way. Tyson became the symbol of the supreme 1980s professional because he emerged as raw material to be moulded into an invincible fighting machine by the white father figure. When the civilising influence of American paternalism was stripped away, he was left at the mercy of new postmodern nightmare blacks, the bejewelled entrepreneur and the scheming bitch.

Missing from these accounts are other uncomfortable readings. The ones which suggest that Cus D'Amato's only interest in Tyson was as a fighting machine, as product. The teenager's evident sexual aggression was allowed to develop unchecked as long as he kept knocking other boys over in the ring. Legal difficulties were smoothed over by the financial muscle and influence of Jacobs and Cayton, who held an exclusive option on all the young fighters emerging from the Catskill gym and took a huge slice from Tyson's early earnings. At the same time Tyson's intellect was deliberately left underdeveloped in order to hone his persona into that of an American pit-bull terrier. When their creation finally slipped its leash, the legal protection was removed and Don King lacked either the will or influence to buy-off those legal forces as effectively as the Jacobs-Cayton cartel.

While the complex truth of the Tyson saga probably lies somewhere between those points, the simple fact remains that at the end of the twentieth century, a black prizefighter emerged who had been bought and bred for raw aggression in a way which directly echoed the slave champions spoken of by Frederick Douglass.

The saga takes on tragic proportions when the fighter emerges into a world where he is an anachronism, never having been equipped to deal with civil laws and constraints. It is an image which feeds directly into the demonisation of black masculinity in contemporary society, and which reinforces the dominant white male ideologies which continue to bombard us.

1 Jeffrey T. Sammons, 'Narrative of the life of Frederick Douglass: An American Slave', (New York: Signet: 1968), *Beyond the Ring, The Role of Boxing in American Society*, (University of Illinois Press: 1990), p.31.
2 Mike Marqusee, 'Sport and Stereotype: From role model to Muhammad Ali', *Race & Class*, (Institute of Race Relations: UK: April-June 1995), Volume 36, p.3.
3 Jeffrey T. Sammons, op. cit., p.31.
4 Paul Magriel, *Tom Molineaux: Career of an American Negro Boxer in England and Ireland, 1809-18*, (Phylon: 1951).
5 Nat Fleischer and Sam Andre, *A Pictorial History of Boxing*, (Bonanza Books: 1987), p.26.
6 Bud Schulberg, *Art in the Ring*, Producer Kim Evans, Omnibus, BBC MCMLXXXIX.
7 Jeffrey T. Sammons, op. cit., p.34.
8 Mike Marqusee, op. cit., p.5.
9 Jeffrey T. Sammons, op. cit., p.37.
10 Ibid., p.35
11 Mike Marqusee, op. cit., p.11.
12 Jeffrey T. Sammons, op. cit., p.35.
13 Ibid., p.35.
14 Mike Marqusee, op. cit., p.13-14.
15 Malcolm X and Alex Haley, *The Autobiography of Malcolm X*, (Penguin Books: 1968), p.417.
16 Jeffrey T. Sammons, op. cit., p.35.
17 Ibid., p.101.
18 Ibid., p.106.
19 Ibid., p.109.
20 Ibid., p.115.
21 John Hennessy, *Mike Tyson*, (Magna Books: 1990), p. 20,
22 Maurice Berube, *Defeat of the Great Black Hope*, (Commonwealth: 1971), p.54.
23 Phil Berger, 'Heavy, Heavy, Heavy: The Days and Nights of Mike Tyson', *Smart Magazine*, (Owen J. Lipsteinp: May-June 1989), p.56.
24 John Hennessy, op. cit., p.17.
25 Reg Gutteridge and Norman Giller, *For Whom the Bell Tolls*, (Star Books: 1987), p.20.
26 James Dalrymple, 'Sorry is the hardest word', *Sunday Times Magazine*, (Times Newspapers Ltd. Sept. 18, 1994), p.21.
27 Phil Berger, op. cit., p.61.
28 James Dalrymple, op. cit., p.22.

Robert De Niro (Jake LaMotta), *Raging Bull*, 1980, 129m, c/bw, UA. Dir. Martin Scorsese.
Courtesy: BFI Stills, Posters and Designs.

The Ring of Impossibility, or, the Failure to Recover Authenticity in the Recent Cinema of Boxing

David Alan Mellor

The filmic, fictional, boxer had long been portrayed as a singular, heroic figure of tested masculinity in a fallen universe. As such, his body and soul were the locus of a variety of metaphysical narratives. This dominant romantic-modernist representation of existential man in all his bleak grandeur attained definition in Hollywood post-World War II, but also in other visual and textual arts. Contemporary counterpart to the *film noir* detective, the cinematic boxer was an involuntary secular saint, ringed by black and white moral situations. Existential choice was compelled as a rigorous induction into the realm of the authentic. Generally, the boxer gained that dimension of authenticity through passages of suffering and sacrificial violence, and despite those corrupt moral forces pitched against him which manipulated the very terms of that test. If a film like Robert Wise's *The Set-Up* (1949) with its milieu of commensurable meanings represents the apogee of this shadowed, tortured ascension, the film takes place in a larger, unmanaged world where the authentic is still achievable despite temptation. Less than a decade later, in *The Harder They Fall* (1956), boxing, like the world at large, has become a deceptive corporate spectacle where press agents and public relations mediate the sport into a state of inauthenticity. Since the mid-1970s attempts have been made to revive modernist boxing narratives within Hollywood, but such a revival has been problematic and cannot usually withstand postmodern conditions. As well as glancing back to the 'high moral' moment of *The Set-Up* and the turning point demarcated by *The Harder They Fall*, this essay concentrates on some recent re-synthesisations of authenticity in this genre. My examples are drawn from the series of *Rocky* films (1975-1990), *Raging Bull* (1980), *Night and the City* (1992) and *Pulp Fiction* (1994). I will argue that in attempting to simulate the values of modernist boxing these films participate in a process of citation which ultimately renders their project impossible.

The Afro-American Manager as Despot

The boxer who faces the vengeance of a thwarted, crooked manager or promoter after refusing to 'take a dive', be a 'tank artist' or do a 'flip-flop' has been one such key motif in boxing films. In its representation of the fading, 'punchy' Butch Coolidge (Bruce Willis), Quentin

Tarantino's *Pulp Fiction* marks what is perhaps an exceptionally perverse (and exceptionally successful) return to the 1940s and 1950s treatment of this theme. His Afro-American manager, Marcellus, confirms customary power relations between manager and boxer, while crucially inverting those of race and colour. To this end he ironically hails Butch: "You're my nigger!" Eventually this pair fight each other in a clumsy way – Butch attempting to run Marcellus over in his car, and Marcellus using a heavy calibre gun to wound him – but then there is a prizefight of sorts, with Butch repeatedly hitting a prone Marcellus and repeating the manager's nostrums about pride. There is, at this point, a view of Marcellus' head which reverses the perspective the audience were first granted of him. In this earlier scene, Butch's thick-set, unemotional face, stares straight into the camera as he hears a bleak and humiliating assessment of his career: "Your days are just about over." The camera then pulls out to render the back of Marcellus' neck and head. Like a Junker satirised by George Grosz, Marcellus appears as the personification of blind authority, while Butch is left small and unfocused. Later in the store brawl, Marcellus' head is shown front on – virtually for the first time in the film – but upside down, nullified.

In a rare dissolution of the unequal partnership between fighter and manager, Marcellus ultimately releases his white 'nigger' boxer from bondage since Butch had released him from literal bondage at the hands of white psychopaths. It is as if all former power relations have been short circuited in this spectacle of extra-ring violence: "There is no me and you. Not no more," says Marcellus. There is the promise throughout *Pulp Fiction* of a rising from the prison-house of the body either through traumatic experience or through an act of moral choice, for instance Butch deciding not to abandon Marcellus to his fate but to rescue him instead.

In *Rocky V* the aspiration to authenticity is distorted to the point of caricature. This film foregrounds the machinations of Duke Washington, a flamboyant, Don King style Afro-American manager who tries to tempt Rocky Balbao back into the fight game even though he has become vulnerable through 'irreversible brain trauma'. On another occasion, Washington imputes loss of masculinity to Rocky, saying that Adrian, Rocky's wife, "looks like she's the one with the *cojones* in the family". The film concludes with Rocky turning on Duke and – in a gesture of 'street justice' which amounts to popular and racial vigilantism – beats him and lays him out across his car bonnet. Notably, the scene is followed by Rocky receiving the blessing of a local Hispanic priest, since Washington is the incarnate black devil as well as an exemplary inauthentic: a coward, a braggart, a walking flourish of excess, a manipulative showman who has denuded boxing of its moral worth.

The Boxer as Sacrificial Beast

In the simple plotting of those earlier cinematic morality plays, the boxer was cast as victim who, like a dumb beast, was prey to managers, women, the world, the flesh and the devil. He was the 'dumb-ox', to reiterate Wyndham Lewis' description of Hemingway's suffering heroes. What amounts to an imaginary bullfight is surely at work in the nomination of the Argentinian fighter Moreno in *The Harder They Fall*. His ring diminutive, once he falls under the cynical management of Nick Branco, is 'Toro', a bull, an imported humanoid, a living slab of corned beef, dubbed Wild Man of the Andes. He is Bataille's Acephale, envisaged by Masson, a hulking muscle-bound 'freak', a 'giant' sacrificial bull in the cinema of boxing. There is also Jake La Motta's self-nomination as minotaur, the 'raging bull' who – through the circuits of Martin Scorsese's film narrative – is redeemed into a graceful humanity. This licenses the sonic animalism that fills *Raging Bull's* soundtrack with the uncannily abstracted noises of elephants during the fight scenes. In the *Rocky* films the device is mimicked visually. Rocky is surrounded by hyperbolised animal imagery: he is discovered among domesticated animals and sides of beef, and first steps into the ring under the name of The Italian Stallion. Abandoning his former brute existence as a small-time leg and hand breaking mafia enforcer, Rocky goes to work in a meat factory where the sides of beef serve as displaced punch bags or imaginary debtors whose frozen ribs he must break. To publicise his fight against the US Heavyweight Champion, Apollo Creed, Rocky conducts a television interview in the factory's refrigeration rooms. It is billed as being "in the meat house with Rocky Balbao". His Dionysian identification with raw meat, animality and *sparagmos*, is intercut with (and stands in contrast to) the purified, refined corporate milieu of his rival, Creed.

Throughout the *Rocky I-V* film series, Rocky is serially raised from these taints of the brutal by citations of a christological narrative of suffering and redemption of the flesh. This might be a cinematic re-phrasing of what Sartre called *la grande affaire,* 'the scandal of theological survivals'.[1] The *Rocky* saga opens at the Resurrection Athletics Club in Philadelphia where the face of Christ and the Eucharistic chalice are prominent as vast decorative images behind the boxing ring in which Rocky is shown winning a fight. The primal sacrificial body of the boxer becomes a sign of the Christic body. In the closing scenes of his films, Rocky is frame frozen in moments of glory, in an expression of exaltation and transcendence which elevates him from carnality. In *Raging Bull* Jake La Motta only dimly apprehends this vision. The sole exception occurs when La Motta is held in solitary confinement – significantly, he is entrapped by stone walls rather than the transparent space frame of the boxing ring – and proclaims: "I'm not an animal."

The attritional degradation of the boxer, and specifically of his brain, returns his body to brute status in the realist 'social issue' melodrama *The Harder They Fall*. In this film, a television reporter – an agent of the new spectacular culture but a figure of journalistic integrity nonetheless – shows *verité* footage of his interview on Skid Row with a gnarled, elderly punch-drunk fighter to boxing press agent Eddie Willis (Humphrey Bogart). Here is ocular evidence of the brutalising effect of boxing: the former slugger barely makes sense as he descants on the transience of boxers and the eternal rule of their managers. Twice framed or ringed by screens and portrayed as raw news, the interview's claim to verisimilitude is sufficiently convincing to dismay Willis. The brain damage motif recurs in *The Harder They Fall* when Gus Dundee, the stumbling, mumbling, recently deposed US Heavyweight Champion, is set-up to fight Toro. Before the match, in a hotel suite of conspirators, Dundee begs Willis to make his defeat look good, that is, to praise him in interviews and press promotions thus ensuring that he goes "out in a blaze of glory". When Dundee then suffers 'irreversible brain trauma' he becomes a dumb martyr to Toro's miraculous (and staged) yet tainted victories: he ends his own tragic career as a despised bum.

Apollo Creed in *Rocky*, 1976, 119m, UA. Dir. John G. Avildsen. Carl Weathers (Apollo Creed).
Courtesy: BFI Stills, Posters and Designs.

The Pompous Boxing Body and National Baroque

The body of Apollo Creed is the object and focus of post-Ali spectacle in *Rocky I-IV*. Creed first enters the *Rocky* narrative in the run-up to the bi–centennial fight in Philadelphia, where he appears amid a blaze of self-manufactured imperial pomp. As a populist ploy, Creed's managers and promoters set about branding Rocky Balbao the "underdog contender". Rocky, who at this point is still marooned in inner-city disgrace, is asked the catechistic question: "Do you believe America is the land of opportunity? Apollo Creed does." On the eve of the fight Rocky visits the empty stadium, where he walks under gigantic banners of himself and Creed portrayed as if they were idealised personifications of American 'opportunity'. Creed arrives for the fight dressed as a white-wigged George Washington in a sparkling tableaux of *Washington Crossing the Delaware*. The boxer then doffs this outfit for an Uncle Sam costume as he appeared in the World War I poster by Montgomery Flagg: "I want you!" he bellows. Rocky's response is mocking: "He [i.e. Creed] looks like a big flag." Creed, as a black fighter, burlesques these two primordial white father figures of American masculinity. The panoply of a newly confident and resurgent national heraldry is strong in the settings for the fight, which appears as a virtualised melodrama set under the Stars and Stripes. The surface of the ring canvas, when seen from overhead, is covered in white stars; the bell which signals the beginning of the contest is a facsimile of the Liberty Bell; while the round card women are dressed as the Statue of Liberty, in spangly silver, wrapping sexualised surfaces over this female personification of national identity.

Creed's hubristic final appearance in *Rocky IV* – at a goodwill exhibition match against the Soviet super-boxer Drago – sees him at the centre of an American culture of techno-entertainment in the Grand Hotel at Las Vegas. It is there that Drago is himself exhibited: dazzled with lights, star-bursts and the ornamented bodies of women, propelled upwards to that blaze of glory which eluded poor Gus Dundee in black and white film stock. For Creed, it's 'show time'. He is preceded by James Brown and the excesses of pop spectacle, of song and dance amid a Reaganite pageantry of flag-waving. (When the fight proceeds, the pomp is abandoned and, in a mimicking of Scorsese's sound effects from *Raging Bull*, the soundtrack is filled with the sampled squawks and roars of brute animal sounds.) The iconography of Soviet power reaches its zenith in *Rocky IV*, in a climactic fight held in a Russian stadium, before the military in all their regalia and under the gaze of Marx, the Politbureau and a Gorbachov look-alike leader. Drago enters the venue, preceded by torch bearers, and is made to look every inch a totalitarian male like those sculpted by Arno Breker. He is a projected phobic fantasy of the Second Cold War. *Rocky IV* deploys a simulative Western *agon*, a heroism recovered in time for the final match, as a timely metaphor for the greater historic and victorious confrontation, on a political level, with the Soviets in the 1980s.

Boxing, Transformed by Promotional Culture, as Agent in the Geography of Moral Corruption

In *The Harder They Fall* the bus in which Toro Morena travels symbolises the boxer's body as a vehicle for promotional corruption. Shiny, in its aluminium shell and giant cut-out effigies of Toro, each time the bus appears in the film it is accompanied by a repeated snatch of folkloric South American music. Like a customised military aircraft, it bears inscriptions of 'kills' and 'raids', which detail Toro's fights and the short number of rounds taken to defeat his opponents. The bus enters cities like a shiny bug bringing the virus of the spectacle with it. First Los Angeles, then small Californian towns, then Reno and Las Vegas – where it is seen amid the illuminated neon sky signs and the giant cowboy figure of the Pioneer Casino. Then, as *The Chicago Herald Tribune's* headline states, it "invades" Chicago, bearing Toro's less than adequate body. The 'fall' of the title is not just the dropping of the fighter's body onto the canvas, it is, arguably, also the fall into an inauthentic sphere of promotion which, during the 1950s wave of moral panics, was perceived as undermining an heroic American culture.

After the diabolical bus has reached Times Square, the narrative shifts to the fight's formal announcement at the New York Boxing Board under the gaze of Washington and Lincoln's portraits. In a scene of utmost irony, the unwitting bum, Moreno, and his

Toro Moreno's promotional tour bus. *The Harder They Fall*, 1956, 109m, b/w, Columbia. Dir. Mark Robson. Humphrey Bogart (Eddie Willis), Rod Steiger (Nick Benko), Jan Sterling (Beth Willis), Max Baer (Buddy Brannen), Jersey Joe Walcott (George), Carlos Montalban (Luis Agrandi). Based on the novel by Budd Schulberg.
Courtesy: BFI Stills, Posters and Designs.

HEAVYWEIGHT
CHAMPION
OF THE WORLD
TORO
THE FIGHTING SENSATION
OF TWO CONTINENTS

Robert Ryan (Bill Stoker Thompson) in the arms of Audrey Totter (Julie). *The Set-Up*, 1949, 72m b/w, RKO. Dir. Robert Wise. Courtesy: BFI Stills, Posters and Designs.

scheming opponent, Buddy Brannen, hear themselves described as: "Fine athletes in that great American tradition of fine sportsmanship [...] fine clean fights." The repetition of the word 'fine' points beyond to some larger irony about the corruption of America through the promotion industry's embrace of boxing – something Eddie Willis, press agent to Nick Banco, the criminal boxing 'czar', seeks to remedy when he returns to his original calling of journalism and begins to type his tract, 'The Harder They Fall' in the closing shot of that eponymous film. The first sentence demands that: "Boxing should be outlawed in the US, even if it takes an act of Congress to do it." Notice that this lapidary, typed, high moral pronouncement is made by Eddie at the moment of his return to moral authenticity as a journalist. He regains his place within a conventional contemporary patriarchy, complete with wife, home, career and a certain existential grandeur.

The fears which haunted the 1950s, that boxing might be re-shaped at the hands of an inauthentic promotions industry, remains a recurrent trope. In fact, anxieties have intensified in the 1990s, as witnessed in this night-terror letter published in *The Ring* in 1994: "It is 4.11 in the morning. I just awoke from a horrible nightmare: Don King was turning the sport of professional boxing into something similar to the World Wrestling Federation!"[2] In recent historical articles printed in *The Ring* comparisons have been drawn between the authentic ethnic and community grounding of urban localism and current boxing promotion methods, which are seen to be garish and effeminate. It cites the practices of past inner-city New York clubs who: "use[d] local fighters and focus[ed] on match-ups between different ethnic groups [...] Neon lights, round card girls and sequinned trunks? Not here."[3] More recently still, Henry Cooper, the ex-British Heavyweight Champion, "quit his boxing commentary job in disgust"[4] – disgust, that is, at the hybrid "silly circus" of pre-fight ceremonials: "For 45 minutes before the boxers got in the ring we were treated to a firework display, there were bands playing and dancing girls. As far as I'm concerned, that's got nothing to do with boxing [...] all this disco dancing into the ring is ridiculous."[5] Here is a gesture of anger and mourning towards a fading masculine and localist culture which is perceived as disappearing.

A Hyper-modernised Simulacra of Boxing

By the mid-1980s *Rocky IV* had come to personify a nationally coded virtualised masculinity far removed from the earthly and bodily manifestations of sweat, blood and saliva, the carnality and pathos which had driven previous boxing films. If the cinematic boxer marks the aspirations of a culture to portray the perfect body, the Cold War saw the carnal body replaced by the technological hyper-real body, transmitted via the media in ever more sophisticated displays of promotion and entertainment. The graphics which open *Rocky IV* stage this disembodied conflict. A lone, scaleless boxing glove rises in slo-mo, metal-plated like the Koonsian simulacra of pathetic bodies and stand-ins (his casts of scuba diving kits, comic bunny balloons). Then, as if weightless in outer space, the glove, emblazoned with 'Old Glory', turns and floats like a space craft or satellite. The glove is met by another glove, embellished with the hammer and sickle; they collide and explode into fragments like the burned-off detritus of a *Star Wars* video simulation. In this film, Rocky is found in an environment of advanced electronic consumer goods, JVC video cameras, Sony Walkmans and a domestic robot, the consumer rewards of Reaganite postmodernity. Similarly, his rival, the Russian athlete, Drago, is represented surrounded by digital displays, heat graphics and technicians. This regime, say the Russians, will build a 'Superman'.

An Ugly Crowd Gendered as Female

The audience constitutes another important and changing motif in boxing films since the mid-1970s. In *Pulp Fiction,* Esmerelda Villa Lobos is sole spectator of Butch's crucial match. A taxi driver by profession, she waits in the alley below the dressing room for the boxer's escape after he refuses to throw the fight. Tarantino chooses neither to show the spectators nor the ring since the action – the drama of the boxer, his relations with his manager and the bizarrely violent world he inhabits – lies elsewhere. This *kenosis* of the boxing crowd is also gendered, given the masculine actants in the ring. It appears only to vanish to those outer recesses of the stadium in the figure of that self-enforced absence and/or blindness of the female spectator. In earlier boxing films women were rendered incapable of watching their partner's defeat. This was conveyed either by their absence (for instance, the vacant seat of the woman

TAURANT

In a halting speech, Rocky Balboa (Sylvester Stallone) thanks the people of Philadelphia for honouring him with a life-size statue in front of the Fine Arts Museum. *Rocky III*, MGM/UA.
Courtesy: BFI Stills, Posters and Designs.

in *The Set Up* and in the late 1940s British boxing film, *The Flanagan Boy*); or by the covering of her face (as shown in *Raging Bull*). In the aftermath of the fight, after a Marian witnessing of the Passion in the ring, women are shown as a comforting presence – see for example, the Pieta arrangement of Julie cradling Bill 'Stoker' Thompson (Robert Ryan) at the end of *The Set Up*. Such women partners exist as points of resistance to the temptations of the world, the flesh and the devil.

In a less Marian mode are those depictions of the woman as ringside tormentor. In *The Harder They Fall* she appears, grotesque and bloated, shouting: "You yellow dog!" when the dying Gus Dundee is carried away on a stretcher at the Chicago stadium. In *Pulp Fiction* Esmerelda Villa Lobos is a more alluring femme fatale witness to the death of a fighter, but she is remote. She has listened to the match on her radio, where the over-excited male commentators avow that the death of Butch's opponent in the ring will "shake the world of boxing to its foundations". She is caught up in that excremental world, paid and tipped by Butch, a prurient, excited spectator who repeatedly asks him during their journey: "What does it feel like to kill a man?" It is the very insistence of her inquiry which re-doubles the uncanniness of her absence at the fight itself. On one level, Esmerelda belongs with that gallery of abject spectators who attend the fights, the very ones which Scorsese chose not to represent: "The very, very important thing about the fight scenes in the movie [*Raging Bull*] was that you never see the audience [...] the overweight woman eating as people are beaten and blood is flying. You know that she's sitting there eating a frankfurter and popcorn. None of that. None of that. Stay in the ring."[6] Within the boxing film genre, stands another type of female, whitened and spectral. Vicki, in *Raging Bull*, is such deadly a vision, a pool-side, undressed temptation, an icy creature of the sun, as opposed to the nocturnal boxer who is denizen of the darkling underground passages and only occasionally emerges into the artificial light of the ring. In *The Flanagan Boy*; Lorna, a boxing promoter's wife, is another shimmering waterside female who blinds 'Sailor' Johnny Flanagan and entraps him in a plot to murder her genial husband. Lorna and Vicki are difficult to place within stabilised domestic surroundings, although Vicki is presented as a housewife, despite her illicit sallies out to the Copacabana Club from the Pelham Parkway suburbs.

The Boxer's Statue and Masculine Apotheosis

In its willed return to authenticity, the *Rocky* series uses the motifs of resurrection to a triumphal end, and also marks the boxer's elevation from the brute carnality of his meat handling job. Rocky's training takes him for runs through a still-darkened Philadelphia at dawn. At the end of a grand axial avenue, he struggles bent double up monumental steps, to stand ultimately on the terrace of the Philadelphia Museum of Fine Arts. He ascends to the temple and enters the pantheon. This *loci* recurs in the narrative as a place of triumphal exaltation (but also debacle). In *Rocky II* it is the site of restoration where Rocky gathers young people around him as he scales the steps in slo-mo during his training. Another populist apotheosis occurs there in *Rocky III*, when a statue to him is unveiled, with all due civic ceremony: "On behalf of all the citizens of Philadelphia [...] to the indomitable spirit of man." The statue is in a triumphal posture, with hands raised, a gesture taken up by the crowd, who punch the air. The dramatic climax – marked by Rocky's congealed 'solidification' as a sculpture and his announcement of imminent retirement – is disrupted by the challenge issued by Clubber Lang – a black fighter nemesis, played by Mr T. as a novelty barbaric 'other'. At Rocky's apparent moment of power, Clubber publicly propositions his wife Adrian ("Bring your pretty little self over to my apartment tonight and I'll show you a real man"), in a taunt intended to cast doubt on Rocky's sexual potency. After the death of his trainer, Mickey, later in the same film, Rocky visits the statue at night, looking at it in anger and throwing his black motorcycle helmet at it. Finally, in *Rocky V*, the series concludes with the boxer and his son Robert Balbao climbing the museum steps to regard the statue, before going to see a Picasso exhibition in the building. Rocky has become legend, a pure sign and sublimely merged with art, he has ascended into some sports Valhalla. Even while portrayed in statue form, he will disarmingly entertain a viewing of Picasso at the behest of his art-loving son. The last shot of this film is a back view of the Rocky statue superimposed on a vista of Philadelphia. Here, it signifies the apotheosis of masculinity still intact, a passage from the shabby, dusty and carnal, to something hardened in a sanctified realm; the white champion of the free western

world, re-ascendant, one who has speeded the conclusions of *perestroika* and the dismantling of the Communist system by his example.

The Procurement of Honour

In its account of Butch Coolidge, *Pulp Fiction* twists and reverses the former roles assigned to boxers within the filmic genre. Butch's story of pride, righteousness, redemption and resurrection dovetails with the picaresque stories recounted in this portmanteau film. He rises from stunned acceptance of dishonour as he wakes from the dream of a talismanic transmission of masculinity found in the short narrative 'The Gold Watch'. When Butch rescues his vengeful manager from anal rape, he adds another instance to that continuing metaphor of masculine humiliation, countering the rape by wielding a samurai sword, sign of oriental power. The prospect of this outlandish Oriental threat, which violates male bodily integrity, circulates; for, as Marcellus says, on discovering Butch's treachery in winning the fight: "I'm prepared to scour the earth. If Butch goes to Indochina, I want a nigger in a bowl of rice [...] to pop a cap in his ass [...] ". Butch joins Rocky as an exemplary re-ascendant white American male, all the while waylaid by picaresque and grotesque circumstance, and viewed by non-Americans and non-whites – Soviets, Columbians – at the times of his testing.

The switch back course of the plot allows Butch to redeem his debt of dishonour with Marcellus for not taking a dive in the fifth, and to kill Vincent Vega, who had insulted him as a punch-drunk wretch. Pride is the key. Marcellus warns him that on the night of the fight: "Pride will fuck with you [...] pride only hurts". Butch colludes in his own humiliation when, on being instructed that "in the fifth my ass goes down", he is forced to repeat: "I have no problem with that Mr. Wallace." Butch thereby earns money, but it cannot compare with the hoard of patriarchal gold condensed in the figure of his father's watch, a focus of pride, made over to him as a sign of his incorporation into a male code of honour. Consider also the moment in *Raging Bull* when, stuck for bail money, Jake la Motta attacks his World Championship belt in order to separate and pawn its encrusted jewels only to be told that the entire belt, in its material and symbolic integrity and rarity, would have realised far more. Here is the play of honour and its valuable symbols in the boxing film, where the recovery of honour and the prickings of pride may entail threat and physical humiliation.

The Gym as Site of Authenticity and Male Presence, to the Edge of Hallucination

Night and the City showed people's attorney and tribune Harry Fabian, endeavouring, but comically failing, to return to what he calls "the good old days", the days of "people's boxing". Harry Fabian glimpses a gym for the first time, and seeing a palimpsest of male bodies says: "This is wild." In among this montage of authenticity are old advertisements for fights, tokens of a pre-electronic epoch, since, as Fabian is warned: "If you want to watch a fight you watch television." But Fabian is a fantasist, registering risibly as a promoter with the trade name of Bullshit Productions, and finding his entry into boxing an unhinging experience. Authenticity, in the shape of the ancient 1950s boxer Al, dies in front of him in an absurd fight with a disco bouncer. As Harry's fortune unravels, boxing undergoes a process of restoration. When he is shot by the dominant promotor's heavies, Harry is put into the ambulance, joking: "Boxing, I must have been out of my mind." Part serious, part comic, this is a confession of loss of control in the face of monumental and fatal corporate interests.

The gym signifies in the boxing genre film as an index of the moral health, status and prospects of a culture which cannot articulate itself. In the *Rocky* series, it is initially the site of realist rhetoric and fits the visual landscape of post-industrial dereliction that is mid-1970s Philadelphia. Mick's Gym is at first sight an unwelcoming place for Rocky, since his locker has been emptied to make space for a "contender". "You put my stuff on skid row," he remonstrates, for he is one step from being a bum himself (indeed, he was addressed as such by a woman in the crowd in his Resurrection Athletic Club match). Intertextually in using the word 'contender' Rocky cites the terms used by Brando in *On the Waterfront* (1952). Like Brando he displays his body in a vest while showing off his inner-city pets to a prospective girlfriend. Rocky's decline is demonstrated by the overblown training camp and gym in *Rocky III*, which is in fact a luxury hotel. This postmodern interior revels in all the decadence of its promotional excess like director Brian De Palma's figuring of his anti-hero's mansion in the film *Scarface.* It is decked out in neon and consumer designer logos, an orchestra and a Baselitz-esque, neo-expressionist portrait of Rocky. This gym is a public relations-friendly extravaganza, full of merchandising. Here, the cynical words of Nick Branco, the corrupt manager in *The Harder They Fall* are recollected: "You drum the names [of products and boxers] in their heads long enough and they buy the label." It generates a carnival, bordello milieu. "How," asks Rocky's trainer Mickey, "can we train in this house of ill repute? Can we go back to the old gym?" Mickey's words suggest that it is a kind of brothel and he has already warned Rocky, in *Rocky*, that "women weaken legs". Meanwhile Clubber Lang is shown exercising strenuously on rough floorboards, while Rocky's masculinity is endangered. "This is a zoo, you know? [...] He [Clubber Lang] is going to kill you," says Mickey. Rocky responds by giving Mickey a burlesque kiss. The gym has become a phantasmic carnival which seeks to exclude, yet incorporates sexual difference. The gendered space of the gym also makes it possible to juxtapose male and female bodies in unique ways: male bodies can be placed on display and the women who are occasionally present during these moments, compose Edenic, yet perturbing, scenarios of temptation.

The gym is a primal, haunted place in *Rocky V*, the doorway to the past. When Rocky returns to the derelicted neighbourhood Mick's Gym in Philadelphia after his discovery that he has 'irreversible brain trauma', he re-encounters the revivifying but grey, shadowed and spectral presence of his dead trainer, Mickey Goldmills, that lost embodiment of integrity. Rocky puts on a dusty glove and then hallucinates Mickey passing on a talisman – the angelic Rocky Marciano's cufflink. In *Rocky III* he had physically encountered Apollo Creed in this same abandoned interior of memory and the past when his former opponent invited him to regain the primordial 'eye of the tiger', 'the edge', through re-encountering authenticity by returning to train in the darkest, grimmest Afro-American gym in all Los Angeles.

Patriarchal Traces, Talismans and Fetishes

In *Pulp Fiction* Butch's narrative is attached to a gold watch, a totemic object secreted and worn and cherished by his father's predecessors and martial generations. Rocky passes on to his son a golden glove cufflink on a chain in a similar circuit – a ring – of transmitted patriarchal power.[7] A complication is found in the gesture of Rocky's son taking these supremely masculine adornments and holding them as if they were effeminising earrings. "You look like the daughter I always wanted," says Rocky. Talismanic signs of masculinity are playfully inverted, but only after Robert has demonstrated his own prowess by reclaiming a stolen jacket (another trophy) in a fist fight, and replacing the duplicitous, false son, Tony Gunn, whom Rocky has adopted. It is, perhaps, in a different modality that Harry Fabian's girlfriend, in *Night and the City*, gives him a pair of miniature silver gloves as personal ornaments. These are reified, an erotic gift, rather than ancestral trophies, and, as such, they connote Fabian's failure of aspiration and lack of grace, but also the failure of his project to revive the authenticity of "the good old days". It is a mission compromised by an oppressive sense of belatedness and impossibility, feelings which surface in the wording of his poster design for the matches: 'HARRY FABIAN PRESENTS THE RETURN OF PEOPLE'S BOXING TO NEW YORK'. But the past cannot return, thus bidden, to the universe of promotion. Nonetheless, Rocky keeps a poster of Rocky Marciano in his crummy apartment above the fireplace. It takes on the significance of an ancestral god of hearth and home, a noble figure among Rocky Balboa's menagerie of dumb tortoises and goldfish. In *Rocky* his gaze moves from Rocky Marciano to his own reflection in the mirror, and finally to a photograph of himself as a child. Mickey, the paternal trainer and his manager-to-be, recognises the Rocky in Rocky and says in his gravel voice: "You look like him [but have you] got heart like him?" – which is to say, can he make corporeal, can he embody that authentic substance, that body of the boxer, from a phantasmic photographic image.

1 G. Hartman, *Saving the Text*, (1981), p.99.
2 'Come out writing', *The Ring*, (Feb. 1994), Vol. 73, No. 2, p.60.
3 R. Cassidy, 'Where have all the fight clubs gone?',*The Ring*, op.cit.., p.25.
4 'Boxing Turns My Stomach', *The Sun*, (23 January 1996), p.26.
5 ibid.
6 M.P. Kelly, *Martin Scorsese*, (1992), p.132-3.
7 These fetishes could be construed as counterparts of the boxing ring itself, composed of enclosing structures with straps or links pulling clothing together.

Will. Hogarth f.
James Figg
Master of ye Noble Science of Defence
on ye right hand in Oxford Road .
near Adam & Eve court teaches Gentle-
-men ye use of ye small backsword &
Quarterstaff at home & abroad

A.M.I. Sculpt.

The Noble Art: Boxing and Visual Culture in Early Eighteenth-Century Britain

Sarah Hyde

Anna Maria Ireland, after a print falsely attributed to William Hogarth, *Ticket for James Figg*, etching, 1794.
Courtesy: The Whitworth Art Gallery,
University of Manchester.

The names of William Hogarth, 'the father of English painting', and James Figg, 'the father of English boxing', have been persistently linked. Early boxing historians such as Henry Downes Miles felt that it was owing to "the pencil [...] of Hogarth" that Figg was "the first public champion of the ring of whom we have authentic record."[1] Surprisingly, however, there is little concrete evidence to consolidate claims that these two figures were associated: none of the recorded painted portraits of Figg can be firmly attributed to Hogarth, and none of the fighters who appear in Hogarth's prints can be securely identified as Figg. It would seem then that the repeated linking of these two men lies less in such shaky evidence of their acquaintance, and more in a number of parallel developments which occurred within both professions during the first half of the eighteenth century. These developments were to mark the beginnings of painting and boxing as professionalised, public spectacles.

Figg's lifetime saw the separation of boxing from other forms of duelling in which he excelled such as backsword and cudgelling (fighting with one or two sticks), and, in the decade after Figg's death, Jack Broughton developed a set of rules which formed the basis of boxing as a spectator sport. Hogarth's lifetime similarly saw the development of 'spectators' or a wider audience for painting through the establishment of the first public art exhibitions in Britain. An equivalent to Broughton's regulations might be seen in the fostering of a particular set of practices in a number of teaching institutions founded during the early decades of the eighteenth century, culminating in the foundation of the Royal Academy in 1768, four years after Hogarth's death.

The apparent neatness of these parallels, however, masks a far more complicated situation: neither boxing nor painting were to follow a smooth path as they became professionalised. The development of both activities involved awkward negotiations between lower class would-be 'professional' practitioners, gentlemanly amateur practitioners and a wider, socially heterogeneous audience. The way in which these problems have frequently been misunderstood is demonstrated by art historian Frederick Antal's reaction to an etching attributed to William Hogarth titled *Ticket for James Figg*.[1] Not only has this etching served as the basis for numerous explorations into the early history of boxing in Britain but, since the late eighteenth century, it has served as evidence of Hogarth's close relationship with Figg.

According to Antal, the etching's crude execution suggested that, although based on Hogarth's design, it was in fact carried out by another less competent hand. Antal insists that Hogarth deliberately chose a less skilled etcher so that Figg's advertisement would appeal to a popular audience. Three years after the publication of Antal's essay the print was convincingly shown to be a fake, produced in the late eighteenth century, several decades after Hogarth's death.[3] Antal's reaction to the print is interesting nevertheless for what it reveals about the misguided assumptions he, and many others, have made about the status of art and boxing in the early eighteenth century.

Antal's interpretation was based on the belief that boxing was a 'popular' sport in early eighteenth-century Britain, which led him to assume that the advertisement must have been designed to appeal to a popular audience. As the text inscribed on the ticket makes explicit however, it is not addressed to working people but to 'Gentlemen'. Figg is known to have taken on pupils who wished to develop their 'skill in the Science of Defence' on an amateur basis, yet these men were sophisticated members of the gentry and aristocracy. Were Figg to have had a shop card produced, it would have been addressed to this class of people. Furthermore, judging by Hogarth's print series aimed at the social elite, *Marriage à la Mode* for instance, when the artist wanted to appeal to a genteel audience he usually employed a correspondingly sophisticated printmaking style. These are a few of the many pieces of evidence which suggest that the work is a fake. Antal's assumption that boxing was an exclusively 'popular' sport in the early eighteenth century is such a common misconception that it merits further investigation.

Captain John Godfrey's *Treaties Upon the Useful Science of Defence* (1747) gives some idea of the social tensions involved in the development of boxing and related forms of combat in the first half of the eighteenth century. For Godfrey, backsword was the most useful part in the 'Science of Defence' since its practice in the armed forces contributed to the defence of the British nation. He conceded that other exercises such as smallsword (fought with a foil), could be useful since: "the meanest of them [...] greatly contributes to inure the Common people to Bravery; and to encourage that truly British Spirit, which was the Glory of our Ancestors."[4] Nonetheless Godfrey also warned that this very involvement of 'the Common people' had caused problems. Having praised Figg's skill with the backsword, he lamented that the practice had 'dwindled and died' after Figg's death, which Godfrey related to the injurious effect of the public fighting displays which Figg himself had organised: "It must be allowed that those Amphitheatrical Practices were productive of some ill, as they gave some Encouragement to Idleness and Extravagance among the Vulgar."[5]

Tensions between the social background of most would-be professional fighters (the majority of whom were former watermen, bakers, paviours and the like) and that of their genteel pupils (who regarded ability in the art of self-defence as an important way of establishing their status as gentlemen), are both reflected and reinforced by portrayals of boxers in early eighteenth-century British prints. Further problems were caused by the heterogeneous audiences attracted to 'amphitheatrical displays'.

John Faber II after James Ellys, *Portrait of James Figg*, mezzotint, c. 1729. Copyright: The British Museum.

John Faber II after James Ellys, *Portrait of John Broughton*, mezzotint, c. 1730. Courtesy: The Whitworth Art Gallery, University of Manchester.

Anonymous, *Ye Roaring Blades...*, etching, date unknown (c. 1750s). Courtesy: The Whitworth Art Gallery, University of Manchester.

Johnathan Richardson the Elder, *James Figg*, black and white chalks on blue paper, 1714. Courtesy: The Ashmolean Museum, Oxford.

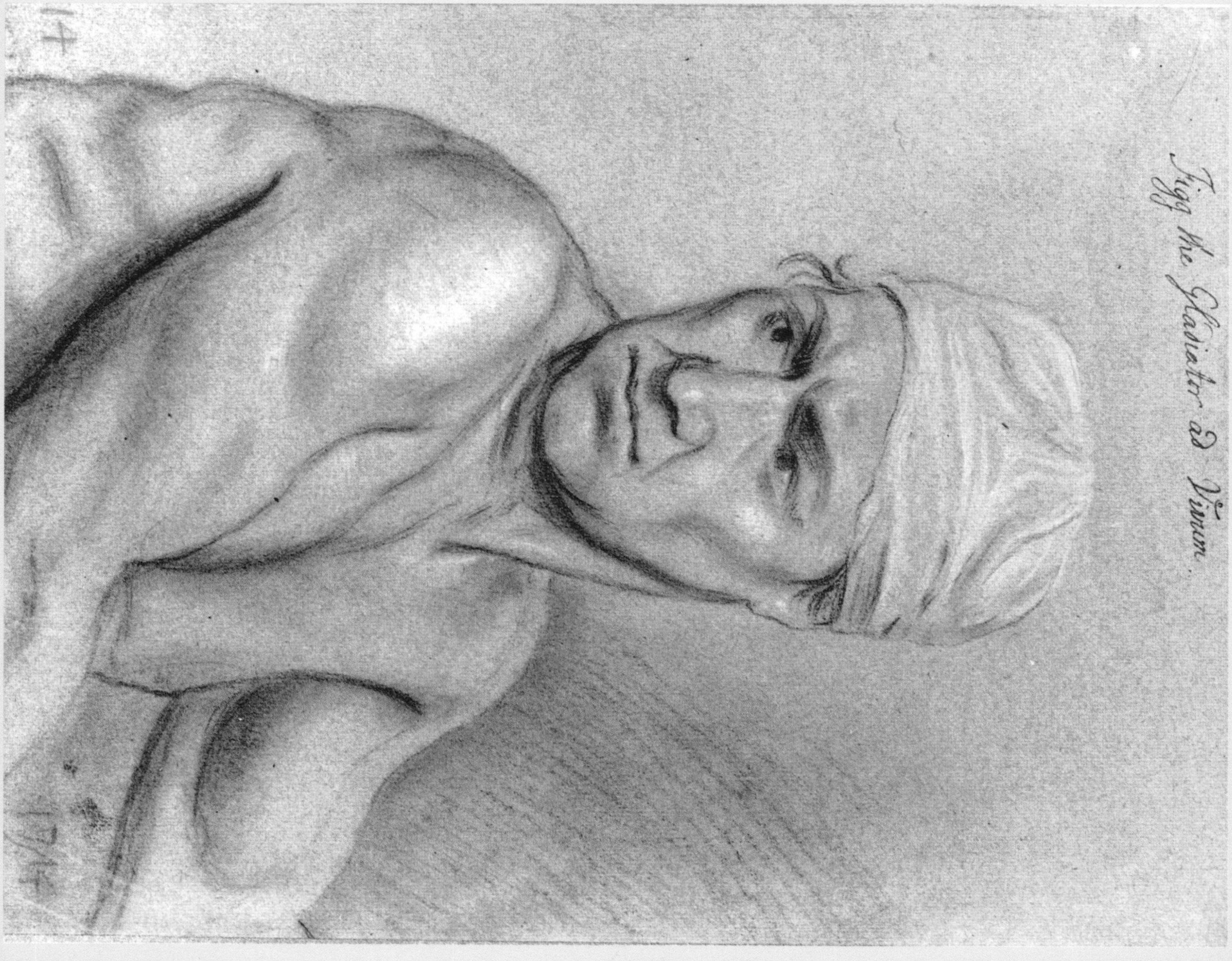

An analysis of a small number of printed and drawn images of boxers from this period gives insight into the complexities which can be glossed over by the tendency to regard boxing as a 'popular' sport, practised by and for 'the mob'.

Images of fighters such as John Faber's mezzotint portraits of James Figg (c. 1729) and John Broughton (c. 1730) were clearly addressed to gentlemen, whether amateur practitioners or boxing spectators. There were considerable difficulties involved in presenting a fighter such as Broughton, widely known to have been a former Thames waterman, in such a way as to suggest that he was worthy of the admiration of a gentleman. John Ellys, who produced the oil painting from which Faber's print was taken, used two main tactics to solve these problems. The first was to ensure that Broughton's pose suggested he had the *manners* of a gentleman despite his lowly origins. Body language was a means of confirming and giving authority to one's social status. The boxer's pose follows almost to the letter the recommendations made by contemporary books on manners and deportment written for educated young ladies and gentlemen. One such book gives the following advice to young men: "To stand genteel, the Head must be erect and turned a little, then put on a manly Boldness in the Face, tempered with becoming Modesty; the lips should be just joined to keep the features regular, the shoulders must be full easy, and be no further drawn back than to form the chest full & round [...] the arms must fall easy, not close to the Sides & the bend of the Elbow at its due Distance will permit the left Hand to place itself in the Waistcoat easy and genteel within two Button-holes of the bottom."[6] The second tactic was to emphasise the noble, classical origins of self-defence. Broughton's pose and the oval frame surrounding his portrait combine to give classical overtones to his shaven head, which polite viewers would have associated with low relief portraits of Roman emperors on coins and medals. Such references to the antique are further reinforced by the verse accompanying the image, which claims that Broughton is more powerful than the ancient Greek 'athletic heroes' described by authors such as Pindar. Ellys was by no means alone in using such methods. Reference to the classical origins of boxing was one of the main ways in which artists and writers gave respectability to an activity which would otherwise have been difficult to disassociate from the undisciplined street brawls with which boxers such as Broughton and Figg began their careers. Ellys was said to have painted Figg in the pose of a celebrated classical sculpture known as *The Gladiator* and both Figg and Broughton were repeatedly compared to subjects of classical art and the heroes of Greek and Roman mythology. Captain Godfrey described Figg as "the Atlas of the sword" and expressed the wish, "long may he remain the gladiating statue".[7]

While contemporary boxers shared the physical prowess of classical heroes, the association of these two classes of people inevitably also drew attention to the huge differences between them, differences which it became increasingly difficult to ignore. Whereas prints such as Faber's mezzotint underlined the classical ancestry of the boxer's skills, contemporary satirical prints mocked Broughton for taking such comparisons too seriously. Broughton was known to have erected a sign bearing a Latin motto above his house. One of a number of satirical prints mocking him after he was roundly defeated by John Slack suggested that he should:

> *"Erase the Motto from your Sign,*
> *Where you in Lattin us'd to Shine."*[8]

This tension between admiration for the physique and physical prowess of the ancients, and the acknowledgement of the lowly social status of most contemporary boxers, was a problem also faced by history painters when trying to find suitable models for their classical or biblical heroes. The well developed musculature of contemporary boxers made them ideal models: John Broughton was widely rumoured to have been the model for the figure of Hercules in J.M. Rysbrack's monument to Sir Peter Warren, now in Westminster Abbey. Jonathan Richardson's chalk drawing of *James Figg* was almost certainly made as a life study. Nevertheless, artists wishing to use life drawings such as Richardson's as the basis for history paintings could not avoid confronting the yawning gap between the social status of their models and that of the exalted heroes they wished to represent. The inscription which was added to Richardson's drawing by his son, *Figg the Gladiator ad Vivum*, highlights these problems. Drawn '*ad vivum*' (from the life), the facial expression, cloth skull cap and stray pieces of hair would have made Figg's low social status immediately legible to contemporary audiences. At the same time however, his musculature – emphasised by white chalk highlights – suggests affinities with Figg's classical guise as 'the gladiator'.

One of the main ways of dealing with the rift between the harsh realities of contemporary life and the idealised representations of classical art was to adopt the mock-heroic tone frequently used in early eighteenth-century art and literature, including Hogarth's 'modern moral subjects'. In print series such as *A Harlot's Progress*, Hogarth made great satirical play on the distance between his lower class heroes and the biblical heroes more commonly seen in history paintings. Plate three of *A Harlot's Progress* has been interpreted as a modern version of *The Annunciation*: in place of the Virgin Mary being interrupted by an angel, Hogarth substitutes a harlot disturbed by a magistrate. Despite the obvious humour of his print series, the artist also wanted to suggest that representations of 'low life' characters could deal seriously with important moral issues. His efforts in this direction were, however, for the most part frustrated: contemporary criticism of his work suggests that, in spite of all his efforts to the contrary, Hogarth was seen as a comic artist, dealing with subject matter which was acceptable and humorous in the lower art form of the print, but which was considered inappropriate in the higher ranking medium of oil painting. The great difficulties which Hogarth experienced in finding buyers for the painted versions of his modern moral subjects suggests that he had failed to convince potential purchasers from the gentry and aristocracy that the activities of working people could be used as a way to explore serious moral issues in the context of 'high art'.

The mock-heroic form and the use of boxers such as Figg and Broughton as models thus emphasises very clearly the twin poles around which the ideology of boxing revolved in the early eighteenth century. While prints addressed to members of the gentry and aristocracy emphasised the noble origins and aesthetic appeal of swordplay and boxing, popular prints emphasised the lowly social origins of boxers in order to suggest that greater honesty may be found at this level of society. A cheap, anonymous etching makes clear the unsavoury connections between boxing and street fights which were obscured by prints such as John Faber's.

Portrayed is John Smith (nick-named 'Buckhorse'), a boxer who according to *The Eccentric Magazine*: "first saw the light in the house of a sinner" in a part of London "notorious" for "eccentric" characters known for their "course amours and bare-faced pilfering". Buckhorse himself was described as a "freak of nature", distinguished not only by his "rude and unsightly appearance" but also by his ability to fight. Unlike Figg and Broughton, Buckie's origins and appearance made it especially difficult for him to be represented in ways which would emphasise the classical and gentlemanly associations of the sport. Indeed, as *The Eccentric Magazine* was not slow to point out, the only way in which Buckie's activities did resemble those of a gentleman was not one which the publishers of fine art prints would want to emphasise: John Smith "like a number of the sporting *gemmen*, was distinguished for his numerous amours with the *gay nymphs* of the town, more by the potency of his arm than the persuasive powers of his rhetoric."[9]

The print's inscription emphasises Smith's lowly origins in order to suggest that honesty is more likely to be found in him than in his social superiors. Apostrophising "Ye roaring blades" who roam the streets at night as 'sons' or followers of the famous John Broughton, it invites viewers to study "poor BUCKY".[10] Judging by Buckhorse's appearance and occupation contemporary audiences would have assumed him to be a blackguard, however the verse goes on to claim that Smith made his living through honest industry (he is shown working as a linkman, lighting the way through the dark streets at night). It also states that unlike "greater blackguards" he did not try to use power and influence to gain a dishonest living. The irony here is focused around the use of the word "greater" since these blackguards are both 'greater' in the sense of having higher social status and 'greater blackguards' in that they were actually bigger crooks. In contrast to such villains, the verse concludes, Buckhorse need not "dread the fatal tree" – in other words, hanging. In spite of these protestations of the boxer's honesty, the image itself – emphasising Smith's ugly face, his ragged and ill-fitting clothes and wig and setting him in the context of the notoriously unsavoury area of Covent Garden – does little to contradict the habitual association of boxing with brawling, bloodshed and thieving.

The print exemplifies the other social extreme with which boxing could be associated in early eighteenth-century Britain. As an early nineteenth-century history of boxing elucidates, displays of boxing and cudgelling – which were staged in the open air at places such as the annual Southwark Fair – frequently "degenerated into down-right ferocity and barbarity [...] from the drunkenness and inequality of the combatants, and the various artifices adopted to get money."[11] In spite of attempts to associate the athleticism of boxing with classical heroes and with gentlemanly accomplishments, the actual barbarity of the fights themselves continued to make its lower class associations particularly difficult to shift. An important attempt to make boxing more acceptable to polite viewers was the introduction of Broughton's famous set of 'rules' – originally conceived as a means to regulate fights at Broughton's amphitheatre in Tottenham Court Road. Not only did they introduce a means of monitoring the sport, but also brought with them the added advantage of placing the betting which accompanied most fights on a much surer footing. Broughton's other main contribution to the development of the sport was the introduction of gloves, or mufflers, which enabled practice fights to be conducted with less danger of injury to the participants. Broughton advertised this development as particularly appealing to gentlemen. *The Daily Advertiser* of 1747 proclaimed that:
"Mr Broughton proposes, with proper assistance, to open an academy at his house in the Haymarket, for the instruction of those who are willing to be initiated in the mystery of boxing [...] and that persons of quality and distinction may not be debarred from entering into a course of those lectures, they will be given the utmost tenderness and regard to the delicacy of the frame and constitution of the pupil; for which reason mufflers are provided, that will effectually secure them from the inconvenience of black eyes, broken jaws and bloody noses."

Nevertheless, the developments introduced by Broughton appear to have underlined rather than resolved the conflict for boxing enthusiasts from the social elite who found it difficult to reconcile their gentlemanly self image with their far from genteel fascination with masculine prowess and gambling. These problems are addressed in three Hogarth prints in which James Figg is reputed to appear. While Figg's identity can not be verified in any of these images, in this instance, it is not the identity of the sportsman which matters as much as the way in which a boxer functions in Hogarth's satire. In plate two of *A Rake's Progress*, the rake conducts a mock aristocratic 'levée' at which a man (frequently identified as Figg) is shown offering to teach the rake self-defence as a badge of his aristocratic status. Boxing is ridiculed as an empty indulgence of the rich. In *A Midnight Modern Conversation*, a man (who has also been identified as Figg) is shown in a drunken sprawl in the foreground. Once more, boxing is associated with the vices of the aristocracy. In contrast stands *Southwark Fair* in which a man (also thought to be Figg) appears outside a booth in which he was said to have organised notoriously disorderly demonstration fights. Hogarth, then, across the broad spectrum of his work, made no attempt to reconcile the twin poles between which boxing swung so uncomfortably in the early eighteenth century. Instead he made it clear that the ideals of sportsmanship and noble ancestry, which could potentially be associated with boxing, were as likely to be transgressed by a gentlemanly audience as by the lower class revellers at Southwark Fair.

1 Henry Downes Miles, *Pulgilistica: Being Forty Years of the History of British Boxing*, 3 vols., (London, 1888), p.7.
2 Frederick Antal, *Hogarth and His Place in European Art*, (London, 1962), p.55.
3 See Ronald Paulson, 'The Joseph Sympson Jr. Etchings', *Hogarth's Graphic Works: First Complete Edition*, (New Haven, 1965), vol. I, Appendix I, for a discussion of the evidence and a possible identification of the faker. The etching was first 'discovered' by Samuel Ireland whose daughter etched the copy used to illustrate the first volume of his *Graphic Illustrations of Hogarth*, (London, 1794), reproduced here as the first image.
4 Captain John Godfrey, *A Treaties Upon the Useful Science of Defence, Connecting the Small and Back-Sword, and shewing the Affinity between them [...] With Some Observations upon Boxing and [...] Boxers*, (London, 1747), p.2.
5 Ibid., p.39.
6 M. Towle, *Young Gentlemen and Lady's Private Tutor*, (London, 1770).
7 Godfrey, op. cit., p.40.
8 *British Museum Catalogue of [...] Political and Personal Satires*, (London, 1873-1883), cat. no. 3081.
9 *The Eccentric Magazine*, not dated, quoted in P. Egan, *Boxiana*, 2 vols., (London, 1818), p.34.
10 A 'bucky' was a perverse person, but in this context it also refers to 'buckhorse'. To 'stag' means to watch or study and 'mun' is slang for 'face'.
11 P. Egan, op. cit., p.9.

Napoleon Sarony, portrait of Oscar Wilde, 1882.
Courtesy: Roger Lloyd Conover.

Round 1: Poet

Enter Arthur Cravan.

First see him as he was in December 1916: a passenger on board an ocean liner flying the neutral Spanish flag for protection. Then imagine the *Montserrat* sailing from Barcelona to New York. Now picture among its passengers the most undesirable characters of war-torn Europe – deserters, adventurers, speculators, prostitutes, defectors and thieves. Drifters and slackers, among whom frequent fights broke out in this sorry vessel's unruly steerage compartment. After one such skirmish, two passengers warily exchanged stories. One was a revolutionist from Bolshevik country – Lev Davidovich Bronstein, a.k.a. Leon Trotsky. The other was "a boxer, also a poet and nephew of Oscar Wilde, who openly pronounced that he preferred to slug Yankees in a noble sport than to get his chest driven in by some ignorant German." Trotsky thus described his shipboard encounter with Cravan in his *Autobiography*.[1]

What names Messrs. Trotsky/Bronstein and Cravan/Lloyd actually gave one another during their mid-Atlantic encounter is anyone's guess, for both were travelling under aliases. The poet-boxer was a slippery figure, who had dodged border patrols and conscription authorities for two years as he tramped through war-torn Europe with a clutch of doctored passports. The Bolshevik was right: Cravan preferred boxing to serving in the armed forces of any country. He would choose his own allies and enemies. And having successfully eluded checkpoints throughout Europe, he was not about to disclose his real name to Trotsky.

Today, we know many things that Trotsky didn't: that Arthur Cravan was born Fabian Avenarius Lloyd in Lausanne, Switzerland, on 22 May 1887. That his parents were British, and that they had moved from London to Lausanne to escape the disgrace that Oscar Wilde, their son's uncle, had visited on the family name. Fabian was forbidden to speak of his uncle. But he openly mocked his parents' wishes; first by boasting of his family connection to Wilde, then by adopting his uncle's dandified manner of dress. His rebellion against house rules didn't end there: he accused his mother of conducting an adulterous affair with Wilde, of which he imagined himself the offspring and openly declared that he was Wilde's son. Whatever the truth of his patrilineage, it was clear that he was, in spirit at least, the Irish aesthete's legacy.

Fabian was possessed from birth, it seems, with a decadent and contrary nature. He lived according to his own rules and was most content when he strayed beyond them. As a teenager, he was a tireless tramp of continents. The scissor-like stride of the future boxer was prefigured by the legs of a runaway youth who, as Mina Loy – his wife-to-be – once explained, masticated space and used experience as a means of transport. He drew his sustenance, she believed, from swallowing oceans and devouring countries. As a poet, he exercised his omnivorous imagination by inhabiting all identities and places at once:

I would like to be in Vienna and Calcutta
Catch every train and every boat,
Lay every woman and gorge myself on
every dish.
Man of fashion, chemist, whore, drunk,
musician, labourer, painter,
acrobat, actor;
Old man, child, crook, hooligan, angel and
rake; millionaire,
bourgeois, cactus, giraffe, or crow;
Coward, hero, Negro, monkey, Don Juan,
pimp, lord, peasant, hunter,
industrialist,
Flora and fauna:
I am all things, all men and all animals!

Years later, Mina Loy, in *Colossus* – her memoir based on Cravan – called his provocations "pantomimic atrocities on the spectator's habitual expectations," and explained his assaults as natural defences on the part of an artist whom the world saw as dangerous.[2] Cravan himself put it somewhat differently: "I am brute enough to punch myself in the teeth, and subtle to the point of neurasthenia." Expelled from the New College of Worthing (West Sussex) as a youngster, and later from boarding schools in Birmingham and Lausanne (Institut Schmidt de St. Gall), he identified most with the part of his family heritage that his parents had tried hardest to cover up. He had not known his Uncle Oscar, but he admired his writing, his knowledge of classics, and most of all his extravagant, dare-all behaviour.

Arthur Cravan impersonating Oscar Wilde, Paris, ca. 1910.
Courtesy: Roger Lloyd Conover.

The fact that Cravan had never met Wilde was remedied by a posthumous meeting. Some years after Wilde's death, Cravan fabricated a story in which he set out to *prove* that Wilde was still alive. The story ('Oscar Wilde is Alive!') provided precise details of the author's reclusive existence after his imprisonment and release from Reading gaol, and explained why he had come out of hiding to grant this exclusive interview to his nephew.[3] Cravan was forbidden, *Wilde* explained, from disclosing any details that might allow others to find him, but offered just enough *evidence* of his underground existence to make the *interview* seem credible and Wilde's survival plausible. Cravan, the interviewer, and Wilde, the subject, were both appropriately circumspect, without being coy. So convincing was Cravan's portrait that the story was picked up by a journalist from the *New York Times,* who ran a straight-faced piece about the rumour, followed by several earnest refutations from readers who, like the reporter, took Cravan's spoof seriously.[4]

At 16, Lloyd/Cravan made his first trip to America, working his way as a stoker aboard a cargo ship to New York, which he later alluded to romantically in his poems. From New York, he drifted to California, between stints as a lumberjack, orange picker and butcher. He first learned to use his fists in America; boxcar hobos competing for blankets and migrant workers trying to steal his wages received the first taste of the itinerant young poet's knuckle. At 17, he returned to Europe via Australia, Greece and Turkey, settling for a couple of months in Berlin before being kicked out of the city for 'excessive' behaviour. His crime: he was too conspicuous. He dressed like a dandy, hung-out in gymnasiums, and enjoyed the company of card-sharpers, pimps, fighters, prostitutes, drug addicts and homosexuals. One night, living it up on the Kurfürstendam with four prostitutes sitting on his shoulders, he was accosted by a group of policemen and given his final warning: *"Sie sind zu auffallend"* [You are too noticeable], they told him. "Get out of Berlin." Cravan was on the road again.

Round 2: Boxer

In 1909, Cravan turned up in Paris and joined the Club Cuny. There he had his first formal lessons as a boxer under the tutelage of trainer Fernand Cuny himself. In February 1910, he entered the Second Annual Championship of Amateur Boxers, sponsored by the Club Pugiliste of Paris. He won his qualifying bouts and became champion of the light-heavyweight division when Eugene Gette, the last opponent slated to go against him, withdrew. It was during these contests that he adopted the practice which later became his trademark as a boxer. Jumping up from his corner when his name was announced by the referee, he shocked his opponents by boasting loudly of his qualifications, inventing titles, and reciting the litany of achievements which established his tramp pedigree. He embellished his colourful biography with half-truths and lies about his colourful identity outside the ring: hotel thief, confidence man, muleteer, orange-picker, logger, charmer, chauffeur, grandson of the Queen's Chancellor, Queen dowager of Iceland, nephew of Oscar Wilde, sailor, gold prospector, poet with the shortest haircut in the world… He sometimes cited as many as 32 credits before he sat down, his loudmouth antics precociously foreshadowing Muhammad Ali and all subsequent fighters who lead with their mouths.

In March 1910, Cravan (still using his 'real' name, Fabian Lloyd) entered the eighth meeting of the Boxing Championships for Amateurs and Soldiers, organised by the French Federation of Boxing Clubs. Through a bizarre series of defaults, disqualifications, and withdrawals on the part of his opponents, he succeeded in becoming Amateur Light-Heavyweight Champion of France without fighting a single round. He was named the division's champion of France in the April 1910 boxing programme of the *Cirque de Paris*, and took advantage of his new position in the world of sports to write an article for *Echo des Sports ('*To Be or Not To Be American'*)* which appeared on 10 June, despite his having been defeated by Frenchman Cussot Brien on 3 May.

The point of his article was to ridicule American behaviour, and at the same time to make fun of Frenchmen for imitating it. This light-hearted polemic ended with a series of didactic prescriptions addressed to Frenchmen wanting to pass as Americans: "You must know how to box, you must despise women, you must wipe your nose with your fingers, chew gum, spit, swear; and you must pretend that you are a Negro. Caps with outrageous brims are tolerable only for boxers or those who wish to be taken as such, which is exactly the same thing."

In 1911, Fabian Lloyd changed his name to Arthur Cravan, and his address to 29, Avenue de l'Observatoire. Across the street from his apartment was the *Closerie des Lilas*, where on any given night he might run into Paul Fort, Guillaume Apollinaire, Blaise Cendrars, Félix Fénéon or the Delaunays. In the same neighbourhood was the *Bal Bullier*, a favourite night spot among boxers and artists, of which Cendrars once provided a vivid if not altogether flattering description of Cravan, from the perspective of a former gang-member. "Cravan, Delaunay, and I were a trio; we used to go to the Bal Bullier, where we danced the tango in silk socks that did not match, Robert sporting a half-red and half-green dinner jacket, Arthur in black shirts with the dickey slit open to reveal his bleeding tattoos and the obscene inscriptions on his skin, his coat-tails flying free and daubed with fresh paint (before going to the dance hall, Arthur invariably managed to sit down on Robert's palette…). The poet, Arthur Cravan, had immense talent, but he used it as badly as he used his immense physical strength. Arthur being a champion athlete, a boxer, but morally weak, like many semi-professional sportsmen who exhaust themselves with intensive training, being slaves to their beautiful bodies, victims of their torsos and the muscles they love to show off, flexing their biceps to seduce women and earn themselves honours, prize money, comfort, luxury, and, ultimately, the flabbiness that overtakes them before they are 30 years old!"[5]

Cravan occasionally performed in public. To advertise his 'lectures', he placed posters outside the *Noctambules*, announcing the subject of his next *conférence.* On one such occasion, he promised with a great deal of bluster that he would commit suicide in public, and persuaded a standing-room-only crowd to pay FF 2.50 each to witness his death. He would replace the standard podium-glass with a bottle of absinthe, he explained beforehand, and, in deference to the ladies, would wear only a jockstrap, drape his balls on the table, and – before chopping them off – read from Victor Hugo. Before another lecture, Cravan promoted himself as the only artist who could "dance as Zambelli boxes, box as Joe Jeanette dances, punch the face of the audience with a punch that will generate laughter, and make *Maintenant* the magazine of the future".[6]

Maintenant was the violently polemical journal that Cravan launched in 1912; it was considered by Breton the forerunner of *391* and other aggressive post-war publications and the precursor of all that was later to represent *l'esprit Dada*. Cravan managed to bring out five issues of the journal between 1912 and 1915; all five numbers consisted entirely of his own writing, some of which appeared under pseudonyms (W. Cooper, E. Lajeunesse, Marie Lowitska, Robert Miradique). He was the magazine's exclusive distributor as well; parking his wheelbarrow outside the entrance to the Gaumont Hippodrome and other arenas, he flogged his pamphlet like a circus barker at sports events and read from it at art openings and receptions. Each issue of *Maintenant* was meant to start a fight, and, in this sense, each issue was an unqualified success. Not only did Cravan deliver his opinion of artists' and intellectuals' work with jabs that went straight to the solar plexus, he also let his contemporaries know what he thought of their soft bellies, rank vaginas and muscleless legs. His editorials were the literary equivalent of bullying; the knock-out instinct dominated his critique.

Maintenant made Cravan famous and unleashed a storm of protests. He insulted the most revered artists of his generation, in what seemed the most insolent and personal terms imaginable. Not only was Cravan's 'review' an exercise in total denunciation; 80 years later, it remains one of the most extreme examples of malignant art criticism ever published, mixing transgression, sarcasm and pugilism with charismatic advertisements and hypocritical praise. To say that Cravan's editorial tactics were precocious is an understatement; no subsequent editorial operation on the art or culture scene has ever been as transgressive. The ostensible subject of his journal was 'art', but as he quickly made clear, his aim was not to discuss paintings, but to ruin reputations. (In France, where Cravan has long been a cult figure, *Maintenant* is one of the scarcest and most sought-after collectibles of the pre-war avant-garde. A compete run of the original magazine recently sold at auction in Paris for FF 250,000. But in the United States and United Kingdom, where Cravan's writings remain virtually unknown, *Maintenant* has very little profile. The Getty recently declined an original set offered them at a much lower price, content with the Jean-Michel Place reprint. No public archive in the UK owns a complete run.) *Maintenant*'s bruising editor described his tactics matter-of-factly: "If I write, it is to infuriate my colleagues; to get myself talked about and to make a name for myself. A name helps you succeed with women and in business […] Moreover, my pen may give me the advantage of passing for a connoisseur, which in the eyes of the crowd is something enviable, for it is almost certain that not more than two intelligent people will attend the Salon […] If I mention a number of names, it is solely for reasons of guile, as the only way of selling my magazine."

Cravan declared that he was too busy developing his muscles in gymnasiums to submit a painting to the 1914 Salon des Indépendents Exhibition in Paris. But, wrote Cravan in his review of the exhibition (*Maintenant* no. 4), had he ever finished the painting he conceived, he would have called it *The World Champion at the Whorehouse*. For that, he said, is what the Salon represents: a whorehouse. Take Apollinaire's mistress, Marie Laurencin: "Now there's one who needs to have her skirt lifted." Cravan was just warming up. "There are fake Roybets, fake Chabats, fake

Fight poster announcing match between Canadian champion Arthur Cravan and Greek Olympic champion Georges Calafatisin in Athens, 16 August 1914.
Courtesy: Roger Lloyd Conover.

Arthur Cravan, publicity photo, Paris, ca. 1910.
Courtesy: Roger Lloyd Conover.

primitives, fake Cézannes, fake Gauguins, fake Maurice Denis, and fake Charles Guérins. Oh those dear fellows […] What a kick in the ass I'd like to give them! […] Let me say right at the start that in my opinion the first requirement for an artist is to know how to swim. I also feel that art, in the mysterious state corresponding to form in a wrestler, is situated more in the guts than in the brain, and that is why it exasperates me when, in the presence of a painting, I evoke the man and all I see is a head. Where are the legs, the spleen and the liver? That is why I feel nothing but disgust for a painting by a Chagall or a Jackal, that shows you a man pouring kerosene into a cow's ass-hole, when even real madness does not appeal to me because it manifests only a brain. Genius is nothing more but an extraordinary manifestation of the body […] Take a few pills and purge your spirit; do a lot of fucking or better still go into rigorous training: when the girth of your arm measures nineteen inches, you'll at least be a brute, *if* you're gifted."[7]

Breton had such lines in mind when he praised Cravan's critique of the Paris Independents Exhibition as a "masterpiece of humour applied to art criticism". But some artists can't take a poke. His comments about individual artists (Marie Laurencin in particular) soon resulted in libel charges, costing Cravan eight days in jail: representing, I'd guess, the only eight days an art critic has spent behind bars (for reviewing an exhibition) in all of the twentieth century. Cravan was unrepentant, and rubbed salt in his detractors' wounds when he published a mock-apology in a subsequent issue of *Maintenant*.

Cravan's sentence immediately followed Jack Johnson's successful defence of his title as Heavyweight Champion of the World. Cravan, who was well aware that Johnson had been the object of a vicious and racist smear campaign ever since the ex-stevedore had become the first black boxer to win the heavyweight title in America, loved everything about the outspoken, flamboyant boxer. The champion who flicked expensive cigars as elegantly as he courted blondes was hated by Jack London, but was loved by Arthur Cravan. "After Poe, Whitman, Emerson, he is the most glorious American. If there is a revolution here I shall fight to have him enthroned King of the United States," Cravan wrote of Johnson. Although Cravan couldn't have known it at the time, Johnson would later be remembered as the most skilled heavyweight in the history of boxing. He was Cravan's age, exactly, stood an inch or two shorter, and was about the same weight. Johnson and Cravan made the club scene in Paris together, boxed in Spain, and later met in Mexico City, where they were hosted by Pancho Villa and monitored by the US Government.[8] Cravan particularly admired Johnson's feint (an art that is now on the wane), and his appreciation of the classics. Like Cravan, Johnson studied literature and practised theatre, brandished non-conformist stances, and had a difficult time training. Both shared a weakness for the good life, or, by puritan standards, the bad life. But unlike Cravan, Johnson died prosaically in a car accident in 1946.

The best of Cravan's Paris pals was Kees Van Dongen, whose studio on Avenue Denfert-Rochereau not only made him a neighbour, but was also a meeting place of painters living in Montparnasse. In Van Dongen's studio, French and American, physical and intellectual culture mixed. Cravan sometimes held boxing exhibitions there. One such sparring session inspired a painting (now lost) by Patrick Henry Bruce, depicting Cravan in life-sized

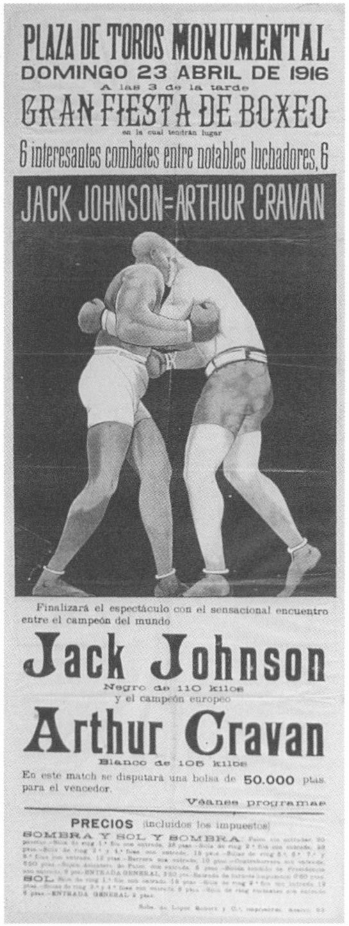

Poster announcing match between Arthur Cravan (105 kilos) and Jack Johnson (110 kilos) in Barcelona, 23 April 1916. Courtesy: Roger Lloyd Conover.

Poster announcing ten round match between Arthur Cravan and Frank aHoche, Barcelona, 26 June 1916. Courtesy: Roger Lloyd Conover.

geometric abstraction; some, if not all, of the surviving portraits of Cravan by Severini, Modigliani, Picabia, Gan and Hayden were likewise inspired by these artists' rendezvous with Cravan *chez* Van Dongen.

In the summer of 1915, American art critic Henry McBride visited Van Dongen's studio. There he encountered Cravan for the first time. Cravan was about to deliver one of his 'performance lectures' at the Sociétés Savantes. The poster announced that on 5 July, at 8, rue Danton:

Le poète ARTHUR CRAVAN
(neveu d'Oscar Wilde)
Champion de Boxe. Poids 125 K. Taille 2 M.
Le Critique Brutale
Parlera
Boxera
Dansera
La nouvelle "Boxing Dance"
LA VERY BOXE

McBride not only attended Cravan's performance, he also described it: "He carried a pistol and fired a few blank cartridges at the floor and into the wings and then endeavoured to read a long poem he had written. He seemed to be aware that he was not in a position to be taken seriously, to loathe the condition he found himself in and at the same time to defy his public with it."[9] Another newspaper account of the same event described Cravan's performance as that of a "tall, young, unshaven man who – dressed in a torn flannel shirt, red belt, black pants, and light pumps – talked, danced, and boxed. Before speaking, he fired several pistol shots into the air, then, half in jest, half-seriously, made the most insane pronouncements against art and life. He praised athletes above artists, he praised homosexuals, those who rob the Louvre, madmen, etc. He read standing, balancing first on one foot and then on the other, and from time to time he insulted the audience. His listeners seemed enthralled by this bizarre performer. Things almost went too far, however, when this Cravan threw his briefcase into the audience. It was only by accident that no one was hit. Some friends of this dancer, boxer, and lecturer put the finishing touches on the evening by dancing, boxing, and declaiming as well."[10]

Cravan rejected anything approximating 'normal' life; he lived outside the law. He favoured underdogs. He took experience in the most extreme doses and sought life in the most extreme conditions he could find. As a boxer, he sometimes took his training seriously, but at other times showed up for prizefights bathrobed and drunk. He may even have done so at the most significant match of his career, which took place on 23 April 1916 in Barcelona. Jack Johnson, disputed World Heavyweight Champion and undisputed European Heavyweight Champion at the time, weighed in at 242 pounds. Cravan scaled 230 pounds. Both fighters were fugitives from so-called 'justice'. Cravan was wanted for evading military service and carrying false identity papers; Johnson had skipped the States when he was found guilty of violating the Mann Act, a trumped-up charge meant to punish him for consorting with Caucasian women, for which he later served a year in Leavenworth.

Spain offered amnesty.[11] Both men needed a fight. Johnson's presence was enough to guarantee a good gate, but Cravan wanted to make sure the Plaza de Toros Monumental was filled in order to increase his take. In the weeks leading up to the fight, he mounted a massive publicity campaign, holding press conferences at sparring

First round between heavyweights Arthur Cravan and Jack Johnson, Plaza de Toros Monumental, Barcelona, 23 April 1916 (previously unpublished).
Courtesy: Roger Lloyd Conover.

Arthur Cravan in a training session, Barcelona, 1916.
Courtesy: Roger Lloyd Conover.

Jack Johnson (seated centre with cigarette holder) and Arthur Cravan (seated to his right), Barcelona, 1916.
Courtesy: Roger Lloyd Conover.

sessions and making a point of being seen with Johnson in public. So avidly did the Barcelona press cover the story that, by the day of the fight, the Spanish public was convinced: Cravan, a virtually unknown boxer in Spain, was indeed "the great white hope" that the heavyweight division had long been waiting for to topple Johnson. Together, Cravan and Johnson had set the stage for a fight whose execution could never equal its hype.

Even before the bell announced the start of the first round, Cravan had achieved his aim: the stadium was full. Whether he won or lost, his percentage of the purse would cover his passage to the States, where friends like AB Frost, Jr., Francis Picabia and Robert Coady were waiting. Contrary to published reports by Gabrielle Buffet-Picabia, Jack Johnson (who stated in his autobiography, "I knocked him out in the first round") and others who later described Johnson's dispatch of Cravan within the fight's first three minutes, newspaper accounts of the fight appearing the next day verify that Cravan did not go down until the sixth round.[12]

Round 3: Poseur

In late 1916, Picabia wrote to Arensberg, Duchamp, et. al., warning of a sensational landing about to take place in the States: "Arthur Cravan too has taken to the transatlantic; he will deliver talks. Will he be dressed as gentleman or as a cowboy? When he left he was in favour of the latter outfit and intended to make an impressive entry on the scene: on horseback and shooting revolvers at the lights."[13]

On 13 January 1917, Arthur Cravan disembarked in New York or rather Paris, New York, for through Picabia's introductions and Cravan's own contacts, Manhattan was cosy with cohorts. Cravan had plenty of choice when it came to beds, and occasionally availed himself of invitations (he found actress Sophie Treadwell's invitations particularly seductive). But his preferred address, for the most part, was Central Park, that is to say, its benches. Within three months of his arrival (19 April 1917), Cravan found himself lecturing at the first annual exhibition of the Society of Independent Artists at the Grand Central Palace, still the largest art exhibition ever held in New York, almost double the size of the 1913 Armory Show. Marcel Duchamp and Francis Picabia had invited him to speak at the Grand Central Palace venue. His subject, 'The Independent Artists in France and America', was natural. Duchamp and Picabia had read his review of the Independents show in Paris, and knew he could be counted on to do something equally scandalous in New York. The hosts agreed on the choice of speaker, but held quite different views of the man. Picabia was drawn to him. Duchamp kept his distance. Duchamp's guard, however, had more to do with his protective feelings toward Mina Loy and with Cravan's seduction of her than with intellectual differences.

Picabia and Duchamp's instincts were correct: Cravan could draw a crowd. If nothing else, the public would come to hear his lecture out of curiosity. When, after all, had a professional boxer – and a recent opponent of Jack Johnson, no less – ever addressed a sophisticated audience about modern art? Some members of the audience, no doubt, had already read the March issue of *Soil* (a journal devoted to arts and sports), in which Cravan's appreciation of Jack Johnson appeared. Even if Johnson's left "droops a bit", Cravan allowed, the man has impeccable style outside the ring: "He's a man of scandal – I like him for that – eccentric, he's lively, good-natured and gloriously vain."[14]

According to one eye-witness report of his lecture, Cravan arrived at the podium drunk, swayed back and forth a few times, began to disrobe and was quickly hauled off the stage.[15] According to other versions of the same event, Cravan was on the verge of urinating on a painting when he was manacled and arrested. Some reports say he spent a week in Sing-Sing. Others say Walter Conrad Arensberg and Marcel Duchamp quickly bailed him out of jail. Rumour and fact cross regularly in sightings of Cravan. He exists for a moment in the crosshairs between them, then splits out of sight.

By August 1917, more threatening forces were closing in on Cravan. His former Paris sparring partner and fellow artist, Arthur Burdett Frost, Jr., suggested that they hitchhike to Canada, camouflaging themselves as soldiers. Cravan approved; he was amused by the idea of donning the uniform of the very war that he was determined to escape. They hitched rides to Hartford, Connecticut; then to Boston, Massachusetts; and finally to Portland, Maine, where they hooked up with a trucker driving through to Nova Scotia. Once across the border, they could relax. But when Frost Jr. suddenly died

Miércoles 12 de Abril 1916
A LAS 10 DE LA NOCHE
Gran Soirée de BOXE
IRIS-PARK.-CALLE VALENCIA
1.° Combate de 5 raunds de 2 minutos
ENRIQUE contra MONTERO
46 K. 49 K.
2.° Combate de 6 raunds de 2 minutos
STANLEY contra ALAIX
54 K. 56 K.
3.° Combate de 8 raunds de 2 minutos
EVELYN KNIGHT contra MIRO
63 K. 65 K.
4.° Combate de 10 raunds de 2 minutos
FRED JAKS contra SUM
62 K. 70 K.
5.° Combate de 15 raunds de 3 minutos
ALLACK contra FRANK HOCHÉ
70 K. 74 K.
El campeón
Jack Johnson
que combatirá proximamente CONTRA
Arthur Cravan
actuará de Referée en esta Soirée.
¡Todo Barcelona podrà admirar el Jack Johnson de todos los tiempos!
Precios de las localidades: 5, 3 y 1'50 ptas.
La Empresa se reserva el derecho de alterar.

Broadside advertising '*Gran Soirée de Boxe*' listing Arthur Cravan as referee, Barcelona, 12 April 1916.
Courtesy: Roger Lloyd Conover.

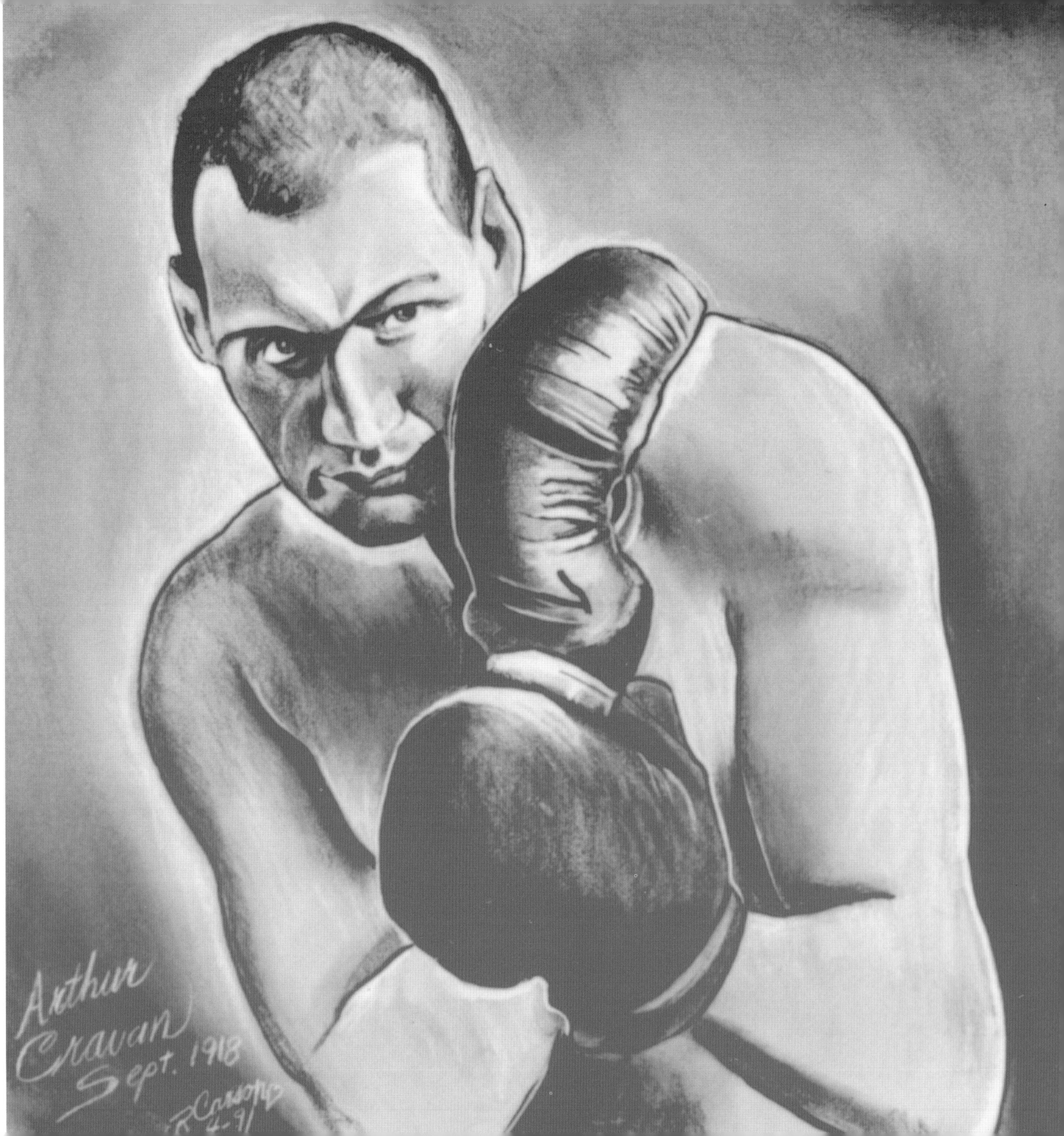

Portrait of Arthur Cravan by Robert Carson, based on pre-fight photo of Cravan's fight with Jim Black Diamond Smith, Mexico City, September 1918. Courtesy: Roger Lloyd Conover.

(probably of pneumonia), Frost Sr. – who had not approved of his son's travelling with Cravan in the first place – accused Cravan of homicide. Cravan felt the heat, and boarded the first ship available – a Danish trawler bound for Mexico – where Mina Loy, the beautiful poet who had been one of his lovers in New York, would join him.

On the 13 September 1918 cover of the Mexico City bulletin *Arte Y Deportes* (*Arts and Sports*), Cravan's mug appeared beneath that of a black fighter, Jim Black Diamond Smith. Cravan was to fight Smith on 15 September in the Plaza de Toros, a municipal arena famous for matadorial events. The magazine predicted a "sensational boxing match of twenty rounds", for the Heavyweight Championship of Mexico. Previously, in the 9 August issue of the same magazine, Cravan had been introduced as "Professor of Boxing and Art" at the Physical Culture Institute ("Escuela de Cultura Physica"), where he had sparred against Honorato Castro, Mexican Champion. The next issue of *Arte Y Deportes* reported that Cravan had been knocked out by Jim Smith in the second round. The fight with Black Diamond Jim Smith, whoever he was, was Cravan's last documented ring appearance.[16]

Round 4: Technical Knock-out

Fast forward: a few years later, Mina Loy was questioning US authorities and searching Mexican morgues, hospitals, and prisons for Cravan, hoping to find some sign, some clue, some indication as to the fate of her missing husband. For in November 1918 Arthur Cravan suddenly vanished without a trace, leaving no corpse, no witness, no note. He appeared to have literally sailed off the face of the earth, leaving no clues as to his whereabouts, no destination, no motive. But this was not new. He had disappeared before, and had sometimes spoken of suicide. His European colleagues assumed that he would eventually resurface, bearing the passport of another country, wearing the overcoat of a new profession, or speaking the language of a new girlfriend. He was a tireless traverser of borders, a sworn resister of order. He was fond of saying that he carried twenty countries in his memory and dragged the colours of 100 cities in his soul. His fists were not his only passport. He is alleged to have forged and traded in Wilde manuscripts, and to have painted and sold fake Picassos. He was in love with illusion, movement, escape, sleight. "He worked to maintain his reality by presenting an unreality of himself to the world – to occupy itself with – while making his spiritual getaway," said Mina Loy.[17] She of all people should know.

Cravan did not wish to be a saint. But he has been claimed as the guardian angel of the Dadaists, the Surrealists, the Pataphysicians and the Sex Pistols. Today, what once appeared to be one of the cleanest getaways in the history of boxing appears to be one of the most perplexing escapes in the history of art, for Cravan's exit has been ghosted by a bizarre sequence of shadowings and revenants not explicable by death. Cravan – or if not Cravan, then an impostor – has continually surfaced under various aliases for more than 75 years: sometimes as the mysterious painter Edouard Archinard,[18] sometimes as the gallerist Isaac Cravan, sometimes as Dorian Hope (the mysterious person behind the unsolved Oscar Wilde forgery case), sometimes as the androgynous amanuensis of André Gide, and most recently, I imagine, as a shadow-boxer in the dreams of a certain American writer who is sympathetic to criminals, loves boxing, and recently wrote a sexography on the life of a Spanish painter.

Round 5: Blanks

Bullet Guy Debord, avant-garde film-maker, founder of the extreme Left-wing magazine *Internationale Situationiste* and guru of the 1968 student revolt, wrote in his autobiography (*Panégyrique,* 1989) that Arthur Cravan was one of the people he most admired in all of the twentieth century. Debord's book was published by his friend Gérard Lébovici, the homosexual Maoist shot dead at point blank range with four bullets from a .22 at the wheel of his Porsche in a car park beneath Avenue Foch in Paris in 1984.

Cartridge Ten years later, Debord, 62, shot himself in his country house where he had lived as a recluse for the past two decades.

Body Two days later (3 December 1994), the body of Gérard Voitey, founder of the French publishing house Quai Voltaire, was discovered dead at the wheel of his car near a deserted lake, a single round from a P38 revolver in his head.

Chamber The following day (4 December 1994), Debord's and Voitey's mutual friend, Roger Stéphane, 75, writer, 'provocateur' and friend of novelist André Malraux, was found dead in the Paris apartment where he lived with his dog. A bullet was lodged in his head, his body covered by a mountain of books.

Suspect Debord, whose suicide was initially investigated as a possible homicide, sued several newspapers in 1984 for implying that he might have had a hand in Lébovici's death. Lébovici, at the time of his death, was working on a film based on the life of Arthur Cravan; the film was never completed, but in 1987 Editions Gérard Lébovici published Arthur Cravan's *Oeuvres: Poèmes, Articles, Lettres*, another project Lébovici had been working on at the time of his death.

Witness In 1982, Arthur Cravan made a fleeting appearance in American novelist John Gardner's *Mickelsson's Ghosts*. Gardner died shortly thereafter in a motorcycle accident. In 1940, the poet Brion Gysin, speaking in confidence to the art dealer Julien Levy about ghosts, revealed that he was, "above all [...] haunted by a man known as Cravan. I feel sure he is not dead, or if he is, he is among my present stars."

Denial In 1882, Oscar Wilde covered the title fight between heavyweight boxers Boston Strong Boy John Sullivan and Trojan Giant Paddy Ryan for a British publication. Ten years later, Sullivan would lose his crown in the first title fight conducted under the Queensbury rules, drafted under the auspices of one John Sholto Douglas, the eighth Marquess of Queensbury, an eccentric Scottish nobleman who is chiefly remembered for authoring the rules which still govern amateur boxing (the Queensbury rules) and for ruining Oscar Wilde. This is the same Marquess whom Wilde once sued for libel; the trials which followed led to the disclosure of Wilde's homosexual affair with the Marquess' son, Lord Alfred Douglas, and ended with Wilde's conviction and imprisonment for sodomy. Might Arthur Cravan – later suspected by Vyvyan Holland, Guillot de Saix, William Figgis and Herbert Boyce Satcher – of being 'Dorian Hope', the con-man who passed himself off as the homosexual secretary of André Gide (and accused of selling forged Oscar Wilde manuscripts in

Europe in the early 1920s) have been exercising Wilde's posthumous revenge on two of his nemeses, Gide and Queensbury?[19] It seems so. There are more than a few facts connecting the dots, not least of which is the bad blood between Gide and Wilde, Queensbury and Wilde, Gide and Cravan, Queensbury and Cravan. Cravan was no doubt aware that Gide, in his youth, had been enraptured by Wilde, but turned on him in his memoirs. Gide, as Cravan's elder, was the subject of an unflattering profile by Cravan in *Maintenant* (1913). Gide immediately retaliated, modelling his most famous character after Cravan. Lafcadio, the hooligan and amoralist in *Les Caves du Vatican* (1914), was based on Cravan.[20] And Cravan was forced to box as a gentleman by the Marquess.

At-large Cravan disappeared four months after he and his bride, Mina Loy, conceived their first and only child, and has never been seen since. The man who invented a father left a daughter. We wait for a faun to re-enter the ring. We dream of the poet-boxer.

Excursus: Cravan Baedeker

This match may be continued, depending on the stores of imagination, evidence, and stamina available. But for now, this is the last round, each having imposed deliberately greater tariffs on writers' lives, readers' patience and editors' tolerance. Those who wish to find other thumb prints of Cravan are first referred to the primary source, Maintenant, but may also identify him via more recently inked whorls. Authors' names are suppressed in order not to place their lives at greater risk. A selection:

1 *'Wanted: Arthur Cravan, 1887-?',* Four Dada Suicides *(London: Atlas Press, 1995).*
2 *'The Secret Names of Arthur Cravan',* Arthur Cravan: Poète et Boxeur *(Paris: Terrain Vague, 1992).*
3 *Mina Lloyd, 'La modernista perduda: Mina Loy, Mina Lloyd, Madame Arthur Cravan',* La Veritable Història d'Arthur Cravan: Poeta i Boxador *(Barcelona: Ajuntament de Barcelona, 1992).*
4 *'Eloge d'un poète pugiliste: Arthur Cravan',* Le Lèrot reveur, *no. 54, February 1992 (Paris).*
5 *Arthur Cravan,* Poesia, *no. 38, 1992 (Madrid).*
6 *Arthur Cravan,* le prophète *(Paris: Actual, 1992).*
7 *Arthur Cravan,* Poeten Med Världens Kortaste Här *(Lund: Bakhall, 1989).*
8 *Arthur Cravan,* Oeuvres: Poèmes, Articles, Lettres *(Paris: Editions Gerard Lébovici, 1987).*
9 *'Mina Loy's 'Colossus': Arthur Cravan Undressed',* New York Dada *(New York: Willis Locker & Owens, 1986). This article originally appeared in the journal* Dada/Surrealism *14 (Iowa City: Association for the Study of Dada and Surrealism).*
10 *Introduction to* The Last Lunar Baedeker *(Highlands, No. Carolina: Jargon Society, 1982; and London: Carcanet, 1985).*

I wish to thank the following people who provided me with leads, information, encouragement, and inspiration in writing this essay: Michael Barson, Robert Carson, Mary Ann Caws, Case Conover, Strand Conover, Rob Ellowitch, Judi Freeman, Martin Hagler, George Garrett, Anna Ginn, Kenn Guimond, Harry George, John Irving, Terry Keller, Angus King, Billy Kluver, Mark Kramer, Alan Lelchuk, Rod MacDonald, Julie Martin, Thomas Moser, Francis Naumann, Floyd Patterson, George Plimpton, John Richardson, Martica Sawin, Vernon Scannell, Budd Schulberg, Ligia Slovic Rave, Jose Torrés, Steven Watson, Allen Wier. I would also like to thank David Chandler, Tania Guha, Gilane Tawadros and the staff of the Institute of International Visual Arts for their editorial courage, curatorial vision and the extraordinary patience it took to produce *Boxer*.
RLC

1 This passage is cited in Leon Trotsky's autobiography, *Ma Vie* ('A travers l'Espagne') (Paris: Gallimard, 1973); the work was originally published in Russian.
2 As of this writing, Mina Loy's *Colossus* remains an unpublished manuscript, but portions of it were excerpted in Roger L. Conover, ed., 'Mina Loy's "Colossus": Arthur Cravan Undressed', *New York Dada* (New York: Willis Locker & Owens, 1986), which originally appeared in the journal *Dada/Surrealism*, 14 (Iowa City: Association for the Study of Dada and Surrrealism).
3 This story first appeared in a special issue of *Maintenant*, 2:3 (October/November 1913) dedicated to Oscar Wilde, under the title 'Oscar Wilde est Vivant!'. An English translation of Cravan's text later ran in two successive instalments of *The Soil* (nos. 4 and 5 April and July 1917). See also 'Documents Inédits sur Oscar Wilde' in *Maintenant*, 1:1 (April 1912) and 2:2 (July 1913) and 'Wilde's Personal Appearance' in *The Soil*, no. 4 (April 1917).
4 'No One Found Who Saw Wilde Dead', *New York Times*, 9 November 1913. Robert Sherard describes this incident in some detail in *The Real Oscar Wilde* (London, 1911).
5 Blaise Cendrars, *Le lotissement du ciel* (Paris: Denoel, 1949). Translated in Cendrars, *Sky: Memoirs* (New York: Paragon House, 1992).
6 Joe Jeannette was one of the most popular black American heavyweights in Paris in the 1910s. He challenged Jack Johnson on numerous occasions and beat Sam McVey in 1909 after 49 rounds.
7 This and the previous paragraph's quotation from Cravan come from *Maintenant* 3: 4, *Numéro Spécial* (March/April 1914), 'L'Exposition des Independents'.
8 I have recently obtained copies of the US Government's surveillance files on Johnson and Cravan under the Freedom of Information Act. These files reveal, among other things, that both men were being watched closely by US intelligence agents in Mexico, that both were considered subversive and dangerous to the war effort, and that their mail was systematically read and its contents reported to bureau chiefs in Washington.
9 *New York Sun*, 18 April 1915.
10 Undated, unsigned newspaper column (Paris). Collection Roger L. Conover.
11 Prior to the fight, Cravan spent some months in Spain: at the Real Club, Maritimo where he worked as a professor of boxing; but also at the seaside resort of Tossa, outside Barcelona, where his acquaintances included Albert Gleize, Francis Picabia, Juliette Roche, and pseudo-Futurist Valentine de St. Point. Cravan also became ring buddies with Frank Hoche (whom he later fought in Paris), Frank Crozier, and Fred Jaks, who were part of the fight scene in Barcelona (Jaks was on the undercard of the Johnson vs. Cravan fight).
12 See for instance the 24 April 1916 editions of *El Mundo Deportivo, La Veu, Illustració Catalano*, and *Diari de Barcelona*.
13 *391*, vol. 1, no. 4 (New York, 1916).
14 'Arthur Cravan vs. Jack Johnson', *The Soil*, no. 4, April 1917.
15 'Independents Get Unexpected Thrill', *New York Sun*, 20 April 1917.
16 No record of Jim Smith exists. He was most likely a black American boxer fighting in Mexico under an assumed name.
17 Mina Loy, 'Arthur Cravan is Alive!', The Last Lunar Baedeker (Highlands, N.C.:Jargon Society, 1982).
18 Cravan's career as the possible double of painter Edouard Archinard was first discussed in 'The Secret Names of Arthur Cravan', *Arthur Cravan: Poete et Boxeur* (Paris: Terrain Vague, 1992).
19 This story is told in much greater detail in 'Arthur Cravan', *Four Dada Suicides* (London: Atlas Press, 1995).
20 Jean Cocteau first identified Cravan as the 'original' Lafcadio in the 'Gide' commemorative issue of *Nouvelle Revue Français* (November 1951). Cravan was later identified as the person upon whom Gide's character, Lafcadio, was based, in Bernard Delvaille's introduction to the first reprint of *Maintenant* (Eric Losfeld, Paris, 1957). *Les Caves du Vatican* (Paris: Gallimard, 1914) first appeared in English as Lafcadio's Adventures (New York: Knopf, 1925).

Raging Bulls: Sexuality and the Boxing Movie

Nick James

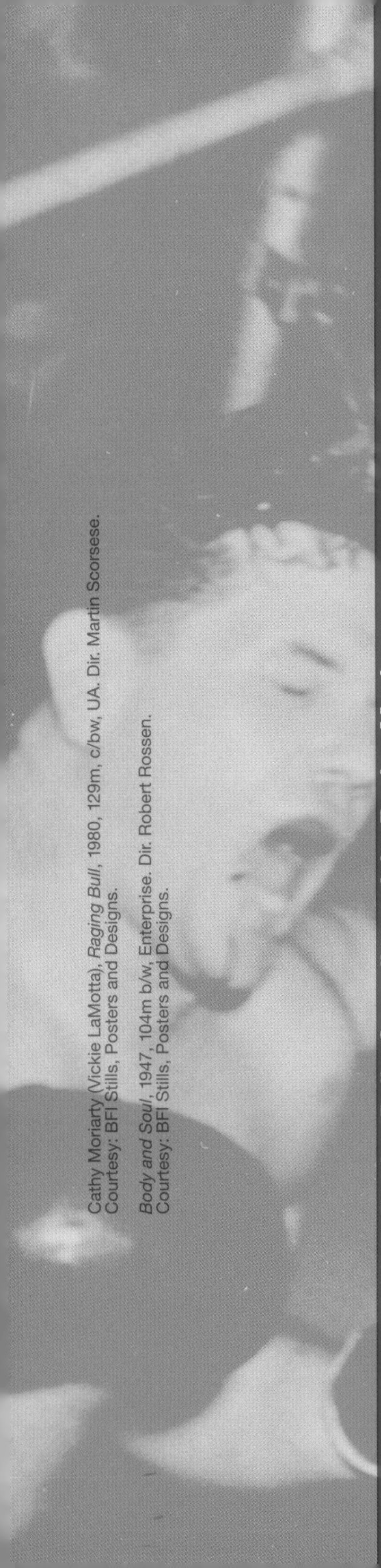

Cathy Moriarty (Vickie LaMotta), *Raging Bull*, 1980, 129m, c/bw, UA. Dir. Martin Scorsese. Courtesy: BFI Stills, Posters and Designs.

Body and Soul, 1947, 104m b/w, Enterprise. Dir. Robert Rossen. Courtesy: BFI Stills, Posters and Designs.

A grey face flattens under a blurred black glove projecting an arc of blood from the smashed nose: "He don't look pretty no more," says ringside gang boss Tommy Carbone of the challenger Janiro, whose sweet looks have been destroyed by the Bronx Bull, Jake La Motta, in the movie *Raging Bull* (1980). La Motta's wife has said Janiro was "good-looking, popular" and sexual jealousy is motive enough for this singular revenge. With this supreme moment of 'aesthetic violence' the director Martin Scorsese follows a familiar pattern in Hollywood's treatment of boxing: framing the brutality, excitement and eroticism of the spectacle within a context of heterosexual validation.

There is a long tradition of boxing movies going back to the early years of cinema, but a fight between two trained boxers involves a set of aesthetic and moral relationships which are often antithetical to commercial movie purposes. The movie business likes its male icons to have primarily a heterosexual appeal, and a homosexual appeal only as a by-product. Yet the erotic content of boxing is exclusively homoerotic. As Joyce Carol Oates has stated: "The confrontation in the ring – the disrobing – the sweaty heated combat that is part dance, courtship, coupling – the frequent urgent pursuit by one boxer of the other […] surely boxing derives much of its appeal from this mimicry of a species of erotic love."[1] For Muhammad Ali's trainer, Bundini Brown, this homoeroticism is inextricable from the need to hurt: "You got to get the hard-on, and then you got to keep it. You want to be careful not to lose the hard-on, and cautious not to come."[2]

Mainstream film producers cannot afford to show this interdependence between animosity and the sexual element in boxing. If "to enter the ring near-naked and to risk one's life is to make of one's audience voyeurs of a kind,"[3] it's the wrong kind of voyeurism for the movie industry. A lead actor may be portrayed as a blatantly sexual presence, a pin-up and a hero, but he must be viably heterosexual. This perceived commercial necessity reflects deeper concerns, as Steve Neal argues: "In a heterosexual and patriarchal society the male body cannot be marked explicitly as the erotic object of another male look: that look must be motivated in some other way, its erotic component repressed."[4] So the violence of boxing presents a problem of sexual and moral representation for film-makers: how to

Robert De Niro (Jake LaMotta), *Raging Bull*, 1980, 129m, c/bw, UA. Dir. Martin Scorsese.
Courtesy: BFI Stills, Posters and Designs.

make a boxer a plausibly savage and obsessive combatant in the ring – to show his 'hard on' – yet keep him as a sympathetic and attractive lover of women outside it? This character conundrum is compounded by the technical problem of reproducing the violence itself. For, despite the magnificent stylised horror of *Raging Bull*, cinema has no convincing equivalent to the pure and brutal animosity sometimes manifest in a real boxing ring – it just can't be faked.

Boxing movies, such as *Raging Bull*, Robert Wise's *The Set-up* (1948), Robert Rossen's *Body and Soul* (1947), or the first three *Rocky* films (1976, 1979, 1982), have their own aesthetic of violence – one that subordinates animosity and eroticism to the hero's narrative redemption – but it's a simulation not a recreation of what happens in a real ring. The difference in pacing, the delivery of blows, the lack of technique and the absence of the less-eventful stretches of a match, all contribute to a choreographed feel. The flash-lit intensity of *Raging Bull* can give an intimate sense of raw power and physical sadism; the *Rocky* movies, with their peculiar unguarded celebration of masochism, can render the soaring emotion of a big fight better than ringside television cameras, but none of these films quite replicates the instinctive ferocity often seen during a real fight, as any comparison with real fight footage will confirm.

It is the absolute necessity of animosity to the sport which accounts for wariness about sexuality within it. Real boxers are supposed to refrain from sex as part of their training ritual, as if the intensity of their desire to punish the opponent can be weakened only by sexual satisfaction. "Every athlete [is] up against the old question – could the refinement of your best reflexes which sex offer[s] be worth the absence of rapacity it might also leave?" writes Norman Mailer.[5] This 'in training' taboo implies that the two states of anticipatory desire – for sex and for combat – are interchangeable. "Instead of focusing his energies and fantasies upon a woman," says Oates, "the boxer focuses them upon an opponent. Where Woman has been, Opponent must be."[6] Thus for a male fighter to retain his mythic power over his opponent, his 'maleness' must be intensified by being cloistered in a hermetic all-male environment.

Nevertheless, boxing movies continually try to invert this process. In Robert Rossen's *Body and Soul*, Hazel Brooks' gold-digging nightclub floozy sits below the training ring, obscured from the camera by a punchbag. As the troubled boxer, played by John Garfield, starts pounding the bag, each blow reveals her, so that the two images blur together. Later she wraps herself around the bag in front of Garfield, obviating the mixture of dislike and desire that he feels for her. The movie is overlaying her image onto that of the opponent-substitute and she invokes the same mixed emotions in Garfield as a fighter would. In *Somebody Up There Likes Me* (1956), the movie based on Rocky Graziano's autobiography, Pier Angeli, the pacifist wife of Paul Newman's Rocky, takes this inversion a step further. When Graziano is about to blow his entire career because the boxing commission has taken away his licence, she hits him in the face. To break Graziano's obsession with his opponent, she must not only offer herself as replacement but also take part in the violence.

The exclusion of women from the boxer's world is a tradition fostered in certain communities in which men and women were neither used nor encouraged to share their leisure time. Typical of these might be the Victorian Irish-American immigrant milieu in which the bare knuckle heavyweight champion John L. Sullivan was raised. According to Sullivan's biographer, Michael T. Isenberg: "Boston's young Irish males, searching for comradeship in their leisure time [...] lived within an ethos of 'gender hostility', with each sex possessing a rationale for the faults of the other [...] [Their] cult of masculinity was tied together by friendships, rough-and-ready camaraderie, tall tales and masculine fantasies."[7] In such a cult, the homoerotic is necessarily invisible. Boxing's hostility towards suggestions of its homoeroticism finds its most obvious incarnation in the Marquis of Queensbury, the sponsor of the Queensbury rules devised by John Graham Chambers in 1867.[8] Such niceties as three-minute rounds, padded gloves and so on were introduced in to legitimise the sport and help promote it as mass entertainment at around the same time that moving pictures were first introduced. In the years between 1892 and 1896, Queensbury sought the ruin of Oscar Wilde for 'corrupting' his son Lord Alfred Douglas and "posing as a sodomite."[9] Yet Wilde himself was a boxing fan. "I do not breathe my prejudices aloud," he said in Philadelphia in 1882, "[but] I'd go further than New Orleans to see a good [fight] like that between [Paddy] Ryan and [John L.] Sullivan is going to be."[10]

The heyday of British prizefighting in the late eighteenth and early nineteenth centuries affords a rich picture of the mutual appreciation of male physique among certain upper-class men. The homoeroticism that echoes through Norman Mailer's writings about boxing first flowered in literature at this time. William Hazlitt's *The Fight* has typical passages: "Hickman might be compared to Diomed, light, vigorous, elastic, and his back glistened in the sun as he moved about like a panther's hide."[11] It was the era of the Regency dandy and it "was the practice when gentlemen fought or sparred with professionals" that "the latter would fight stripped to the waist, but the gentleman always fought somewhat hampered by ruffled shirts, sashes, collar buttons and so forth."[12] The future George IV as Prince of Wales backed prizefights, and among his entourage was Wilde's great antecedent Beau Brummell (of whose coat Lord Byron once said, "you might say the body thought.")[13] Byron, himself a dandy and a bisexual,[14] was taught to box by the pugilist John Jackson at 'Jackson's Rooms' in Bond Street, as was the Prince of Wales.[15] Whatever vestiges were left of this dandyism after the moralist repression of the Victorian era, the Marquis of Queensbury's eventual victory over Wilde made any appreciation of boxing's homoeroticism unthinkable.

In the 1890s, the emergence of legitimised boxing and cinema as public spectacles went hand in hand. Films of real boxing bouts were a hugely popular genre of their own. Some 100 were made from 1894 to 1915 and they were among the first multi-reel entertainments, well before dramatised films. Nevertheless, after a long campaign against this "popular yet controversial cycle"[16] by women's organisations and religious groups opposed to such "brutal and degrading performances,"[17] and racist groups anxious to suppress evidence of black heavyweight champion Jack Johnson's physical supremacy, they were outlawed by the US government in 1912. That these filmed fights made moving images of the naked male torso regularly available to mass audiences, including women, might also be supposed to have fuelled the campaign. Institutionalised boxing has since retained the sexually repressive demeanour of the late nineteenth century, whereas films of real boxing matches can be seen to have prepared audiences for easily accessible sexual images of the male body, a familiarity that drama film-makers and actors would soon exploit.

The boxing movie became a generic staple of Hollywood in its heyday. The opportunity that they offered male actors – to strut a taut and burnished musculature – is one that few could resist. The list of those who succumbed includes a good many anxious to confirm a macho reputation: Errol Flynn, John Garfield, Kirk Douglas, William Holden, Robert Ryan. Also the dominating influence of the pugilistic Ernest Hemingway on the pre-World War II generation of Hollywood scriptwriters ensured that there was a steady diet of tough dramas set in the boxing world (a situation satirised in the Coen Brothers' movie *Barton Fink* (1991) when neurotic New York dramatist Fink is given a Wallace Beery boxing project as his first Hollywood commission). These hard-nosed studio pictures enabled male stars to put their physical desirability beyond question.

Out of this covertly objectifying atmosphere of 'men's men' competing for the spotlight, some perhaps unlooked for aspects of homoeroticism leaked into the boxing movie. Directors didn't bother trying to reproduce the often slow and relentless pace of a real fight and they knew that they couldn't fake the actual malevolence. Instead, fight movies of the 1930s and 1940s are often boyish, knockabout affairs, partly designed, it would seem, to coyly show off the torsos of their lead actors. In *Kid Galahad* (1937), tall, blonde but obscure movie star Wayne Morris, keen no doubt to charm the camera in the few scenes he could steal away from his co-stars Edward G. Robinson and Humphrey Bogart, keeps a flirtatious smirk on his face through every fight. As the violin player who turns to the ring in desperation in *Golden Boy* (1939), William Holden is sensitive and naive until finally he is brutalised. Errol Flynn, playing the last of the big time bare-knuckle pugilists in *Gentleman Jim* (1942), gives a peacock display of erect and concentrated elegance more dashing than any of his swashbuckling roles. An 'innocent' rumbustious eroticism inflects many of these fight scenes, although they are usually brief and, by modern standards, unbloody.

The fight movies of the late 1940s and 1950s are more pessimistic, brooding affairs. If a fighter wakes up sweating in the night with a man's name on his lips, as John Garfield does at the beginning of *Body and Soul* (1947), it is not that of his opponent, but of a fighter whose health he once destroyed. The post-war era, with its "rampant inflation, unemployment, labour strife, shifting social patterns and the […] anxieties of the cold war,"[18] had after all spawned *film noir* and laid bare more complex existential predicaments. According to Deborah Thomas: "What was normal during the war – close male companionship, sanctioned killing […] and more casual sexual behaviour – became deviant in the context of post-war calm."[19] The passive heroes of *film noir* were beset by vampiric women, parasitic criminals and aggressive government agencies and the boxing movie proved the perfect arena for projecting this crisis of masculine powerlessness. In such socially-conscious films as *Body and Soul* (1947), *The Set-Up* (1948), *Champion* (1949), *The Harder They Fall* (1956) and *Somebody Up There Likes Me* (1956), the climactic bout becomes a moral arena where nothing and no one is 'innocent'. There has to be a motive greater than the simple desire to crush an opponent: John Garfield in *Body and Soul*, Robert Ryan in *The Set-Up* and Paul Newman in *Somebody Up There Likes Me* all have a burden of responsibility towards the women they exclude from their working lives.

They refuse to lose rather than need to win. Each of them is fighting to redeem himself from his own violent career, and arguably from its implicit sexuality.

The role of the boxer's wife or girlfriend in these movies often follows a routine generic trajectory. She must avoid the ringside and suffer at a remote distance via radio reports, until the final bout where she appears, reluctantly, at the ringside to flinch in close-up as counterpoint to her lover's receiving of blows. In these movies, boxers enjoy established relationships with women, yet their relationships conform to mythic archetypes that reinforce the idea of heterosexuality as a threat to a boxer's ability to perform. A sympathetic woman, such as Audrey Totter in *The Set-Up*, is cast as Beauty to the boxer's Beast, her domesticating feminine intelligence striving to bring out the gentility beneath the savage breast. A more obstructing influence, such as Hazel Brooks in *Body and Soul*, is a Delilah to Garfield's Sampson. Totter's insistence on a 'normal' life is just as destructive to the boxer's will to win as Brooks' expensive hedonism. However, in the final bout – which in most boxing movies constitutes the only concentrated fight footage – the process is again inverted. The boxer is no longer fighting through animosity. Physical intimacy with his opponent becomes an irrelevance and there's never much of it on camera. The hero wants to win only to subordinate the hermetic male world which made him a boxer to a domestic order and to proclaim himself a responsible husband and/or community hero.

If the late 1940s and 1950s still constitutes the 'golden era' of boxing movies, then the 1960s, with its popular avowal of pacifism, was not conducive to their production. When the next wave finally came along it was the self-conscious product of the 'movie brat' generation. Films such as Walter Hill's debut *Hard Times* (1975), John Avildsen's *Rocky* (1976) and Scorsese's *Raging Bull* (1980) deliberately refer back to the post-war classics that the film-makers grew up with and which they felt resonated with the 1970s mood of pessimism. The crucial figure for these directors, and especially for the conception of *Rocky*, was Marlon Brando's Terry Molloy from *On the Waterfront* (1954). Only peripherally a boxing movie, *Waterfront* does away with boxing scenes altogether. Molloy's career is already over when the film begins and his struggle centres on his new role as a dockyard stevedore and mob errand boy.

Molloy's significance in the 1970s is partly a matter of due reverence. As Scorsese has suggested, *On the Waterfront* is the iconographic equivalent of Shakespeare for his generation.[20] In the film Brando and Eva Marie-Saint enjoy a halting intimacy that leads the washed-up ex-boxer to brave a terrible, disfiguring beating from dockside racketeers. Their relationship – a fragile, sentimental and desexualised affair, set in the Beauty and Beast mould – is transplanted almost whole into the story of Rocky Balboa and his wife Adrian. Like Molloy, Rocky has difficulty expressing himself and a predilection for masochistic self-sacrifice. Stallone has encouraged the idea that Rocky's rags-to-riches story parallels his own, which makes it all the more poignant when in *Rocky II* (1979) he equates his profession with his masculinity. "I never asked you to stop being a woman," he says to the pregnant Adrian who has insisted he retires. "Please don't ask me to stop being a man." Once again, the real boxer's dilemma – to be a man in this context is to be obsessed with another man – is turned inside out for the cinema icon. To portray a boxer is to be a man, but to be a pin-up and the object of the look, is not. Joyce Carol Oates has dismissed the *Rocky* films as being "scarcely about boxing as we know it," noting that Stallone and his opponents are, "ludicrously encumbered with bodybuilders' physiques."[21] This overblown musculature only compounds Stallone's dilemma. "Bodybuilding is […] taken to signal a disturbing narcissism," argues Yvonne Tasker, "inappropriate to familiar definitions of manhood. In other words the bodybuilder, obsessed with his appearance as he is, is not a real man."[22]

Questioning what it means to be a real man is what fires the post-Molloy movie boxer, it is the one thing that sets him apart from the movie boxers of the golden era and gives a desexualised credence to the violence of his profession. With Molloy, Brando made the boxing role a holy site for the method actor (according to Gerald Early, Graziano, who had hung out with Brando, Newman and James Dean, was a huge influence on method mannerisms.) A halting way with words was seen as somehow truer and more poetic an embodiment of the outsider, the "misunderstood, anti-social youth".[23] Most post-1970s boxing movies refer in some way to this Brando archetype, especially the *Rocky* cycle, Jon Voight in *The Champ* (1979) and Mickey Rourke (a former boxer)

The Set-Up, 1949, 72m b/w, RKO. Dir. Robert Wise.
Courtesy: BFI Stills, Posters and Designs.

Body and Soul, 1947, 104m b/w, Enterprise. Dir. Robert Rossen.
Courtesy: BFI Stills, Posters and Designs.

Body and Soul, 1947, 104m b/w, Enterprise. Dir. Robert Rossen.
Courtesy: BFI Stills, Posters and Designs.

in *Homeboy* (1988), in which the hero's mode of expression is an unintelligible whisper. The one film that tries to build on the Brando performance, using the boxing movie as a site in which to examine the crisis of masculine identity at the heart of *On the Waterfront*, is Scorsese's *Raging Bull*.

The movie starts with Jake La Motta in his latterday post-boxing persona as a nightclub host. Here we have the physical equivalent of Molloy's inarticulacy, the muscle turned to blubber of the old bruiser with the cauliflower ear. In La Motta's own words he's become "a bum"[24] and, according to the film-maker Lizzie Borden he has "walled himself in against his own sexuality".[25] To play La Motta, De Niro took method acting beyond all limits, putting himself through a physical ordeal of weight gain and loss that is as impressive as any body weight manipulation achieved by a real boxer. Unlike the *Rocky* movies, *Raging Bull* is undeniably about boxing as we know it, as well as a knowing tribute to the great boxing movies of the 1940s and early 1950s.

La Motta, in his autobiography *Raging Bull*, locates his own loss of animosity and power to the moment when, on the night that he became middleweight champion of the world, he discovered that Harry Gordon, a man he thought he'd beaten to death in his youth, was still alive,[26] stripping him of the guilt that had motivated him throughout his boxing career. Scorsese's movie makes La Motta's story a wider matter of male impotence, tying La Motta's guilt and his facility with violence to a recurrent inability to perform sex with his female partners. Scorsese even makes a symbolic comparison between penis and fist. A scene showing La Motta fending off his second wife Vicky's advances ("I love the smell of the gym," she says, "I can't fool around" he replies) and pouring iced water into his 'boxer' shorts is soon followed with one of him cooling his fists in a bucket of ice. The director is here forcing us to think about the sexuality of boxing, about La Motta's deliberate shunning of women. Homoeroticism nonetheless remains a matter of ringside insult: one of the local gangsters watching La Motta and his brother Joey sparring whispers: "They look like two fags, don't they".

In *Raging Bull*, Jake La Motta's slow transformation from a lean and vicious destroyer to the sad, fat, unfunny, comic beating his head against the wall is the paradigm of all tragic boxing careers. As such it remains firmly within its tradition, despite all the aesthetic risks taken. For the feminist critic Pam Cook: "*Raging Bull*, like its predecessors in the boxing genre, presents the powerful male body as an object of desire and identification, but moving towards the loss of male power. This loss activates the desire to call it up once more."[27] So *Raging Bull* becomes a film of nostalgia for the pre-impotent lethal fist-fighter version of masculinity.

It is clear that most boxing movies attempt to sublimate their erotic content to wider narrative ambitions. However, in doing so, these films foreground such ambivalent and contradictory images that it is precisely the erotic power of the male body that consistently emerges and is reinforced. For the viewer these tensions often lead us to experience the spirit if not the exact terms of Jake La Motta's confusion in *Raging Bull* when he looks at his 'pretty' opponent Janiro before their fight and says: "I don't know whether to fight him or fuck him."

1 Joyce Carol Oates, *On Boxing*, (London, Pan Books, 1988), p.30.
2 Quoted in Norman Mailer, *The Fight*, (London, Penguin, 1991), p.129.
3 Oates, op. cit., p.8.
4 Steve Neal, 'Masculinity as Spectacle', *The Sexual Subject: A Screen Reader in Sexuality*, (London, Routledge, 1992), p.281.
5 Mailer, op. cit., p.60.
6 Oates, op. cit., p.30.
7 Michael T. Isenberg, *John L. Sullivan and His Times*, (London, Robson, 1988), p.48.
8 Derek Birley, *Sport and the Making of Britain*, (Manchester University Press, 1993), p.286.
9 Richard Ellman, *Oscar Wilde*, (London, Penguin, 1988), p.142.
10 Quoted in Isenberg, *op. cit.*, p.105.
11 William Hazlitt, 'The Fight', from *William Hazlitt Selected Writings*, (London, Penguin, 1982), p.91.
12 George Plimpton, *Shadow Box*, (reprint New York, Lyons and Burford, 1993), pp.55-56.
13 Edith Sitwell, *English Eccentrics*, (reprint London, Penguin, 1976), p.115.
14 Leslie A. Marchand, *Byron, a Portrait*, (reprint London, Pimlico, 19??) pp. 89-90.
15 Plimpton, op. cit., p.53.
16 Dan Streible, 'A History of the Boxing Film' *1894-1915*, from *Film History*, Volume 3, pp.235-257.
17 Editorial, *New York Tribune*, 22 March1897, quoted in Streible, *History of the Boxing Film*, p.235.
18 J.P. Telotte, *Voices in the Dark: the Narrative Patterns of Film Noir*, (University of Illinois Press, 1989), p.4.
19 Deborah Thomas, 'How Hollywood Deals with the Deviant Male', *The Movie Book of Film Noir*, (London, Studio Vista, 1992), p.60.
20 *Scorsese on Scorsese*, (London, Faber, 1989), p.77.
21 Oates, op. cit., p.58.
22 Yvonne Tasker, *Spectacular Bodies: Gender, Genre and the Action Cinema*, (London, Routledge, 1993), p.78.
23 See Gerald Early, *The Culture of Bruising*, (New Jersey, The Ecco Press, 1994), p.90.
24 Quoted in Early, ibid., pp.97.
25 Lizzie Borden, 'Blood and Redemption', *Sight and Sound*, February 1995, vol. 5, issue 2, p.61.
26 Description quoted in Early op. cit., pp.95-96.
27 Pam Cook, 'Masculinity in Crisis: Tragedy and Identification in Raging Bull', *Screen* Oct/Nov 1982, p.45.

EXIT
EXIT
EXIT

Dawn Davies and Forrester Joseph at a female boxing/kick boxing night at York Hall, London. Photograph: Gillian Allard, 1994.

Bruising Peg to Boxerobics: Gendered Boxing – Images and Meanings

Jennifer Hargreaves

A Symbol of Masculinity

Proponents of boxing characterise it as 'the noble art of self-defence', 'the sweet science', a channel for courage, determination, and self-discipline – the sport which, above all others, combines fitness with skill, and strength with artistry. In the following quotation, poet and ex-professional fighter, Vernon Scannell, compares the role of a great artist with that of a boxer: "But what it [boxing] can do – and here it is like art – is give a man a chance to behave in a way that is beyond and above his normal capacity. The great artist may be, outside the confines of his art, cruel, weak, arrogant and foolish, but within them he can transcend his own condition and become noble, passionate and truthful beyond the range of ordinary men. Something similar happens to the great fighter, too. He may be stupid, vain, ignorant and brutish – though he is not, in fact, these things nearly as often as popular belief imagines – but in the exercise of his art he becomes the embodiment of transcendental courage, strength and chivalry. I have seen it happen and I have experienced the Aristotelean catharsis as powerfully in the boxing stadium as in the theatre."[1]

In contrast, opponents of boxing claim it to be a brutalising experience which is blatantly savage and destructive, resulting in acute and chronic injuries, mostly to the eyes and brain, and sometimes causing massive haemorrhaging and even death.[2] The following excerpt from Irvin S. Cobb's graphic account in the *New York Times* of 3 July 1921, of the World Heavyweight Championship fight between Jack Dempsey and Georges Carpentier, describes the sort of incident used to support the anti-boxing lobby: "I see the Frenchman staggering, slipping, sliding forward to his fate. His face is toward me and I am aware at once his face has no vestige of conscious intent. Then the image of him is blotted out by the intervening bulk of the winner. Dempsey's right arm swings upward with the flailing emphasis of an oak cudgel and the muffled fist at the end of it lands again on its favourite target – the Frenchman's jaw. The thud of its landing can be heard above the hysterical shrieking of the host. The Frenchman seems to shrink in for a good six inches. It is as though that crushing impact had telescoped him. He folds up into a pitiable meagre compass and goes down heavily and again lies on the floor, upon his right side, his face half covered

BE
BOXING

Previous page: Lorraine Farley vs. Cheryl Robinson, British Bantamweight Title contest, York Hall, Bethnall Green, 19 February 1994.
Photograph: Brian E Rybolt. Copyright: Brian E Rybolt.

Barbara Buttrick, Cottingham, Yorkshire, England, World Fly and Bantamweight Boxing Champion 1950-1960.
Courtesy: Jennifer Hargreaves.

by his arms as though even in the stupor following that deadly collision between his face and Dempsey's fist, he would protect his vulnerable parts. From where I sit writing this, I can see one of his eyes and his mouth. The eye is blinking weakly, the mouth is gaping, and the lips work as though he chewed a most bitter mouthful. His legs kick out like the legs of a cramped swimmer. Once he lifts himself half-way to his haunches. But the effort is his last. He has flattened down again and still the referee has only progressed in his fateful sum of addition as far as 'six'."

In both these accounts, however, one can recognise a conventional sporting ideology – that boxing is an essentially masculine activity, associated with the male physique and psychology, and with no organic connection with femaleness. Blood, bruises, cuts and concussion, which accompany boxing's intrinsic aggression, violence and danger, are popularly considered to be legitimate and even 'natural' for men,[3] but absolutely at odds with the essence of femininity. Boxing, as Wacquant argues,[4] is deeply engendered, embodying and exemplifying, "a definite form of masculinity: plebeian, heterosexual and heroic".

In lower working-class communities, and particularly in America in immigrant and African American families, fighting prowess provokes powerful images of machismo and virility. Dominance in combat is at the same time feared and admired. In boxing subcultures maiming or even killing an opponent is rationalised, and contempt for punishment and pain is a sign of being a 'real' man and a good boxer. Because the boxer's body is both weapon and target, it is constantly under surveillance and highly disciplined in order to become strong and tuned for the fight. If Foucault's analysis is applied to the male boxer,[5] his is a subjected body, heavily invested with power and, furthermore, in a manner which produces a distinctly gendered form of embodiment.[6] The investment of power in the male boxer's body can also be understood as a form of cultural capital, or, more specifically, as Pierre Bourdieu conceptualises, a symbol of physical capital highly valued for males in working-class communities.[7]

It seems surprising, therefore, that in recent years there has been an increase in the numbers of Western women who box, and, in particular, of those with middle-class and highly educated backgrounds. One such boxer is Dierdre Gogarty, a contender for a world title. She comes from a middle-class Irish family – her father is a mouth surgeon, her mother is a dentist, she has a sister who is a doctor and a brother who directs an orchestra. Rene Denfeld, author of *The New Victorians*, is another aspiring world champion. There are accountants, attorneys, nurses and doctors, teachers and business women, all of whom box competitively and choose to ignore the dangers. Their attraction to the sport has nothing to do with money, and their participation is stamping a new character on a sport which has the essence of maleness and, more specifically, of working-class masculinity. Not surprisingly, women's boxing in the 1990s is characterised as a radical activity which blurs traditional male and female images, identities and class alliances.

Fighting Women

Few people are aware that women's boxing – or more correctly, prizefighting – can be traced back to the eighteenth and nineteenth centuries. The early bare-knuckle contests were crude and bloody – fights to the finish in a harsh world in which the bodies of working women were imbued with strength and aggression, similar to the physical capital of working men. In London from the 1720s onwards, bouts were staged between women from labouring trades in search of money and status. Some of them became well-known and their feats are recorded – for example, we read about The Famous Boxing Woman of Billingsgate, The Fighting Ass-Driver from Stoke Newington, A Female Boxing Blacksmith, The Vendor of Sprats, The Market Woman, The City Championess, The Hiberian Heroine and Bruising Peg.[8] The contests were vicious free-for-alls, either topless or in tight-fitting jackets, short petticoats and Holland drawers. They involved punching, feet- and knee-kicking to all parts of the body, mauling, scratching and throwing, and usually resulted in serious injuries. Large crowds and large bets were commonplace, and lucrative purses were often donated by members of the nobility.[9] A bout between two women in 1794, was described as follows: "Great intensity between them was maintained for about two hours, whereupon the elder fell into great difficulty through the closure of her left eye from the extent of swelling above and below it which rendered her blind through having the sight of the other considerably obscured by a flux of blood which had then continued greatly for over forty minutes […] not more than a place even as large as a penny-piece remained upon their bodies which was free of the most evident signs of the harshness of the struggle. Their bosoms were much enlarged but yet they each continued to rain blows upon this most feeling of tissue without regard to the pitiful cries issuing forth at each success which was evidently to the delight of the spectators since many a shout was raised causing each female to mightily increase her effort."[10]

A century later, women's prizefighting was continuing on both sides of the Atlantic. Because there were relatively few women competitors, exhibition matches were often against men and sometimes women were the victors. More usually, women were seriously injured and on occasions were killed. On-the-spot stitching of large cuts was sometimes carried out so that a bout could continue, and women fought on with broken noses and jaws, smashed teeth and swollen eyes.[11] The betting economy and the lure of a fat purse, meant that women's fights continued to be staged as brutal spectacles. Although from the 1880s regulations were applied to the sport and in some contests punching or boxing with the hands only was allowed, 'savate' fights (strikes with the feet as well as the hands) continued to be popular and sometimes girls as young as twelve-years-old headed the bill. Here is an extract from an article about the history of women's boxing in the *Police Gazette* (1924). It describes a fight between a woman of 25 and a girl of seventeen: "One snapshot showed the woman shooting a kick at the girl's head; the girl was warding it off with her left arm and sending in her right fist to the woman's stomach. This fight ended in a victory for the woman. Another such fight was won by Mlle. Fari, who, soon after an hour of bloody and bruising battle, broke the other girls' jaw by a savage kick […] About 1902 Mlle. Augagnier beat Miss Pinkney of England in a savage fight. It was boxing and savate against straight boxing. Pinkney was better with her fists and looked like a winner after about one and a half hours of bloody fighting, but Mlle. A. cleverly managed to kick Pinkney in the face. This blow made a terrible scar and stunned the English girl, then the French girl shot a smashing kick to Pinkney's stomach and knocked her out. The French girl was carried by her admirers in triumph from the ring."

By this time, the status of local champion had been replaced by national and even international titles. In 1884, Nellie Stewart of Norfolk, Virginia, claimed to have

Kenwood UK Ltd. print advertisement, originally run with the caption: “Don’t give up the day job, Cathy. Cathy Clark, administrator, Communications division, Kenwood UK. Works in Watford. Puts her feet up in the evenings. Kenwood, it’s the people who make it.” Courtesy: James Abelson, London. Ad. Agency: Buckfield Lord & Co.

won the first 'Female Championship of the World'.[12] The following year the title was claimed by Miss Ann Lewis of Cleveland, Ohio, following an advertisement in the *Police Gazette* (1924), challenging any woman in the world to fight her for $1,000. The first properly advertised Championship probably took place two years later in 1886. Neither of the contestants had ever been beaten in a fight, and together they had accumulated 76 knock-outs. On this occasion, Hattie Leslie was battered around the ring, knocked down for a count of eight, had her nose broken and one eye practically closed, but then, miraculously, turned things around and became the first officially recorded 'Female World Champion'.

Feminine Capital

The development of women's boxing was quite separate from that of other women's sports. From the turn of the century through to the 1960s, it was associated with showbiz and spectacle, with the 'low-life' worlds of travelling booths, brothels, carnivals, circuses, fairs, night-clubs, saloons and theatres. It could be ugly and brutish, invoking images of bruised and battered female bodies, untamed and unprotected. At the same time, in another sphere, middle-class women were struggling to get into the 'respectable' world of organised sports, but found themselves seriously constrained by dominant medical ideologies about the innate physical limitations of females and their unsuitability to take part in vigorous exercise.[13] Whereas the development of mainstream sports for women was based upon notions of sexual difference, and male and female bodies in most sports are signifiers of those differences, the basic symbolism of women's boxing seemed to contradict this trend. In its most pure form, it was a celebration of female muscularity, physical strength and aggression. Power was literally inscribed in the boxers' bodies – in their actual working muscles – an expression of physical capital usually ascribed to men. But however serious the women were about their sport, because of its low-class, disreputable image, it remained 'underground', or at best marginalised. Working women who used their bodies freely and powerfully were characterised as uncivilised and vampish, in distinct contrast to the listless, weak and sexually repressed image of the well-bred, middle-class Victorian lady. For that reason women's boxing always attracted male voyeurs – not only working men, but also local dignitaries and businessmen. Its explicit sexualisation through bare breasts and the ripping of clothes, the scope for male fantasies, and potential as a surrogate for male brutality against the 'weaker' sex, increased the entertainment value of women's boxing into the twentieth century.

Opposition and Advances

During the 1930s there seemed to be a surge in the popularity of women's boxing in different countries around the world: reports of bouts came from Western Europe, North America, South America, the Antipodes and the Indian sub-continent, and even during World War II there were public matches and competitions, including those between women from the armed forces. But, in common with other female sports that experienced a growth during the inter-war years, such as football and water-polo, after World War II women's boxing faced harsh and widespread opposition.[14] It was argued that hard hitting could harm the ovaries, womb or breasts and thus affect women's abilities to bear and suckle children. In fact, the female reproductive organs are firmly positioned and thoroughly protected inside the body cavity and are probably less susceptible to injury than those of men. And, of course, women, like men, can wear protective apparatus to protect vulnerable parts.[15] The ethics of arguments to ban boxing are as appropriate to men as they are to women, but the differential treatment of the sexes in boxing provides an example of the way in which biological arguments have been applied systematically to women's bodies in order to control cultural practices. The repression of women's bodies in boxing symbolised powerfully the repression of women in society. In contrast, the possession by men of physical capital in boxing was transformed and exploited as cultural capital. (Ironically, part of this process was the exploitation of male boxers themselves.)

In spite of opposition, the 1940s, 1950s and 1960s produced a number of female boxers – in North America, England, France, Germany (and in Australia until 1948 when it was made illegal). One of the most famous of all time was Barbara Buttrick, 'a little toughie' originally from Yorkshire, England, who was the undefeated Women's World Fly and Bantamweight Boxing Champion from 1950-1960.[16] Battlin' Barbara Buttrick, as she became known, learned her trade in the fairground boxing booths of England and France where, it was claimed: "She not only pulverised every woman she met, but swapped punches with over 1,000 men in exhibition bouts."[17] Barbara Buttrick has been eulogised in boxing circles for her understanding of the very essence of the noble art. She was not an uncontrolled slugger, or a vamp, but, in Vernon Scannell's terms, a civilised and disciplined 'artist of the physical'. Admired for her "speed, finesse and knowledge of boxing" and the way she moved "with the rhythm of a ballet dancer",[18] she became known as the Female Jimmy Wilde.[19] In 1960, Barbara Buttrick became the first woman boxer to be elected to the International Boxing and Wrestling Hall of Fame and in 1995 she became the first President of the newly founded Women's International Boxing Federation (WIBF).

Barbara Buttrick and other female boxers were unlicensed fighters, and boxing was only recognised as a professional sport for women in a few US states as recently as the 1970s. In 1974 in America, there was a publicity drive for women's boxing which coincided with International Women's Year and the strengthening of radical feminism. Although the Men's International Boxing Association has recognised the amateur female sport, and the WIBF was inaugurated in order to promote and co-ordinate women's boxing on an international scale, it remains commonplace for women to struggle for recognition and resources at both amateur and professional levels, and to compete for unofficial titles amid hostile controversy. In some countries female boxing at all levels is outlawed. In spite of the obstacles, 1994 marked a watershed when the powerful promoter, Don King, signed up his first female boxer, Christie Martin, and promoted a Women's Championship event. Then, in 1995, the first ever fully sanctioned Women's World Championships in professional boxing history took place. Women's boxing is developing at a remarkable rate.

Non-Combat Boxing

Since the late 1980s there has been a huge escalation of interest in, and demand for, female boxing and associated activities, such as 'boxerobics' ('boxercise' and 'boxtraining'). At one level this can be understood as an aspect of the commercialisation of exercise, feeding off the modern obsession with body maintenance and its surface representation or the 'look' of the body.[20] Part of

Bodo Goeke, *Next one Please*, 1978. Westfällische Rundschau, published in 1987 under the auspices of the World Press Photo Holland Foundation.
Courtesy: Bodo Goeke.

the power of consumer culture derives from its ability to harness for profit people's desires about their bodies – a form of "control through stimulation" as Featherstone has written.

An advertisement for 'Pony's Exerbox' range of sportswear recommends boxerobics by claiming it "really sorts out the women from the girls". The advert promises that: "After the first few rounds of training you'll start to lose weight and gain strength. You'll develop long, lean muscles, not bulk. Your body will feel firm and look hard." We see an image of a strong, muscular young woman, sitting in a changing room in a manly pose with her legs apart. She is wearing Exerbox gear – boxer shorts, vest and trainers. Her hands are strapped, her boxing gloves beside her on the bench. As the advert points out, she looks more like Mike Tyson than a Cindy doll. Certainly, this representation supports Susan Bordo's contention that in recent years the athletic and muscular image of femininity, although quite solid and bulky-looking, has become highly desirable. This, she argues, is because tautness and containment have become more valued than thinness, and that any form of excess sagginess or wrinkling – even on the skinny body – is considered to spoil its line and firm appearance.[21] Whereas in the past muscularity has been associated with masculinity, the new androgynous look acquired through work-outs has become a symbol of both control and desirability. In the same way that muscularity has always symbolised the empowerment of men, representations of the athletic female body can also be understood as symbols of empowerment and reconstructions of traditional images of femininity. By appropriating male symbols of physical capital, women are shifting gender relations of power and empowering themselves.

The burgeoning popularity of boxerobics has made it something akin to a cult activity. It attracts women who explicitly reject the 'ultra-feminine' image of aerobics and who want more exciting and demanding forms of exercise. Evolving from 'Executive boxing', originally devised by actor Mickey Rourke (once an amateur boxer) to relieve stress, and coinciding with the new female muscular and aggressive image popularised through Linda Hamilton's performance in *Terminator II*, it spread to gyms in Hollywood and New York, before becoming an international phenomenon. Screen actresses like Jodie Foster, Michelle Pfeiffer, Cindy Crawford and Claudia Schiffer have become devotees, and after it was introduced into England, the former Page 3 Girl, Samantha Fox, made a boxercise video. Modelled on a boxer's work-out, exhausting routines of skipping, shadow boxing and pummelling punch-bags are performed to funky tunes. Unlike 'real' boxing, this mode of exercise severs the female agent from the worrying relationships between combat, aggression, pain and injury. It is boxing without an opponent – a non-contact form of exercise during which, the Exerbox advert *reassuringly* tells us: "The only pain you inflict is on yourself." The new feminine body is represented as an ascetic and disciplined one that subjects itself to a self-imposed physical regimen. This introspective approach reflects widespread insecurities about the body and self, but also reveals how anxieties are mediated and perpetuated through dominant modes of consumption such as advertising. The discourse surrounding female boxing training nevertheless remains contradictory. Cole and Hribar discuss the ways in which power and lifestyle intersect, arguing that images of the "new [more athletic] woman" are suggestive of independence and of a body produced "for oneself", rather than as "the object of male desire."[22] In the open embrace of rigorous physicality, muscularity and firmness, they see a broadening of femininity and a radicalising of the link between the public female body and hegemonic heterosexuality.

Dismissing Danger

Competitive boxing has a dimension which separates it from other forms of exercise which are non-aggressive and non-combative. It is an intrinsically vicious and potentially lethal sport and to disregard this in analyses is implicitly to support or idealise it. The main purpose of boxing is to disable or render an opponent unconscious as a result of injury to the brain caused by a punch to the head. One consequence is death, and it has been known for many years that the 'punch drunk syndrome', which is a debilitating neurological disease (and has features in common with Alzheimer's dementia and Parkinson's disease), is an occupational hazard in the men's professional game.[23] Serious eye injuries and arthritis are the other most common injuries sustained by fighters. Recent research on amateur boxers has more worrying implications for practitioners of the sport.[24] It shows that there is an accumulative build up of brain damage over time which goes undetected if untested. Further research has been carried out at the Royal London Hospital following the death in the ring of a 23-year-old man who had been boxing since the age of eleven, but had previously shown no signs of brain dysfunction. He suffered a massive brain haemorrhage and was found to have "long-standing brain damage, and some of the structural abnormalities common in the brains of elderly Alzheimer's patients".[25] This report confirms that: "Young boxers can develop permanent brain damage early in their careers without any signs or symptoms of injury," and at a time in their lives when the power of their punches is less than that of adult female boxers. Although no research has been carried out on female boxers, there is no reason to suppose that their brains are less prone to injury than those of men. Ann Parisio, director of *Raging Belles*, puts it bluntly: "Boxing is much more brutal than wrestling. They are pumping the grey matter into jelly, but a lot of people make a lot of money out of it; that's why it's respectable."[26] The recent promotion of women's boxing is, without doubt, due to its profit-making potential, yet this neither explains the growing penchant for participation, nor the apparent lack of concern among female boxers about the likelihood of injury.

Supporters of boxing for women are quick to point out that it is only thirtieth on the list of dangerous sports, and that because women's upper bodies are less strong than men's, and there are regulations about wearing protective apparatus, the risk of serious injury is minimal. The death of Bradley Stone in 1994 reopened the debate about the safety of boxing, but, ironically, coincided with an accelerating interest in the sport from women and an increasingly vehement and irrationally defensive stance by female boxers.

In Love with the Sport

All female boxers are required to sign the following declaration: "I understand and appreciate that participation in sport carries a risk to me of serious injury including permanent paralysis or death. I voluntarily and knowingly accept and assume this risk." Justifications nevertheless remain varied, and resistance to a serious appraisal of the problem is commonplace. One boxer claimed that the risk of being hurt is minimal, and explained that being the centre of attention in the ring is hugely appealing. Young boxers simply disregard the chronic (long-term) effects of boxing and argue that if they are well trained, they can avoid being hit. The deep feelings of pleasure and empowerment experienced by them is linked to their denial of danger. It is in particular because "women are taught *not* to be physical," another female boxer explained: "It feels good to be in a context where it is *acceptable* to be physical and to discover a side of ourselves we never knew we had. Getting rid of aggression in a *physical* way is really liberating and attractive." Women fighters are excited, as well, about overcoming personal fear; fear of being hit, and fear of hitting someone else. Perversely, they actually enjoy the sense of vulnerability, it: "sends up the adrenaline and releases power". Few of the fighters find problems with their own sense of femaleness, they just want to push their own limits, and in contradiction to popular conceptions of femininity, they claim that they possess an 'innate fighting talent'.

Part of the love of boxing is precisely because it is seen to have a 'feminine side', to be like ballet, requiring skill, speed, lightness, grace and co-ordination. This is reflected in the following description of a successful competition fighter: "People just naturally expect an Amazon when they find out Angel Rodriguez is a boxer. Massive muscles. A few broken teeth. A bashed nose. Maybe a cauliflower ear or so [...] That's why the petite, slender body and unlined face are such a surprise. At five feet four and 107 pounds, it is the body of a ballet dancer, not the top flyweight boxer that Angel Rodriguez actually is [...] With her quiet self-assurance, fine-tuned body and angelic features, she's most certainly the best advertisement there could be for the sport."[27]

In general, promoters and boxers alike want to present an essentially feminine, clean, tidy sporting image. They oppose those women who take a radical feminist position, who argue that boxing makes them more sensuous, and who wear khaki shorts and shirts and 'look like blokes'. Dierdre Gogarty expresses the fear that most boxers have. "I'm always afraid people think I'm butch," she says, "that's my main fear. I used to hang a punch bag in the cupboard and bang away at it when no-one was around, so nobody would know I was doing it. I was afraid people would think me weird and unfeminine."[28] The potential radicalisation of the female body in sport is contradicted by the ever present expression of compulsory heterosexuality and the attempt to justify female boxing on the grounds that it has an authentic feminine element.

Ian Wooldridge rejects the idea that boxing can be feminised: "Boxing is about vehement aggression as much as ring craft and self-defence [...] Do not for a moment fall for the delusion that if two women were released into the same ring with a gold medal at stake we would witness some choreographed balletic performance with mild sporting undertones. It would be bloody. As bloody awful, in fact, as those few disgraceful occasions when women have been lawfully sanctioned to fight one another on a professional bill."[29] Certainly, at the end of an international contest between Dierdre Gogarty of Ireland and Stacey Prestige of America in 1994, although the American was the victor on points, she fought the last rounds with a bruised and battered face, and a bleeding, broken nose. Although there is no justification for moral arguments against boxing to be gendered, the deep desire that some women have to enter a sport which highlights aggression and abuse can be viewed as a worryingly reactionary trend rather than a radical reconstruction of the feminine.

Research carried out at the University of Michigan and at the US Centre for Media and Public Affairs suggests that there have been an increasing number of aggressive female role models in film and on television – *The Avengers, Thelma and Louise, Charlie's Angels* and *Wonderwoman* for instance.[30] It is argued that women seem to be more aggressive than they used to be and that when aggressive acts carried out by media heroines are portrayed positively, girls view this type of behaviour as acceptable. Boxing could be seen as one element of this trend. A characteristic of the blurring of gender divisions in sport is that girls and women move in the direction of boys and men to a far greater extent than occurs in the opposite direction. Coinciding with the rising numbers of women in boxing are rising numbers of women taking part in other traditional male contact and combat sports. There is no similar movement of men into 'feminine appropriate' sports.

The Seedy Side

As predominantly middle-class women move into boxerobics, boxing training and competitive fighting, it is mostly working-class women who continue to play the more traditional boxing roles, with organic links to Bruising Peg and her associates. Although serious boxing is gradually replacing explicitly sexualised women's events, it is probably still true that many aspiring women fighters wind up on the seedy tough girls' circuit (popularised in the American South and Midwest) to provide sadistic spectacles for crowds of jeering men and women. They are peepshow fighters, kick-boxers and wrestlers, often topless, shrieking, kicking, biting, and yanking each other round the ring by the hair while splattering themselves with hidden blood capsules that burst on impact.[31] Pseudo-serious topless boxing and foxy boxing (which originated in singles bars in California and involves bikini-clad women wearing huge foam gloves and prancing about for male voyeurs) are regular events associated with working-class venues, pubs, bars, nightclubs and boxing gyms. Descriptions of topless contests, accompanied by photographs, are found in boxing-style magazines. They are a titillating mixture of the languages of boxing and sexuality: "Round One. The girls were unaware of each other's skills, so they feinted around for the first few seconds. Then Zanabe landed a nice punch to Geraldine's breasts and that got Geraldine going. She concentrated on her younger black opponent's beautifully developed tits, hitting them again and again."[32]

Topless boxing is one tiny element of a huge structure of gender relations of power. Sexualised images of female boxers are part of the general bombardment of sexual imagery relating to the female body, and in this context the message that female sexuality is more important than boxing ability is clear. This is further consolidated by other female roles in the broader boxing context. For example, traditionally, women have been accoutrements to, or have provided side-shows for men – as spectators, hostesses, show openers, or by holding up counter-boards between rounds. These women are displayed as stereotyped, heterosexual commodities in swimsuits, high-heeled shoes, Lycra tights and black silk stockings. The severing of women from the 'real' sport also happens in advertising and in sports photography. Women wearing boxing gloves have become a popular sporting image in advertisements that use sexual imagery to promote the sale of products – whether or not they have anything to do with sport. Through the convention of sexualisation, women's real involvement in sport is again trivialised. Boxing is used simply as a channel for the commodification of the female body in order to encourage clients to spend money – on hair products, deodorants, sports shoes or vitamins. In a recent advertisement for 'Haliborange' vitamin tablets, a young woman's head is just visible above a huge boxing glove which dominates the picture. The eyes bore purposefully into the viewer, signifying that Haliborange, in common with female boxing, is a form of self-defence. Here we have a strong woman taking up a male sport, connoting the power and 'extra PUNCH' of Haliborange. But an alternative reading of the advertisement is also possible. The eyes of the woman, highlighted because they are the only visible part of the face, and because they 'speak' to the reader with intensity, could be saying, 'I am sexy. Come and get me'. In this case, the message is that behind the boxer is the 'real' woman. Rather than a subject of pleasure, the body here is an object of desire. In sport, as in advertisements, the body is fundamentally semiotic, a place where meaning is both created and enacted, a place for the inscription of multiple signs.[33]

Boxing photography has also become part of the mass market in pornography. Because boxing gloves are potent symbols of masculinity, for topless, Page 3 girls, to be wearing them, "suggests a provocative sexual message, that 'real' sports are for men and women are there to provide excitement and arousal. It is as if women's bodies are part of the equipment – apparatuses for male 'sporting' pleasure – 'playthings' for men."[34] Because boxing is commonly believed to be a distinctly masculine sport, to mix it with images which exaggerate the insignia of female sexuality produces a provocative illusion.[35]

Contradictions

Images and meanings surrounding women and boxing are complex and contradictory. Novelist Joyce Carol Oates in her book, *On Boxing*, explicitly rejects the idea that women's boxing could be a subversive activity when she declares that: "The female boxer [...] cannot be taken seriously. She is parody, she is cartoon, she is monstrous."[36] But the increase in the numbers of female boxers from different social backgrounds is a lived example of the way in which women construct a sense of self in relation to their personal bodies, and they, in turn, reject Oates' polemic. The body is the most important signifier of meanings and, in the case of women and boxing and associated activities, these are constantly contested and are changing according to the broader contexts of boxing discourse and gender relations of power. Although strength and muscularity in boxing have symbolically been a source of physical capital for men, the diversity and complexity found in representations of the female body in boxing make it difficult to assess the extent to which the sport is a subversive activity for women or an essentially assimilative process with a radical facade. For now, female boxing remains riddled with contradictory cultural values.

This paper is based in large part on information gathered from various people who sent or loaned me material – for example, articles from old magazines, letters, newspaper cuttings and videos. Some of the material was undated and the sources were not identified, and for that reason, this paper is not comprehensively referenced. It also contains information and ideas obtained from interviews with women boxers and others involved as coaches or promoters of women's boxing. I am most grateful to everyone who so generously contributed time, money and ideas. JH

1 V. Scannell, *The Tiger and the Rose*, (London, Hamish Hamilton, 1971), pp.48-9.
2 British Medical Association, *The Boxing Debate*, (London, Chameleon Press, 1993).
3 M. Messner, *Power at Play: Sports and the Problem of Masculinity*, (Boston, Mass., Beacon Press, 1992), pp.67.
4 L. Wacquant, 'Pugs at Work: Bodily Capital and Bodily Labour Among Professional Boxers', *Body and Society*, Vol. 1, No. 1, March 1995, pp.65-94.
5 M. Foucault, *Discipline and Punishment,* (New York, Vintage, 1979), pp.26.
6 J. Sawicki, *Disciplining Foucault: Feminism, Power and the Body*, (New York, Routledge, 1991).
7 P. Bourdieu, *Distinction: A Social Critique of the Judgement of Taste,* (London, Routledge, 1984); P. Bourdieu, 'The Forms of Capital', 1986, reprinted in J. Richardson (ed.), *Handbook of Theory and Research for the Sociology of Education,* (New York, Greenwood Press).
8 R. Park, 'from "Genteel Diversions" to "Bruising Peg": Active Pastimes, Exercise, and Sports for Females in Late 17th and 18th Century Europe', 1994, reprinted in D. Costa and S. Guthrie (eds.), *Women and Sport: Interdisciplinary Perspectives*, Campaign, Il: Human Kinetics, pp.27-43. See also A. Guttmann, *Women's Sports,* (New York, Columbia University Press, 1991) pp.74-77.
9 Ibid.
10 Ibid.
11 *Sunday Dispatch,* 15 December 1946.
12 L. Eskin, 'Complete History of Women's Boxing', *Boxing Illustrated,* August/September 1974, pp.25-32.
13 J. A. Hargreaves, *Sporting Females: Critical Issues in the History and Sociology of Women's Sports*, (London, Routledge, 1994).
14 Ibid.
15 K. Dyer, *Catching Up the Men: Women in Sport*, (London, Junction Books, 1982).
16 L. Eskin, op. cit., p.30.
17 R. Philip, 'Memoirs of a Happy Left Hooker', *Sport 7*, 28 April 1993, p.39.
18 The Dallas Morning News, 1955.
19 R. Philip, op. cit., p.39.
20 M. Featherstone, 'The Body in Consumer Culture', 1982, reprinted in M. Featherstone, M. Hepworth and B. Turner (eds.), *The Body: Social Process and Cultural Theory*, (London, Sage Publications, 1991).
21 S. Bordo, 'Reading the Slender Body', M. Jacobus, E. Fox Keller, and S. Shuttleworth (eds.), *Body/Politics: Women and the Discourse of Science*, (London, Routledge, 1990).
22 C. Cole and A. Hribar, 'Celebrity Feminism: Nike Style, Post-Fordism, Transcendence, and Consumer Power', *Sociology of Sport Journal*, Vol.12, No.4, 1995, p.361.
23 P. Kemp, A. Houston, M. Macleod and R. Pethybridge, 'Cerebral perfusion and psychometric testing in military amateur boxers and controls', *Journal of Neurology, Neurosurgery and Psychiatry*, No. 59, 1995, p.368-174.
24 Ibid.
25 L. Hunt, 'Boxing damages young brains', *Independent*, 18 January 1996, p.2.
26 M. Downes, 'Raging Belles', *City Limits*, 9-16 March 1989, pp.14-16.
27 J. Krieg, 'The Angel of the Ring' .
28 Channel 4 television documentary, *Champions: Hard Hitting Women.* Transmitted on 9 May 1994.
29 I. Wooldridge, 'Keep boxing clear of the gender trap', *Daily Mail,* 26 October 1994, p.61.
30 K. Whitehorn, 'What little girls are really made of', *Observer*, 2 February 1996, p.6.
31 V. Hennessy, 'Punching Judy Show', *You Magazine, The Mail on Sunday,* 1990, p.16-20.
32 J. Laird, 'Wrestling and Boxing', *Amazons in Action,* No. 62. May 1993. p.4-15.
33 P. Brooks, *Body Work: Objects of Desire in Modern Narrative*, (London, Harvard University Press, 1993), pp.38.
34 J.A. Hargreaves, op. cit., pp.167.
35 J.A. Hargreaves, op. cit., pp.167.
36 Joyce Carol Oates, *On Boxing* (The Echo Press, New Jersey, 1994) pp.73.

Notes on Contributors

David Chandler is Projects Manager at the Institute of International Visual Arts. Formerly Head of Exhibitions at The Photographers' Gallery, London, he is a writer, editor and curator. He has published widely on photography and twentieth-century visual culture contributing to a variety of magazines including *Creative Camera* and *Portfolio*.

Roger Lloyd Conover has been responsible for the avant-garde art, architecture and theory books published by MIT Press (Cambridge, Massachusetts) for the past 20 years . His published works include: *The Lost Lunar Baedsker: Poems of Mina Loy* (1996); 'Introducing Mina Loy' in *Mina Loy: Woman and Poet* (1996); 'Wanted: Arthur Cravan, 1837 - ?' in *Four Dada Suicides* (1995); 'The Secret Names of Arthur Cravan' in *Arthur Cravan: Poète et Boxeur* (1992); introduction to *The Last Lunar Baedeker* (1985) and the introduction to *Insel*, a novel by Mina Loy (1991). He is currently writing a biography of Arthur Cravan.

Jean Fisher is an artist and writer on issues of contemporary art and the debates on multiculturalism. She teaches at the Jan van Eyck Akademie, Maastricht, and the Slade School of Fine Art, London. She is the co-editor of the international journal *Third Text*.

John Gill is a freelance curator currently developing the South East Exhibitions Project for South East Arts in England. Formerly Curator of Exhibitions at the Royal Festival Hall Galleries, London his recent curatorial projects have included *A Room Full of Hungry Looks* for the Stedlijk Museum, Amsterdam and *Offside! Contemporary Artists and Football* for Manchester City Art Galleries in collaboration with the Institute of International Visual Arts. He also curated the exhibition *Boxer* for Walsall Museum and Art Gallery which provided the impetus for this anthology.

Tania V. Guha is a London-based writer and editor. She was Assistant Editor of *Artscribe International*, the journal *Third Text* and deputy to the editor of *City Limits*. She is a regular contributor to *Time Out* and *The Face* and has written for *Vogue*, *The Independent*, *The Guardian*, *The Evening Standard* and *Portfolio*. Forthcoming publications include contributions in *Beyond Frontiers, South Asian Art and Culture* published by Serpent's Tale in July 1996 and a book for the Public Art Development Trust, co-authored with Jeremy Millar.

Jennifer Hargreaves is Professor of the Sociology of Sport and a Co-Director of the Centre for Sport Development Research, Roehampton Institute, London. Her books include: *Sporting Females: Critical Issues in the History and Sociology of Women's Sports* (1994) and *Sport, Culture and Ideology* (Editor). She is currently engaged in research on women's sport in South Africa.

Sarah Hyde is currently Curator in the Department of Prints and Drawings at the Courtauld Institute Galleries, University of London. She is a member of the editorial board of *Art History* and has co-edited a number of exhibition catalogues including: *1966 and all that: Design and the Consumer in Britain 1960-1969* (1996); *Walter Crane: Artist, Designer, Socialist* (1988) and *Prints (Re) Presenting Poussin* (1994). Her forthcoming book on gender and museum collections will be published by MUP in 1996.

Nick James is the Deputy Editor of the British Film Institute's *Sight and Sound* magazine and has previously acted as Film Editor for *City Limits* magazine. He has contributed to a variety of publications including *The London Review of Books*, *The Guardian*, *The Literary Review* and *The Modern Review*.

Ian Jeffrey is an art historian, writer and exhibition curator. Recent published works include the exhibition catalogues *Bill Brandt* (1994) for the Barbican Art Gallery, London and *German Photographs* (1995) for the Royal Festival Hall, London. He is a regular contributor to the *London Magazine*, and is currently a part-time tutor on the M.A. Photography course at Goldsmiths College, London.

Glenn Ligon is a New York-based artist who has shown in *Black Male: Representations of Masculinity in Contemporary Art* at the Whitney Museum of American Art, New York (1994), the Whitney Biennial (1993), *Mistaken Identities* at the University Art Museum in Santa Barbara, California (1992), *Double Take: Collective Memory and Current Art* (1992) at the Hayward Gallery in London and *Mirage: Enigmas of Race, Difference and Desire* at the ICA in London (1995). His recent solo shows include *Glenn Ligon: To Disembark* at the William College Museum of Art in Williamstown, Massachusetts (1995); *Glenn Ligon* at the Des Moines Art Center in Iowa (1995) and *Good Mirrors Art Not Cheap* at the Whitney Museum of American Art in New York (1992).

David Alan Mellor is a writer and curator and is currently Reader in History of Art at the University of Sussex. He has written extensively on photography and widely about twentieth-century visual culture. His published works include co-authoring with Phillipe Garner *Cecil Beaton* (1994) and *The Sixties Art Scene in London* (1993). He has also contributed to *Paris Post-War: Art and Existentialism* (1993), *Figurabile, Francis Bacon* (1993), and a variety of magazines including *Art and Design* and *Portfolio*.

Joyce Carol Oates is a celebrated author of fiction and literary criticism, her recent novels include *Blackwater* (1992) and *Foxfire* (1993). A National Book Award Winner for her novel *them*, she lives in Princeton, New Jersey, and since 1978 has been a member of the American Academy of Arts and Letters. *On Boxing* was first published by Dolphin/Doubleday in 1987.

Keith Piper is a London-based artist and writer who completed his MA in Environmental Media at the Royal College of Art, London in 1986. He has exhibited internationally including in the touring exhibition *Boxer* (1995/96); *The Masculine Masquerade* at the MIT List Visual Arts Centre in Cambridge, Massachusetts (1995); *Cocido Y Crudo* at the Museo Nacional Centro de Arte at the Reina Sofia (1995); *Interrogating Identity* at the Museum of Fine Arts in Boston (1991) and *The Other Story* at the Hayward Gallery, London (1989-1990). His solo shows include *A Ship Called Jesus* at the Ikon Gallery in Birmingham, Britain (1991) and *Exotic Signs* at the Gallery Theesalon in Arnheim, Holland (1993).

Marcia Pointon is Pilkington Professor of Art History at the University of Manchester. She has written extensively on British and French Art in the eighteenth and nineteenth centuries, on portraiture and on patronage and issues of gender in visual culture. Her recent published works include *Naked Authority; The Western Body in Western Painting 1830-1908* (1990); *The Body Imagined: The Human Form and Visual Culture since the Renaissance* (1993) and *Hanging the Head: Portraiture and Social Formation in Eighteenth Century England* (1993). Her forthcoming book, *Strategies for Showing: Women, Possession and Representation in English Visual Culture 1650-1800*, will be published by Oxford University Press in 1997.

Gilane Tawadros is Director of the Institute of International Visual Arts. She is an art historian and critic who has published widely on the contemporary visual arts. She is a member of the editorial boards of *Third Text* and *Art History* and is a Trustee of the Artangel Trust in London.

The Set-Up, 1949, 72m b/w, RKO. Dir. Robert Wise.
Courtesy: BFI Stills, Posters and Designs.

Ian Geraghty, *Bright Lights, Cameras, Bloody Action and Flashes of Brilliance*, 1996. Photograph 20 inches x 30 inches.
Courtesy: The Artist.

Rocky Marciano vs. Archie Moore, November 1955. Stanley Weston Collection.
Courtesy: The Ring Magazine.

Introduction: the Pictures of Boxing

David Chandler

If, as Joyce Carol Oates has so persuasively argued: "Each boxing match is a story," then it is also surely a picture.[1] The boxing match is neatly framed, squared-off by the ring; it is a set piece, a scene to be deciphered, a tableau alive with coded messages that tests our powers of interpretation. Like a pictorial narrative, boxing is composed from patterns of stylised movements, gestures and expressions that draw heavily on historical rules and precedents. In a sense boxing has evolved into a form of representation. It is a formalised rendition, a replaying of all the many fight forms past and present, one that has now come to offer a visual formula for every impulse to fight. Boxing is thus removed, conceptually and formally, from the mindless scrap in the street and yet preserves intact the unpredictable dynamic of angry conflict. The art of boxing, it seems, is based on how this tension is controlled and articulated by the boxers through a taut matrix of disciplined action, repetition and improvisation, on how they combine physical power and psychological manoeuvre.

The Marquis of Queensbury rules, first introduced in Britain in the 1860s, laid down a new representational framework for boxing. Ostensibly an attempt to civilise the sport, to remove it from its side-show, street brawling, low-life associations and so make it more appealing to the growing number of enthusiasts from the gentry and upper classes, the Queensbury rules not only gave boxing the basis for its current structure but perhaps more significantly transformed its visual imagery, its character as spectacle.

The Queensbury rules encouraged a more uniformly upright contest, disallowing all the holds and throws now associated with wrestling, it directed boxers to stand and fight only with their fists. The rules also specified that gloves, previously used only in sparring, should henceforth be worn for the fight itself. Most importantly the Queensbury rules brought boxing firmly under the authority of time. The imposition of three-minute rounds interspersed with one-minute rest periods (previously rounds often lasted only half as long), and the limit of ten seconds within which a knocked-down fighter was allowed to rise and continue (previously thirty seconds had been allowed), gave boxing a new tempo, a new rhythm and a new segmented *time-frame*. Yet it submitted boxers to a more

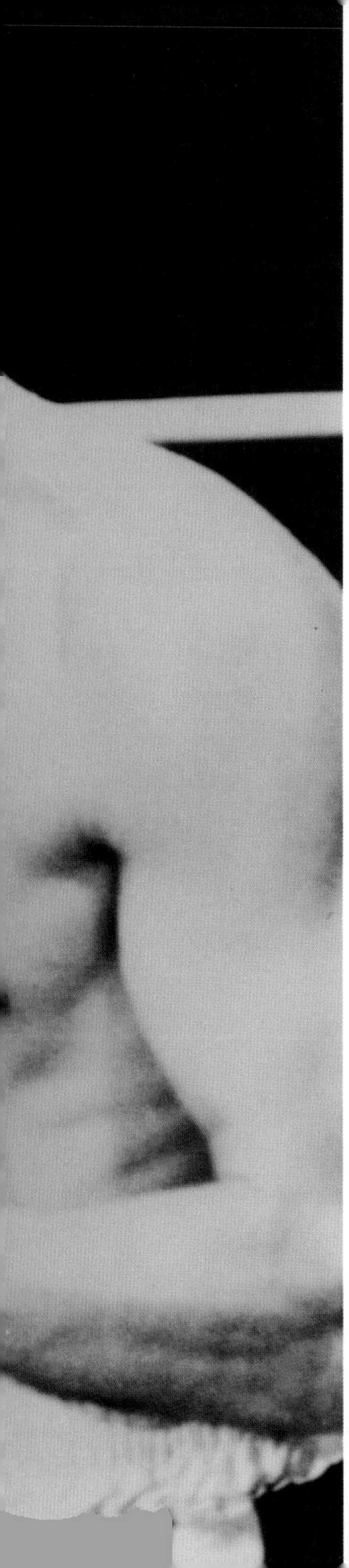

Raging Bull, 1980, 129m, c/bw, UA. Dir. Martin Scorsese. Robert De Niro (Jake LaMotta). Courtesy: BFI Stills, Posters and Designs.

relentless and ironically more dangerous contest (in the long term) over which they had much less control. "[...] the Queensbury rules took control over the pace of action away from the fighters. Like factory whistles, boxing's new rhythms mandated regular periods of work and rest. With a referee now inside the ring urging them to fight, boxers could no longer steal a few minutes to glare at each other, tacitly agreeing to slow down, return to their corners for a drink, and regain their strength."[2]

As the newly industrialised societies of the nineteenth century increasingly inflicted the rigours of controlled and standardised time on private and public experience (World Standard time was first introduced in 1884), removing culture from the cycles of nature to those determined by mechanisation and productivity, so boxing lost its grappling, pre-industrial form and its Arcadian associations as described so vividly by William Hazlitt in his famous essay *The Fight* of 1821: "The crowd was very great when we arrived on the spot; open carriages were coming up, with streamers flying and music playing, and the country people were pouring over hedge and ditch, in all directions, to see their hero beat or be beaten."[3] During the nineteenth century as time became, in EP Thompson's words: "A currency: not past but spent" so boxing promoters and controllers, too, placed more value on time. Time became, as Joyce Carol Oates has said, the boxer's 'invisible adversary' from which he could be 'knocked-out': "While the standing boxer is *in time* the fallen boxer is *out of time*."[4] In this way, as boxing became tuned to the pulse of modernity, to the palpable fact of time passing, and as it compelled its competitors to remain more *in time*, its challenges kept pace with modern demands and aspirations and its image beckoned a new emerging audience. "Above all, the Queensbury rules emphasised quick, dramatic blows. In important respects, boxing became simpler and faster-paced, essential qualities if it was to appeal to a wide if not particularly knowledgeable audience [...] the most important result of the Queensbury rules was not to make the ring less violent but to make it more assimilable to the entertainment industry and to mass commercial spectacles."[5]

The specific character of the new boxing spectacle was also crucially shaped by another facet of the Queensbury rules. The new regulations allowed the boxing ring to be elevated on an indoor stage rather than pitched outside on turf as had been the tradition. This immediately introduced a new commercialism to the sport by allowing promoters to charge admission, and enforced a new regimented form of crowd control by police and private security officers.[6] Symbolically, boxing had traded its open, rural and festive heritage for a new containment and an urban context which has since become embedded in the mythology of the professional prizefighting milieu.

Representations of the modern world of boxing pivot on two extraordinary and contrasting urban spaces – the ring and the gym – that mirror and intensify the bright and dark spaces, the light and shade, central to the mythic terrain of the city. The ring and the gym lay at the core of boxing's layered narrative because they accommodate a transition, a preparatory journey to fitness, to readiness, and to a form of consciousness the final recognition of which Joyce Carol Oates has linked to "the ceremonial ringing of the bell" at the beginning of the fight: "A summoning to wakefulness for both the boxers and spectators."[7]

The gym is dark, claustrophobic, reverent, hypnotic, sexual; a space of intersecting rhythms, sounds and images. In his classic boxing novel *The Harder They Fall* (1947), Budd Schulberg offers a definitive picture of the gym environment, and in a sense of boxing culture: "A large stuffy, smoke-filled, hopeful, cynical, glistening-bodied world. The smells of this world are sour and pungent, a stale gamey odor blended of sweat and liniment, worn fight gear, cheap cigars and too many bodies, clothed and unclothed, packed into a room with no noticeable means of ventilation. The sounds of this world are multiple and varied [...] the tap-drum beating of the light-bag, counterpointing other light-bags; the slow thud of punches into heavy bags, the tap-dance tempo of the rope-skippers; the three minute bell; the footwork of the boys working in the ring, slow, open-gloved, taking it easy; the muffled sound of the flat, high laced shoes on the canvas [...] the hard breathing of the boxers, the rush of air through the fighter's fractured nose, in a staccato tuned to his movements [...]"[8] Here encapsulated is the primal urban territory of boxing, an overtly male preserve of grimy authenticity, a space defined as an organism, as one body. The trained boxers' ritualistic emergence from this space is a progress into light, into the glare and harsh scrutiny of the ring and into another of boxing's essential and enduring images.